WORKING WITH SMALLHOLDERS

WORKING WITH SMALLHOLDERS

A HANDBOOK FOR FIRMS BUILDING SUSTAINABLE SUPPLY CHAINS

International Finance Corporation

CONTENTS

BOXES

FIGURES

FOREWORD

One of our greatest challenges is meeting society's growing food needs while simultaneously reducing agriculture's environmental footprint. This will require the "sustainable intensification" of agriculture: producing more food on less land, with less water, and in a more sustainable way. This challenge is exacerbated in low- and lower-middle-income countries, where 95 percent of all farms are smaller than five hectares. There are about 475 million smallholder farms, predominantly in Asia and Africa. The overwhelming majority of them have low productivity and face constraints in accessing inputs, finance, knowledge, technology, labor, and markets.

Growth in emerging markets and rising demand for higher-quality food products create new opportunities for private firms along the entire agricultural value chains. In parallel, emerging technologies are making it possible to lower costs and dramatically reshape these value chains. However, technologies are also introducing new risks of disruption and redundancy. To counter these forces, ingenuity, innovation, and considerable investments will be needed for decades to come.

The future of agriculture requires new and pioneering partnerships between different stakeholders in the food system. Achieving the

Sustainable Development Goals to end extreme poverty by 2030 will require an estimated $4.5 trillion annually—far more resources than multilateral development banks or donors can provide by themselves. To meet this challenge, International Finance Corporation (IFC) is actively participating in designing the new "Maximizing Finance for Development" (MFD) and "Cascade" approach; this approach entails working with governments to crowd in the private sector while optimizing the use of scarce public resources, including those in the agribusiness sector.

Since the first edition of this handbook was published in 2014, IFC has doubled its agribusiness investment program from around $2 billion to $4 billion annually. Together with our development partners and private sector clients, we are also scaling up advisory programs that improve the livelihoods of smallholder farmers by linking them to modern supply chains, and we are creating opportunities to increase their productivity and improve their farming practices through greater access to financing, technology, and high-quality inputs. IFC supports innovative partnerships among agribusiness, financial institutions, technical assistance providers, governments, donors, and other stakeholders in building new systems of sustainable food production.

Firms increasingly need to establish and expand ways of working with consumer groups, governments, research institutes, civil society organizations, and the millions of smallholder farmers—especially in emerging markets—that are critical to the future supply of many agricultural products, including livestock, coffee, cocoa, vegetables, dairy, and oil palm. Based on our experience, we believe firms can accomplish this while significantly contributing to better economic outcomes for all.

This handbook is a practical guide for firms who wish to expand their supply chains by working with smallholder farmers. The purpose is to enable more productive interactions between private firms and smallholders, creating value in all parts of the chain. This handbook is also a part of IFC's larger contribution to the development of the agribusiness sector, with the aim of shifting our global food system to one in which sustainable production is the norm and food and nutritional security is secured for future generations.

Tomasz Telma
Director and Global Head
Manufacturing, Agribusiness, and Services
International Finance Corporation

CONTRIBUTORS

Eline Arnoldy

Andi Wahyuni Baso
Ernest Bethe
Christopher Brett
Thuong Minh Bui

Victoria Chang
Meei Shi Child

Karen Feeley
Dieter Fischer
Maaike Fleur

Katerina Gladkova
Ann Gordon
Mandy Grant

Mehnaz Haider
Andrea Holtkamp

Alan Johnson

John Lamb
Hannah Leupold

Edward Raphael Limon
Tania Lozansky
Patrick Luternauer

Natalie Macawaris
Rosemary Mahoney
Catalina Ale Monserrat
Gene Moses

Kalyan Neelamraju
Mark Nielsen
Donald Nzorubara

Sarah Ockman
Toshiaki Ono
Jane Onoka

Caitriona Mary Palmer
Valentina Paskalova
Liudmila Pestun
Ian Pringle

Fanja Ravoavy
Loraine Ronchi

Rachel Sberro
Hannington Sebaduka
Alex Serrano
Alex Skinner

Colin Taylor

Rick Van der Kamp
Panos Varangis
Maria Verena Spohler Kouoh
Laura Villegas

Amy Warren
Bruce Wise
Jim Woodhill

Carla Mae Zamora-Galinato
Heidrun Zeug

ABBREVIATIONS

CSA	climate-smart agriculture
DFS	digital financial services
FAO	Food and Agriculture Organization of the United Nations
FI	financial institution
GHG	greenhouse gas
GMOs	genetically modified organisms
GPS	Global Positioning System
ICS	internal control system
ICT	information and communication technology
IFC	International Finance Corporation (World Bank Group)
IPM	integrated pest management
MFD	Maximizing Finance for Development
M&E	monitoring and evaluation
NGO	nongovernmental organization
PO	producer organization
PPP	public-private partnership
SDG	Sustainable Development Goal

INTRODUCTION

KEY MESSAGES

⇒ Meeting the food needs of the world's 9.8 billion people in 2050 and reducing the numbers of malnourished will require an estimated increase of almost 50 percent in agricultural production.

⇒ This objective will be all the more challenging given the limited scope for expansion of cultivated area, the effects of climate change on agricultural production, and competing pressures on natural resources, including water.

⇒ An estimated 475 million smallholder farms worldwide can help meet this target through stronger market links and productivity improvements.

⇒ More vibrant smallholder agriculture, with enhanced participation of women and youth, holds the key to reduced poverty and hunger.

⇒ International Finance Corporation (IFC) of the World Bank Group is working with global agribusiness firms to develop new and efficient ways of working with smallholder farmers (as discussed in box I.2).

⇒ Intended to support the sustainability and sourcing managers of global brands, off-takers, input companies, service providers, and banks, this updated *Working with Smallholders* handbook explores new developments and best practices in working with smallholders.

Purpose of This Handbook

Smallholder farmers are becoming more important players in global food chains as agribusiness companies seek to secure future food supplies for the world's growing population. For some crops, smallholders are already an important source of production, but their role is expanding as land constraints limit the potential for growth in plantation agriculture and as the locus of future food market growth shifts to emerging markets. Those markets face increasing demand for affordable, nutritious foods for low-income urban populations.

These shifts offer opportunities—particularly for economic growth and poverty alleviation in rural areas—but also pose challenges to upgrade and integrate smallholder agriculture against a backdrop of climate change and increasing water scarcity. Moreover, agribusiness companies, under increasing pressure from consumers, shareholders, governments, and other stakeholders, are making important public commitments on sustainability, including adoption of environmental and labor standards. Meeting these competing demands will require new ways of working and new partnerships to deliver change.

This handbook is written for the operational managers in agribusiness companies responsible for integrating smallholder farmers into value chains as suppliers, clients, or customers. These managers include the following:

- Product and sales managers for input manufacturers, distributors, wholesalers, and retailers

- Field managers for financial institutions and their small business clients

- Training service providers working with smallholders

- Supply chain and sustainability managers for off-takers

- Sustainability managers for processors and food companies

- Company managers responsible for engagement via public-private partnerships.

Although written principally to outline training and assistance needs and opportunities for the private sector—whether in high-income, frontier, or low- and middle-income markets—the handbook may also be useful to the staffs of governmental or nongovernmental agricultural development programs working with smallholders, as well as to academic and research institutions.

Supply-Side Challenges Facing Global Food and Agribusiness Companies

Agribusinesses operate in a rapidly changing world. Agricultural production more than tripled between 1960 and 2015 (FAO 2017). Meeting the demand for food, feed, and biofuel in 2050, when the world's population is expected to reach 9.8 billion (UN DESA 2017), will require an almost 50 percent increase in production relative to 2012—and more than double the current production in South Asia and Sub-Saharan Africa (FAO 2017). Despite progress in reducing the prevalence of hunger, there are still an estimated 800 million undernourished people, for whom agriculture must provide sufficient carbohydrates, protein, and fats.

Nations worldwide will increase their focus not only on food *quantity* but also on food *quality*—the need for safe, healthy, and nutritious foods—as the health costs of too much, too little, and the wrong types of food become more evident. Reducing food losses and addressing logistical issues should also be an important focus: globally, around one-third of food production is lost or wasted each year at different stages in the food chain (FAO 2017). Balancing these needs will become even more critical as concurrent rises in incomes and urbanization drive increased consumption of meat, dairy, and biofuels.[1]

Climate change will add further challenges, causing shifts in weather patterns and increasing the frequency and severity of extreme weather events that can disrupt or even shock the entire food supply chain. Moreover, the agriculture, forestry, and other land use sector is the second largest emitter of greenhouse gases (behind the energy sector)—thus both contributing to climate change and underlining the need for action on both the mitigation and adaptation aspects of climate-smart agriculture (FAO 2017).

Meeting the world's food needs will not be easy. The remaining unused arable land is concentrated in a few countries and is difficult to access. Average yields for staple crops such as rice, maize, wheat, and soybeans have seen modest annual increases of 1 percent or less since the 1990s (FAO 2017). Moreover, climate change, water scarcity, and an aging rural population all contribute to the challenging context for agribusinesses seeking solutions to raw material sourcing.

However, this context also presents opportunities. Agribusinesses are increasingly working directly with smallholder farmers in emerging markets in win-win arrangements that can help secure a sustainable supply of key agricultural commodities while boosting rural incomes and economic growth. These arrangements are partly driven by necessity because, in many countries, smallholders dominate the production (70–90 percent) of certain traditional export crops such as tea, coffee, cocoa, and cotton.[2] Smallholders also represent an increasing part of the supply base for high-value horticultural and floricultural exports, where they have an advantage in labor supervision for precise, labor-intensive tasks. The key concern for agribusinesses is to secure and stabilize future supplies and markets in an uncertain and recently volatile market.

Sourcing directly from smallholders can expand a firm's supply base, reduce margins paid to collectors and middlemen, facilitate improvements in quality and yield, and sometimes deliver premium prices for a certified fair trade or sustainably produced product. Smallholders also represent a growing market for farm inputs, information, and financial services. Working closely together, agribusiness firms can help smallholders to

- Raise productivity and improve crop quality

- Access know-how to mitigate social and environmental impacts

- Develop farm management skills and bulk up their produce with other farmers to achieve sufficient scale to be effective market players

- Meet growing demand for demonstrably safe, sustainable food by improving practices and introducing traceability and certification systems.

In addition, rapid developments in information and communication technology (ICT) are creating new avenues for agribusiness companies to engage with smallholders through advances in traceability; in precision agriculture (at the level of vast tracts of land and regarding the availability of micro detail on soils and weather); in the scope for training and communication efficiencies; and in the ability to aggregate output and to disperse demand for inputs.

In many countries where smallholder production and low yields dominate, large areas of land present an important opportunity to increase production of food and feed. Nonetheless, the task is challenging and will require action on multiple fronts among multiple players. As further discussed in the following section, smallholder farmers represent a fragmented and diverse supply base that can be difficult to reach.

Demand-Side Challenges: A Changing Market Landscape

Not only is the world population growing—with implications for the volume of food required—but the locus and nature of market growth is also shifting. Globally, annual population growth rates have been declining for almost 50 years, but the combined population of Africa and Asia is expected to increase by roughly 2 billion by 2050 (UN DESA 2017). That growth will drive large and expanding markets for affordable, nutritious food for low-income populations in those regions.

Moreover, the current 54 percent share of world population that is now urban is expected to grow to around two-thirds by 2050, including large urban populations in low- and middle-income countries (UNCTAD 2017). Urbanization affects food consumption patterns in several ways. Higher urban income tends to increase demand for processed foods as well as for animal-source food, fruits, and vegetables as part of a broad dietary transition. This in turn drives increased demand for animal feed. Urban living is also associated with more fast food, store-bought convenience foods, and foods prepared and marketed by street vendors. With these changes, the nutrient content of diets is changing (typically becoming higher in salt, fat, and sugar—with associated health consequences). These shifts lead to fewer people working in agriculture and more people working in transport, wholesaling, retailing, food processing, and vending.

As food and agribusiness companies face these growing urban markets, especially in Asia and Africa, demand will increase for processed convenience foods (and the associated retail infrastructure), animal-source food and feed, and large markets offering more-traditional foods at affordable prices. When all of these trends are added to increased demand for biofuels and growing consumer expectations in high-income markets that their food be sustainably produced (but not necessarily more expensive), the result is a particularly interesting and challenging market outlook—requiring adaptation and foresight on the part of global agribusiness as well as strenuous efforts to secure sufficient supply.

Understanding Smallholder Farmers

Smallholders are a fragmented and diverse group (as further described in box I.1)—factors that contribute to the challenges in working with them. Nonetheless, they share some common characteristics. Most smallholders work and live within traditional support and power

---

BOX I.1

Smallholder Farmers, by Definition and Location

There are an estimated 475 million smallholder farms in low- and middle-income countries (FAO 2017). Rapid growth in agribusinesses' interest and experience in working directly with small-holders underscores the potential they offer, but efforts to improve the quality and productivity of smallholder agriculture can only be sustainable if such efforts explicitly address farmer incentives.

A smallholder farm is widely defined as a family-owned enterprise that produces crops or livestock on 2 hectares or less. In some countries and sectors, smallholdings can exceed 10 hectares, and there is considerable variation in how countries define smallholders or categorize farms. The key factor is a limited asset base. Although family members provide most of the labor and derive their primary means of support from the farm, the household may nonetheless derive income from multiple sources. Many smallholders are not farmers by choice, but rather because they lack more lucrative opportunities.

Of an estimated 570 million farms worldwide, almost 475 million are smallholder farms, rep-resenting 84 percent of all farms and operating about 12 percent of all farmland. Using less than 2 hectares of farmed land as the key criterion, almost 80 percent of smallholder farms are in low- and middle-income regions in Asia and the Pacific (excluding Central Asia), followed by Sub-Saharan Africa (9 percent), Eastern Europe and Central Asia (5 percent), the Middle East and North Africa (2 percent), and the Americas (1 percent). (In the Americas, where average farm size is much higher, this share increases to 3–4 percent if farms up to 10 hectares are included.) The remainder (3 percent or less) is in high-income countries. Over the past 50 years, the broad trend in high-income countries has been toward increased consolidation in farm holdings, while low- and middle-income countries have generally shown a trend toward smaller average farm size.[a]

FIGURE BI.1 Global Distribution of Smallholders (millions)

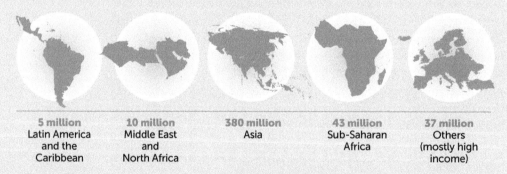

| 5 million | 10 million | 380 million | 43 million | 37 million |
| Latin America and the Caribbean | Middle East and North Africa | Asia | Sub-Saharan Africa | Others (mostly high income) |

Source: https://www.sciencedirect.com/science/article/pii/S0305750X15002703.

structures, but increased access to information is changing the way smallholders organize and interact with markets. For example, the rapid spread of cell phones among farmers and their families is improving real-time information on marketing opportunities and prices, changing the way farmers do business (Luxton 2016) (map I.1).

Smallholders also generally sell their crops through local supply chains, which typically begin with village collectors or producer organizations and continue through a series of traders who aggregate volumes as the crops pass along the supply chain. Smallholders may wait by the roadside with their crops, hoping to sell to traveling traders. Village collectors (and sometimes producer organizations or cooperatives) may extend credit and loan agricultural inputs such as fertilizer, with the repayment expected at harvest time.

Smallholder farming is predominantly a household enterprise, and hence household dynamics affect farm decision making. Men often make the major decisions about farming and selling crops, especially when cash crops are involved, but women may manage their own plots, particularly for food crops. The number of female-headed farms is increasing, particularly in Asia, where women head more than 20 percent of smallholder households in some areas (FAO 2011)—an increasing trend where men out-migrate in search of employment. In low- and middle-income countries, the share of women in the agricultural labor force is growing. It averaged 43 percent in 2010 (FAO 2017), but in many high-value horticulture supply chains, their participation exceeds 50 percent (Maertens and Swinnen 2009). Moreover, among low- and middle-income countries for which data are available, 10–20 percent of all landholders are women (FAO 2011). However, unequal access to necessary resources results in gender-based yield gaps of 20–30 percent (FAO 2011).

The global population is aging and the next 15 years will see particularly sharp growth in the older population in low- and middle-income regions. For example, a 64–66 percent increase is expected in the population aged 65 years and above in Africa and Asia (FAO 2017). An aging rural population poses two challenges: first, to upgrade and modernize smallholder agriculture, and second, to find ways to make agriculture—and related services—sufficiently attractive to absorb some of the unemployed youth. The number of young people aged 15–24 years will rise from about 1.2 billion in 2015 to 1.3 billion by 2030 and 1.4 billion by 2050. Unchecked youth unemployment may hamper development and destabilize economies worldwide. In common with some other aspects of smallholder agriculture (as discussed throughout this handbook) the solutions cannot come from the private sector

MAP I.1 A Global Snapshot of Smallholder Farming in Selected Countries

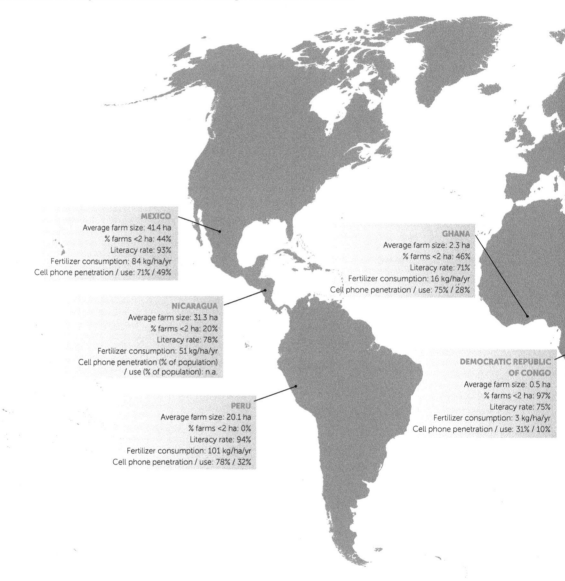

MEXICO
Average farm size: 41.4 ha
% farms <2 ha: 44%
Literacy rate: 93%
Fertilizer consumption: 84 kg/ha/yr
Cell phone penetration / use: 71% / 49%

GHANA
Average farm size: 2.3 ha
% farms <2 ha: 46%
Literacy rate: 71%
Fertilizer consumption: 16 kg/ha/yr
Cell phone penetration / use: 75% / 28%

NICARAGUA
Average farm size: 31.3 ha
% farms <2 ha: 20%
Literacy rate: 78%
Fertilizer consumption: 51 kg/ha/yr
Cell phone penetration (% of population)
/ use (% of population): n.a.

DEMOCRATIC REPUBLIC OF CONGO
Average farm size: 0.5 ha
% farms <2 ha: 97%
Literacy rate: 75%
Fertilizer consumption: 3 kg/ha/yr
Cell phone penetration / use: 31% / 10%

PERU
Average farm size: 20.1 ha
% farms <2 ha: 0%
Literacy rate: 94%
Fertilizer consumption: 101 kg/ha/yr
Cell phone penetration / use: 78% / 32%

Sources: ©World Bank. Further permission from World Bank required for reuse. Data from Deloitte 2015; Huang, Wang, and Qiu 2012; Khalil et al. 2017; Lowder, Skoet, and Raney 2016; Luxton 2016; Nagayets 2005; literacy rates from UNICEF, https://data.unicef.org/topic/education/literacy/.
Note: kg/ha/yr = kilograms per hectare per year; n.a. = not available. Cell phone data are for 2015.

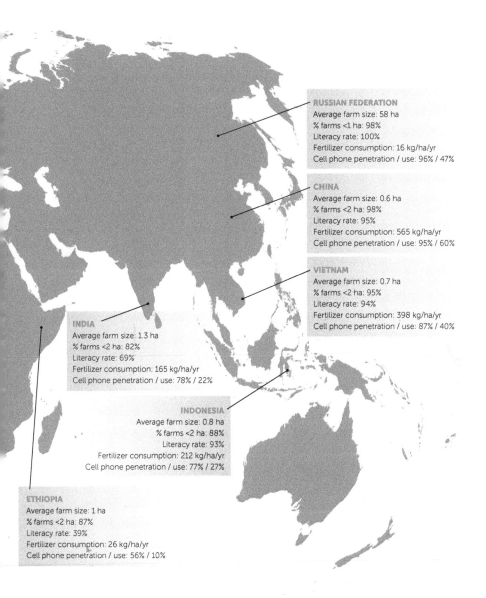

RUSSIAN FEDERATION
Average farm size: 58 ha
% farms <1 ha: 98%
Literacy rate: 100%
Fertilizer consumption: 16 kg/ha/yr
Cell phone penetration / use: 96% / 47%

CHINA
Average farm size: 0.6 ha
% farms <2 ha: 98%
Literacy rate: 95%
Fertilizer consumption: 565 kg/ha/yr
Cell phone penetration / use: 95% / 60%

VIETNAM
Average farm size: 0.7 ha
% farms <2 ha: 95%
Literacy rate: 94%
Fertilizer consumption: 398 kg/ha/yr
Cell phone penetration / use: 87% / 40%

INDIA
Average farm size: 1.3 ha
% farms <2 ha: 82%
Literacy rate: 69%
Fertilizer consumption: 165 kg/ha/yr
Cell phone penetration / use: 78% / 22%

INDONESIA
Average farm size: 0.8 ha
% farms <2 ha: 88%
Literacy rate: 93%
Fertilizer consumption: 212 kg/ha/yr
Cell phone penetration / use: 77% / 27%

ETHIOPIA
Average farm size: 1 ha
% farms <2 ha: 87%
Literacy rate: 39%
Fertilizer consumption: 26 kg/ha/yr
Cell phone penetration / use: 56% / 10%

alone but will need shared investment from government in the public-good components of sector growth.

Quality and productivity vary widely among smallholder farmers depending on their ability to invest. The productive assets of a smallholder farm could be as basic as a hand hoe or as sophisticated as a tractor. Some farmers may have no knowledge of postharvest processing; others may be capable of highly detailed grading and sorting. In some African countries, fertilizer consumption is near zero; in China, it exceeds 500 kilograms per hectare (Huang, Wang, and Qiu 2012). Literacy rates, which tend to be lower in rural areas, also vary considerably.[1]

Overall, these farmers face a variety of challenges, ranging from limitations in agricultural practices, market access, and other capacities to legal, financial, and various other resource constraints, as described below.

Traditional cultivation methods. Farmers usually learn agricultural techniques from their parents and peers. Many traditional practices (including slash-and-burn agriculture), although once sustainable, can degrade soil fertility and cause erosion as a result of increasing land pressure and shorter fallow periods. Moreover, in frontier and low- to middle-income markets, government extension and input support have declined significantly in the past 30 years, leaving smallholders with fewer resources to improve agricultural practices. Many farmers, particularly in parts of Africa, live too far from agro-retailers or can ill afford improved inputs—and are also wary of the widely available counterfeit and poor-quality products (FAO 2017; Kelly, Vergara, and Bammann 2015).

Limited market access. Many smallholders lack physical and economic access to lucrative markets for their crops. Distance, poor roads, and reliance on bicycles or motorbikes for crop transport cause physical isolation from markets. Small quantities of crops to sell, a need for immediate payment, limited capacity to safely store crops, and poor knowledge of prices and quality requirements beyond the farm gate are important economic constraints that limit their power to negotiate with buyers. As a result, most smallholders sell their crops on the roadside near their farms.

Lack of producer organizations. Globally, agriculture and food is the lead sector in numbers of cooperatives and second (to insurance) in cooperative business turnover (COOP and Euricse 2016). Many household names are farmer-owned cooperatives (for example, FrieslandCampina, Land O' Lakes, Arla Foods, Blue Diamond, and Sunkist). Smallholders in some countries are well organized; cooperatives in India have a 36 percent share of the fertilizer market, while those in China have 60–80 percent shares in the agriprocessing, fertilizer, tea, and cotton markets. In many countries, however, cooperative business is less developed: less than 3 percent of the population in Africa are cooperative members, compared with approximately 13 percent in Asia and in the Caribbean, and 8 percent in Latin America (COOP and Euricse 2016; Dave Grace and Associates 2014; Mayo 2012). Recent developments, however, are demonstrating that it is possible to objectively assess the business capacities of producer organizations and support their development with targeted training and coaching.

Informal landholding. Most smallholders lack formal title to the land they farm. They may own the land through traditional structures, or they could be sharecroppers or renters. This means they cannot use land as collateral for financing—or buy or sell and consolidate landholdings. If farmers are sharecropping or renting their land, they may not be willing to invest in inputs.

Poor access to credit. Financial institutions often consider smallholders to be unattractive clients because of insufficient collateral, lack of written records, small loan sizes, and high transaction costs. In contrast to small loans in urban settings, agricultural loans are typically paid off after the harvest, possibly 8 to 12 months after the loan is taken. Few formal financial institutions will lend to smallholders, and suitable products for small-scale farmers are rarely developed. So, smallholders make scant use of formal credit and may be obliged to use informal moneylenders, with high rates of interest.

Poor soil fertility. Most smallholders live in tropical zones with naturally low soil fertility. Although many farmers use traditional practices to manage soil nutrition (for example, using animal manure and natural mulches, intercropping, and burning of stubble), increasing intensification means that such techniques no longer sufficiently replenish soil nutrients. Many smallholders have neither the knowledge to address specific nutrient deficiencies nor the resources to do so, and they rarely have access to soil testing services.

Limited ability to adapt to climate change and water scarcity. Smallholders who rely on traditional cultivation techniques face enormous challenges as they try to adapt to changing weather patterns. Rainfed agriculture is still the norm in most of Sub-Saharan Africa and in poorer rural areas in Asia. Unpredictable rainy seasons reduce farmer confidence in planting crops at the traditional time. The crop varieties they are familiar with may produce low yields or fail during drought or flooding.

Changes in temperature and humidity increase pest and disease prevalence. Even in those regions where smallholders use groundwater for irrigation, they face increased salinity and falling water tables. Although new crop varieties can help them overcome these constraints, particularly if there is irrigation, they also cost more, so many farmers feel such a change will increase their exposure to risk.

Wide use of intercropping. Subsistence and cash crop cultivation are often combined on the same plot. Farmers commonly intercrop food crops with cash crops such as cocoa and coffee, or they may consume a portion of the food crop harvest, such as maize or rice, and sell the remainder. Such practices affect marketable yields and need to be understood and factored into the design of smallholder programs.

Low literacy and numeracy. Many smallholders have little formal education, which limits their ability to keep adequate written records or educate themselves about improved agricultural practices. With output sold and consumed, and production often harvested bit by bit, smallholders may have only a vague idea of basic metrics (such as farm size, crop yield, and real costs) on their own farms.

Aging population. As the population of smallholder farmers ages and youth are drawn to urban areas, farming is losing its appeal among the next generation.

Despite these challenges, a wealth of evidence now indicates that smallholders respond positively to opportunities that enable them to join global supply chains and contribute to food security, poverty reduction, and economic growth (Dixon, Tanyeri-Abur, and Wattenbach, n.d.). Rapid advances in ICT are transforming the way in which smallholder supply chains can be monitored and managed and are creating opportunities for more cost-effective use of inputs based on site-specific analysis. Digital technology is helping provide timely and global access—to local weather forecasts, for example—as well as entirely new sets of tools and opportunities for communication and training.

The main goal of this handbook is to demonstrate that potential while exploring key practical considerations—ultimately helping to multiply those opportunities where both farmers and firms can benefit from greater engagement.

Inclusive Business Models That Integrate Smallholders into Value Chains

As companies increasingly source directly from smallholder farmers, the characteristics and circumstances that define these producers will

FIGURE I.1 Integrated Agribusiness Value Chain Approach

Market context

Enabling environment

Infrastructure, PPPs

Input producers & distributors → farmers → food processors → distributors → retailers   **Consumers 7 billion+**

Financial services

Advisory/technical services

Environmental and social
ecosystem services

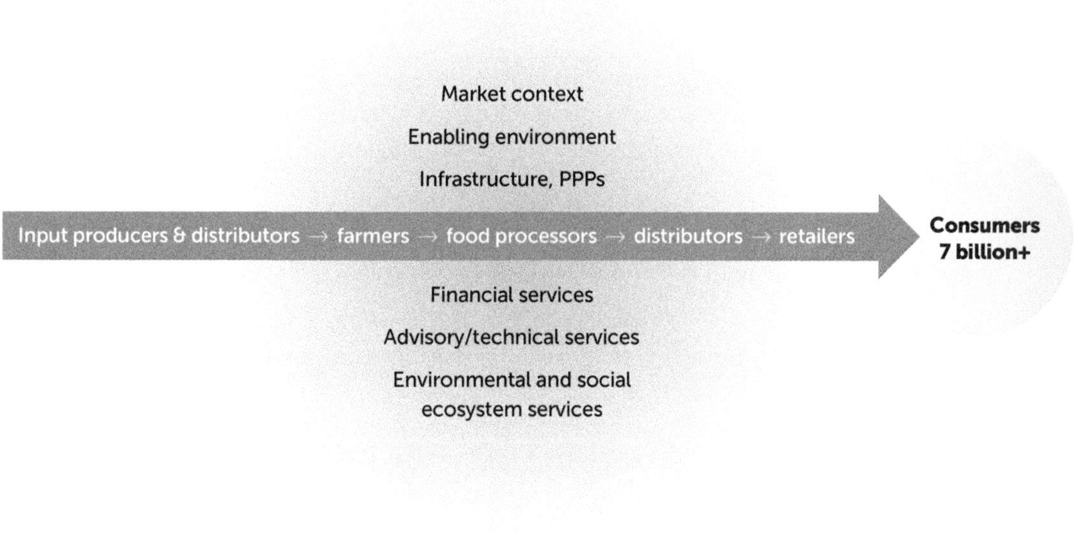

Note: PPP = public-private partnership.

pose particular challenges, requiring agribusiness to adopt approaches that differ from those used in other contexts. Using an integrated agribusiness value chain approach (figure I.1), this handbook focuses on issues that are particularly relevant to smallholder value chains.

Value chain integration can generate mutual benefits for smallholder farmers and the business community. There is increasing convergence between the private sector and the development community in their interest in inclusive business models (IBMs). This handbook touches upon many points of focus for IBMs (Kelly, Vergara, and Bammann 2015):

- Does the enterprise provide a living wage for vulnerable groups, such as smallholders, small enterprises, and women- and youth-run enterprises, while also enabling buyers to profit?

- Are there flexible trading arrangements that make it easier for smallholders or micro or small enterprises to supply a buyer, such as cash on delivery, accepting small consignments, and providing reliable and regular orders?

- Does the enterprise support farmers and small enterprises to establish a stronger negotiation position through skills development, collective bargaining, and access to market information and financial services?

- Does the enterprise build on the skills and expertise of existing market players (including traders and processors) and promote value chain collaboration, transparency in pricing mechanisms, and risk sharing?

- Is the enterprise scalable in the medium term so that the number of small actors involved can be increased or the business model replicated in other value chains or parts of the sector?

- Does the approach allow for diversified income streams in the long term, enabling the dissemination of upgraded skills to the rest of the sector and avoiding overdependence on any single buyer or market outlet?

A parallel development is the growing interest in the multilateral Principles for Responsible Agricultural Investment (as noted in chapter 4).[3]

How the Handbook Is Organized

Serving as a primer on key elements of a smallholder intervention strategy, this handbook leads companies through the prior considerations in working with smallholders (the business case), continues with eight chapters addressing various implementation topics relating to smallholder value-chain integration, and concludes with perspectives on emerging development and future directions (figure I.2).

In summary, the handbook is structured as follows:

- Chapter 1 presents the business case for working with smallholders.

- Chapter 2 explores key aspects of agrifinance that impinge on the development of smallholder supply chains.

FIGURE I.2 Elements of Smallholder Supply Chain Interventions in This Handbook

Implementation

Prior considerations →
- Finance
- Aggregation
- Standards
- Training
- Yield gaps
- Women in supply chains
- Partnerships
- Results measurement

→ Outlook

BOX I.2

IFC Expertise in Agribusiness and Support of Smallholder Supply Chains

International Finance Corporation (IFC) has made agribusiness a priority because of its potential for broad development impact and its especially strong role in reaching rural areas—where about 70 percent of the world's poor live. Through investments and advisory services, IFC helps the private sector address higher global demand for food, fuel, and fiber in an environmentally sustainable and socially inclusive way. In the year ending June 2017, IFC investment in agribusiness sectors totaled US$4 billion, resulting in an overall agribusiness portfolio of US$6.5 billion. These investments include direct investments in agricultural production and processing, fertilizers and other agricultural inputs, forestry and wood products, food retail, and agrifinancing projects via financial institutions, equity funds, and financial mobilization.

IFC also supports global initiatives for sustainable production of agricultural commodities. It works with the multilateral Global Agriculture & Food Security Program, where it manages the "Private Sector Window" identifying private funding and financing aimed at increasing the commercial potential of small and medium-size agribusinesses and farmers by connecting them with local, national, and global value chains. The main avenues through which IFC pursues these goals are its investment and advisory work with off-takers, input companies, financial institutions, and service providers.

Working particularly in low-income countries, IFC seeks to improve smallholders' access to markets, financing, technical assistance, and inputs like fertilizer and seeds. These initiatives include efforts to strengthen firms' supply chains by helping smallholder farmers increase productivity and apply appropriate environmental, social, and quality standards. IFC aims to bring land into sustainable production, to improve the use of inputs by transferring technologies and practices, and to make the best use of water and other resources. It seeks commercially viable solutions and helps companies set benchmarks for responsible production in line with industry best practice.

In summary, IFC's agribusiness work of direct and indirect financing and investment, plus advisory input undertaken with the support if its development partners, addresses the following objectives:

- Improving practices of farmers and small businesses
- Supporting increased knowledge and access to agricultural inputs
- Facilitating market development by helping farmers meet quality and quantity requirements
- Strengthening approaches to food safety
- Promoting climate-smart agriculture
- Working with banks and other financial institutions to provide access to credit and insurance
- Raising standards of corporate governance and business transparency, including work with cooperative smallholder organizations
- Supporting the development and uptake of eco-standards for global commodity value chains.

box continued

BOX I.2

IFC Expertise in Agribusiness and Support of Smallholder Supply Chains *(Continued)*

An increasing amount of IFC's advisory work is taking place in the context of public-private partnerships. Chapter 8 includes discussion of public-private partnerships and funding opportunities for such initiatives.

- Chapters 3 through 8 examine different elements of working with smallholders, covering business rationale, solutions, strategies, and best practices as well as partnerships and other important considerations for firms intervening in these areas.

- Chapter 9 presents tools and strategies to help firms incorporate results measurement into their smallholder engagement strategies.

- Chapter 10 looks at key trends that will influence the way firms engage smallholders over the coming decades to build resilient agricultural value chains and meet the needs of future populations.

Throughout the handbook, boxes titled "In Practice" highlight effective approaches implemented by firms and service providers when working with smallholder farmers. These examples are drawn from projects that IFC and other firms or nongovernmental organizations have implemented in Latin America, Africa, and Asia. IFC's expertise in agribusiness and smallholder supply chains is described in box I.2.

This updated edition of the handbook builds on the rapidly growing experience of working with smallholders, expanding the scope of the case studies. It includes new sections on agrifinance and partnerships as well as new material on the assessment and development of rural enterprises (including farmer organizations) as business partners, principles and standards, the potential offered by rapid advances in digital technology, women's role in supply chains, and results measurement.

Notes

1. All data are from FAO 2017a.
2. Coffee production data from Panhuysen and Pierrot 2014. Cocoa production data from the International Cocoa Association (ICCO) https://www.icco.org/faq/57

-cocoa-production/123-how-many-smallholders-are-there-worldwide-producing
-cocoa-what-proportion-of-cocoa-worldwide-is-produced-by-smallholders.html.
Cotton and tea data from the commodities data pages of Solidaridad (accessed
April 11, 2017) at https://www.solidaridadnetwork.org/supply-chains/cotton and
https://www.solidaridadnetwork.org/supply-chains/tea, respectively.
3. The Principles for Responsible Agricultural Investment (PRAI) were jointly
developed by the United Nations Conference on Trade and Development
(UNCTAD), the Food and Agriculture Organization of the United Nations (FAO),
the International Fund for Agricultural Development (IFAD), and the World Bank.
For details, see the UNCTAD PRAI http://unctad.org/en/Pages/DIAE/G-20/PRAI
.aspx.

References

COOP and Euricse (International Co-operative Alliance and European Research
Initiative on Cooperative and Social Enterprises). 2016. "World Co-operative
Monitor. Exploring the Cooperative Economy: Report 2016." Annual data report,
COOP, Brussels.

Dave Grace and Associates. 2014. "Measuring the Size and Scope of the Cooperative
Economy: Results of the 2014 Global Census on Co-operatives." Report for the
United Nations Department of Economic and Social Affairs, New York.

Deloitte. 2015. "Digital Inclusion and Mobile Sector Taxation in the Democratic
Republic of the Congo." Final Report for the Groupe Speciale Mobile Association,
London.

Dixon, J., A. Tanyeri-Abur, and H. Wattenbach. n.d. "Framework for Analysing
Impacts of Globalization on Smallholders." http://www.fao.org/docrep/007
/y5784e/y5784e02.htm.

FAO (Food and Agriculture Organization of the United Nations). 2011. *The State of Food
and Agriculture 2010–11. Women in Agriculture: Closing the Gender Gap for Development.*
Rome: FAO.

———. 2017. *The Future of Food and Agriculture: Trends and Challenges.* Rome: FAO.

Huang, J., X. Wang, and H. Qiu. 2012. *Small-Scale Farmers in China in the Face of
Modernisation and Globalisation.* London: International Institute for Environment
and Development; The Hague: Hivos.

Kelly, S., N. Vergara, and H. Bammann. 2015. *Inclusive Business Models: Guidelines for
Improving Linkages between Producer Groups and Buyers of Agricultural Produce.* Rome:
Food and Agriculture Organization of the United Nations.

Khalil, C. A., P. Conforti, I. Ergin, and P. Gennari. 2017. "Defining Small Scale Food
Producers to Monitor Target 2.3 of the 2030 Agenda for Sustainable Development."
Working Paper Series ESS 17-12, Statistics Division, Food and Agriculture
Organization of the United Nations.

Lowder, S., J. Skoet, and T. Raney. 2016. "The Number, Size and Distribution of Farms,
Smallholder Farms, and Family Farms Worldwide." *World Development* 87: 16–29.

Luxton, E. 2016. "There's a Global Divide in Smartphone Use. But These Countries
Are Closing the Gap Fast." World Economic Forum website article, May 25
(accessed July 14, 2017), https://www.weforum.org/agenda/2016/05/smartphones

-are-closing-the-digital-divide-and-these-countries-have-made-the-most
-progress/.

Maertens, M., and J. Swinnen. 2009. "Are African High-Value Horticulture Supply
Chains Bearers of Gender Inequality?" Paper presented at the FAO-IFAD-ILO
"Workshop on Gaps, Trends and Current Research in Gender Dimensions of
Agricultural and Rural Employment: Differentiated Pathways Out of Poverty,"
Rome, March 31–April 2.

Mayo, E. 2012. "Global Business Ownership 2012: Members and Shareholders across
the World." *New Insight 9* report, Co-operatives UK, Manchester.

Nagayets, O. 2005. "Small Farms: Current Status and Key Trends." Information
brief for The Future of Small Farms Research Workshop, Wye College, Kent, UK,
June 26–29.

Panhuysen, S., and J. Pierrot. 2014. "Coffee Barometer 2014." Report, Hivos, The
Hague.

UNCTAD (United Nations Conference on Trade and Development). 2017. *Handbook of
Statistics 2017.* New York: United Nations.

UN DESA (United Nations Department of Economic and Social Affairs). 2017.
World Population Prospects: The 2017 Revision. New York: United Nations.

Additional Resources

Endean, E., and K. Suominen. 2014. "International Trends in Aid for Trade in
Agriculture." Prepared by Carana Corporation for the Food Systems Innovation
initiative. Report number: 0052-20140924. September 14.

GIZ. 2012. "Growing Business with Smallholders: A Guide to Inclusive Agribusiness."
GIZ, Bonn.

The Practitioner Hub for Inclusive Business. 2015. "Business Call to Action
for Agribusiness and the Smallholder Farmer." http://www.inclusivebusinesshub
.org/business-call-to-action-agribusiness-and-the-smallholder-farmer/. Accessed
November 15, 2017.

Woodhill, J., J. Guijt, L. Wegner, and M. Sopov. 2012. "From Islands of Success to Seas
of Change: A Report on Scaling Inclusive Agri-Food Markets." Centre for
Development Innovation, Wageningen UR (University & Research Centre),
Wageningen, Netherlands.

CHAPTER 1
THE BUSINESS CASE

KEY MESSAGES

⇒ Firms are engaging more with smallholder farmers, principally to secure supply.

⇒ Other drivers for working more closely with smallholders include expansion into new food markets in low- and middle-income countries, consumer demands for sustainable sourcing, and food safety.

⇒ For input companies and service providers, smallholders offer potential for significant market expansion.

⇒ Smallholders are already key players in some supply chains, providing 70–90 percent of volumes in beverage crops and cotton.

⇒ Yet working with smallholders is often considered risky, particularly because of multiple constraints on smallholder productivity and the potential for side-selling.

⇒ Nonetheless, there is mounting evidence that carefully designed programs can deliver enhanced quantity and quality of supply at lower procurement cost.

⇒ The public sector is promoting private sector engagement, support, and collaboration with smallholders via funding for public-private partnerships.

The Drivers for Working with Smallholder Farmers

Firms can source from or sell to smallholder farmers by working through traders or other intermediaries, but a decision to engage more closely with small farms is driven by several types of incentives:

- *The need to secure sourcing*—in terms of volume, quality, and stability of supply—for agricultural value chains, with smallholders representing the only significant means for increased sourcing

- *Smallholder dominance or advantage* in the production of certain crops

- *The business opportunity* offered by new markets for inputs, services, and output

- *Consumer demand* for increased sustainability, responsible sourcing, or food of known origins

- *Food safety concerns*, specifically the need to prevent and manage contamination and foodborne illness.

In sum, agribusinesses have many reasons to work with smallholders, including enhancing the quantity, quality, and traceability of supply while reducing procurement costs. Different types of business benefit from working with smallholders in different ways—and a longer time horizon expands the scope of what can be achieved by developing that relationship (table 1.1).

TABLE 1.1 Benefits of Working with Smallholder Farmers

Firm type	Short-term benefits	Medium-term benefits	Long-term benefits
Input manufacturers and suppliers	Increased sales	More efficient distribution through groups	Markets for new products designed for smallholders
Financial institutions	Large numbers of potential customers	Development of outgrower arrangements to facilitate repayment	• Market for new financial products • Loyalty among emerging medium-scale farmers
Agricultural information and training providers	Large numbers of potential customers, who can be reached via ICTs at low cost	Partnership with off-takers or input suppliers who pay for services	Information needed to develop new products and services
Off-takers and processors	• Greater production from the same area • Better quality • More efficient logistics	• Traceability • Certification • Reduced environmental and social risk	• Stability of supply • Increased supplier loyalty

Note: ICTs = information and communication technologies.

Meeting Global Demand for Food and Raw Materials

The volatility of commodity markets over recent years—after approximately three decades of relative stability—has driven many firms to reevaluate what they can do to secure future supplies of raw material and develop greater supply chain resilience to climate change and other risks to their supply chains.

World demand for staple crops is projected to grow by 60 percent by 2050 (compared with 2010), while crop area is likely to grow by only 10 percent (Fischer, Byerlee, and Edmeades 2014). Globally, 1.45 billion hectares of land are used for crop production, and another 0.45 billion hectares are theoretically available and suitable (excluding forests and protected areas). However, almost all of this potentially arable land is concentrated in just seven countries (Angola, Argentina, Brazil, China, the Democratic Republic of Congo, Mozambique, and Sudan), much of it far from ports and roads. In the Middle East, North Africa, East Asia, and South Asia, there is little "new" (that is, available and suitable) land available.

With increasing pressure to meet growing demand for raw materials through higher yields and cropping intensity, smallholder agriculture—where there is considerable scope to increase yields—will become more important in global supply chains. Smallholders' share in input markets will also grow, as will their need for technical advice. The lack of "new" land and, in many places, local resistance to large-scale privatization of land means that firms seeking to expand volumes will have to work with smallholders. Moreover, even if it were possible for firms to acquire land, it is often less costly, both financially and socially, to source from smallholders for a defined and profitable market opportunity than to invest in farming directly.

Agribusiness companies are working more closely with smallholder farmers principally to ensure the security and stability of a larger share of their sourcing. The annual reports and sustainability statements of the world's largest global food and agribusiness companies reveal many prominent statements about their work with smallholders, including the following examples:

- "[Our commitment:] Roll out rural development baseline assessments to understand the needs of farmers." (Nestlé 2017, 10)

- "We are working to accelerate growth and social development across our value chain, from growers to retailers." (AB InBev 2017)

- "For many years, we've listened to and worked with smallholder farmers to promote sustainable supply chains." (Mondelez International n.d.)

Smallholder Dominance or Advantage in Production of Certain Crops

In some sectors, such as coffee and cocoa, smallholder farmers dominate production, so firms must work with smallholders to secure supply. In other sectors, such as cut flowers, tree fruits, and other labor-intensive crops, smallholders may be more efficient than large farms.

Smallholders can be competitive against larger suppliers when they bring a differentiated product to the market, such as a higher-quality grade or a niche-market product destined for fair trade, organic, or boutique markets. One reason for this is their lower costs for labor supervision (that is, they are their own supervisors).

Expanding into New Markets—for Inputs, Services, and Output

For global firms seeking to tap into the food or feed sales potential of emerging markets, local sourcing may be their most competitive option (a dynamic that is, moreover, potentially reinforced by regional trade agreements and tariff regimes).

For providers of inputs, financial services, or information, the business case is driven by an expanded customer base at acceptable service delivery costs. Input companies registered increases in sales volumes and grew their client base threefold to fivefold in a study of companies extending their reach to cover smallholders (Hystra 2015). Although individual farmers' needs may be small, as members of farmer cooperatives, they can command significant buying power.

Responding to Demands for Increased Sustainability

Growing consumer concern for sustainably sourced food drives the expansion of the market for certified products from both specialty and high-volume retailers. Interest in sustainable sourcing—"the integration of social, ethical, and environmental performance factors into the process of selecting suppliers" (EcoVadis n.d.)—has increased over the past 20 years, particularly since the 2008 global economic crisis.

About 20 percent of coffee is sustainably sourced, and the shares of sustainably sourced cocoa and tea are also rising. In addition, the market share for organic foods, a category of sustainably sourced products, is approaching 7–10 percent in North America and in several European countries (Ecovia Intelligence 2017). Key agribusiness players are placing transparency and traceability on a par with convenience and choice as a key trend affecting the food industry. As Cargill executive Brian Sikes states, "People are making choices to protect the planet. . . . They want to know the story of where their food comes from and feel good about what they eat" (Schraeder 2016).

Agribusinesses also face potentially damaging environmental and social risks, whether from facilities directly under the firm's control or further up the supply chain on smallholder farms. For example, a food manufacturer could face reputational risk if it purchases palm oil grown on deforested land or cocoa grown using child labor. Financial institutions lending to agribusinesses face the same risks as their clients. By working more closely with smallholder farmers, firms create opportunities to identify potential environmental and social risks in the supply chain, allowing them to proactively respond to issues before they become liabilities or crises.

Now that almost all global agribusinesses emphasize responsible sourcing, many have partnerships with nongovernmental organizations and researchers and make clear sustainability commitments. Many refer to the development of indexes, assessment tools, and other methodologies.

Responding to Food Safety Concerns

Consumers in many parts of the world expect their food to be safe. Nevertheless, unsafe food causes more than 200 diseases, ranging from diarrhea to cancer, each year affecting more than 600 million people and causing many deaths (WHO 2015). The reputational risk for agribusiness firms and the potential for economic losses are significant. Understanding and mitigating risks to food safety are priorities and often legal requirements as well. International Finance Corporation (IFC) has launched an advisory platform—the IFC Food Safety Toolkit—to help its agribusiness clients build capacity in food safety globally (IFC 2017), as further discussed in chapter 4 on standards.

Food contamination can occur during production, postharvest, or processing. For example, a common concern is unapproved or improperly used pesticides, resulting in import bans or additional requirements for selected products from certain countries (for example, European Union imports of okra from India) (FSA UK 2014). Another common concern is aflatoxin, a carcinogen produced by mold that grows on improperly dried or handled crops. This carcinogen can also be transmitted to livestock through contaminated feed. In 2004, maize contaminated with aflatoxin caused 317 cases of liver failure and 125 deaths in Kenya and presented a liability to both suppliers and buyers

(Probst, Njapau, and Cotty 2007). In 2013, animal feed was withdrawn from hundreds of Dutch farms because of an aflatoxin risk (*DutchNews.nl* 2013). Reputational damage can persist long after the problem has been solved.

Firms that engage with smallholders to develop traceable supply chains are better able to monitor all the steps involved in production, harvest, and processing. When problems are detected—such as improper crop drying that could result in mold growth and aflatoxin formation—such firms will already have systems in place to address the issue rapidly and effectively (as further discussed in chapter 4).

A separate but related issue concerns nutrition, which affects agribusiness in two quite separate contexts: (a) at the level of their markets, and (b) with smallholder farmers. With mounting global concern about the costs of ill health linked to being overweight or obese, consumers increasingly want assurances that their food is not only safe but is also health-promoting and nutritious.

Similarly—and this links to the discussion of sustainable sourcing above—firms are aware that by working with relatively vulnerable smallholder farmers, supply chain interventions can potentially affect farm household food and nutrition security, positively or negatively. IFC works with its clients to better understand these impacts (see the

FIGURE 1.1 The Multiple Dimensions of Malnutrition

- ⌄ 800 million people undernourished
    - o Mostly in poor countries
    - ⇨ Childhood stunting
    - ⇨ Lifelong low productivity

- ⌄ 2 billion people obese or overweight
    - o Mostly in wealthy countries
    - ⇨ Diabetes, heart disease, high blood pressure, cancer

- ⌄ 2 billion people with micronutrient deficiencies
    - o Affects all income levels
    - ⇨ Numerous health problems

- ⌄ 600 million people affected by foodborne illness
    - o Affects all income levels
    - ⇨ Can contribute to undernutrition and micronutrient deficiency

Source: WHO 2015.

discussion of food security assessment in chapter 9) and, where necessary, to develop mitigating strategies. (More information is also provided in the "Additional Resources" listed at the end of this chapter.)

Why Do Firms Hold Back from Working More Closely with Smallholder Farmers?

Global agribusiness now has considerable experience engaging with smallholder farmers, but some companies still hold back. That reticence is often linked to risk and the expectation that such engagement would be costly.

The Bigger Picture: The Investment Climate

If frontier and emerging markets—and their smallholder farmers—are to play a greater role in global supply chains, there must be a favorable investment climate, that is, a set of policy, regulatory, and institutional factors sufficiently robust to encourage private sector investment.[1] Important factors include taxes and regulations, financing, policy stability, inflation, exchange rates, corruption, street crime, anticompetitive practices, organized crime, the judicial system, and infrastructure. Weak contract enforcement mechanisms, shifting foreign exchange policies, lack of official (and legal) recognition for farmer cooperatives, poor roads, or high levels of crime can all constrain a firm's scope to engage with small farmers and increase costs.

These factors affect the business climate and economic context more widely and, as such, are the focus of considerable attention by governments and donors, with some countries rapidly improving the "ease of doing business" (World Bank 2016a). To support these efforts, multiple datasets have been developed that are readily accessible to help businesses evaluate potential risks and highlight where new opportunities are opening up. (See, for example, the World Bank's *Doing Business* and *Enabling the Business of Agriculture* series [World Bank 2016a, 2016b]. Also see the "Additional Resources" listed at the end of this chapter.)

In recognition that the development of smallholder agriculture is important for global food supplies and the reduction of poverty and malnutrition, governments and corporations have developed a growing number of public-private mechanisms to promote agribusiness engagement by sharing the risks and funding aspects of sector development (as further discussed in chapter 8 on partnerships). Examples include the muliti-donor Global Agriculture and Food Security Program (GAFSP) and the World Economic Forum New Vision for Agriculture.

Risks Associated with Smallholder Production and Procurement

Agribusinesses have always operated in an uncertain world and have adapted to deal with the inherent risks and price shifts associated with the unpredictability of weather and crop production. Just as there are ways to minimize those risks, so can the risks associated with smallholder procurement be managed.

Smallholders are not a uniform group with a single risk profile. From region to region, country to country, and even within a single country, smallholder farmers and farms vary significantly in capability and capacity. Segmenting smallholders into different categories to evaluate risk and design engagement strategies is important.

Side-selling, low adoption of new practices, or farmer failure to persist with new practices are common risks of working with smallholders—risks that can be reduced through careful program design.

Side-Selling

One of the greatest risks for off-takers is failure to recoup the cost of their investment because farmers divert part or most of their increased production to other buyers—a practice known as side-selling. The structure of the supply chain greatly affects the risk of side-selling. Risk is reduced in a "tight" supply chain where there are relatively few buyers and a high degree of supplier farmer loyalty. In a "loose" supply chain, where many buyers exist and supplier farmers are fickle, investment is riskier because farmers are more likely to side-sell.

Price volatility and the inability to store produce can also create an incentive (and opportunity) to side-sell. Very poor farmers may sometimes find themselves in situations where an immediate financial need can only be met by selling to the highest or first bidder, even if that jeopardizes a higher, more secure income developed over the long term with another firm.

Chapter 6 discusses strategies to reduce side-selling and promote supplier loyalty.

Failure to Adopt New Farming Practices

Another risk for firms is that farmers don't adopt improved agricultural practices despite investments by off-takers or input suppliers aimed at helping them do so. Farmers may not be sufficiently convinced that new practices will benefit them or find they cannot afford new practices or consider them too risky.

Lack of access to financing or, when financing is available, high interest rates can also contribute to the perceived high price tag of improved practices. Experience suggests farmers are more likely to adopt new practices that are *reversible*—that is, where it is not difficult (or expensive) to return to the status quo (Hystra 2015).

Unsustainability of Improved Farming Practices

Some improved agricultural practices are not sustainable for smallholder farmers. After initial enthusiasm, they may decide that practices aimed at increasing productivity are not cost-effective options for their businesses. For example, smallholders will reduce or stop using fertilizer if the required product and labor costs are higher than the additional income generated.

With new inputs, smallholders often look for dramatic and quick yield gains, partly because they do not measure their results closely enough to detect small gains. However, dramatic gains are rarely possible because smallholder yields are constrained by multiple factors that are difficult to address simultaneously.

Efforts to incorporate farmers into a certification program run a similar risk. If farmers determine that the premium for certification is not enough to cover the additional labor requirements or more expensive inputs, they will discontinue the practices, and a firm's investment will be wasted.

The Business Case for Smallholders

It is important to consider the business case from the perspective of smallholders. What motivates and enables their engagement with agribusiness companies? Certainly, smallholders are interested in securing and increasing their incomes.

In general, for smallholders to adopt a new practice, it must be unambiguously beneficial—and preferably quickly. Smallholder farmers can link successfully to vertically integrated value chains if they can engage via fair and transparent contracts with processors and other actors (FAO 2017). They may need access to credit and training, and there may be institutional barriers (formal or informal) that need to be addressed (for example, when a smallholder farmer opens a bank account or when a rural woman attends a training course where most of the participants, or trainers, are men). Moreover, good infrastructure and strong farmers' organizations are important factors that influence smallholder value-chain integration (FAO 2017).

As noted earlier, smallholders might fail to adopt a technology for a variety of reasons. In estimating how farmers will receive a new technological package, outsiders often pay insufficient attention to labor, cash flow, and risk implications. Household labor may be "free" (uncosted), but depending on the season or on whom those additional tasks fall, the opportunity cost may be very real—that is, new tasks can only be taken on if something else is dropped. Hence, understanding how labor is shared within the household can be important.

Cash flow is another issue: rural households face irregular cash flows, with marked seasonality to income and outgoings (including the beginning of the school year), so the impact of additional expense on cash flow (not just net income) may be a key consideration. (Conversely, a technology with perhaps only marginal benefits but that yields income at a cash-scarce time of year may be welcomed). Risk aversion is important, too: even if a new technology delivers better returns *on average*, smallholders may have insufficient savings or other coping mechanisms to survive a bad year (Wiggins 2016).

Assessing Smallholder Constraints to Better Align Farmer and Firm Incentives

This section describes some of the constraints to value chain integration that smallholders may face. Strategies to address those constraints in win-win arrangements—promoting sustainability for both firms and farms—are explored in chapters 2 to 7, which cover finance, aggregation, standards, training, yield gaps, and women's participation.

Ensuring that smallholder farmers adopt improved agricultural practices is a challenge even when the benefits seem obvious to an outsider. Understanding smallholders' constraints when presented with new techniques can help firms design successful interventions. The constraints to be addressed—and proposed mitigating strategies—encompass the areas of education, information, access to high-quality inputs, records and collateral, labor, risk tolerance, climate change adaptation, and attitudes toward success.

Education

Literacy and education levels in rural populations vary widely across regions and within individual countries. Young men tend to have the most formal education, while women and older populations have less. Education levels influence farmers' ability to access and understand training material. Higher education levels correlate with a greater capacity to experiment with improved agricultural techniques and to appropriately assess risk.

Mitigating strategy: Adapting training to participants' education levels increases their ability to access and retain knowledge. Lower literacy levels require more rudimentary explanations and visuals. Chapter 5 elaborates on strategies for adapting training.

Information

The gap between smallholders' knowledge of agricultural practices and the knowledge available at agricultural research institutions is huge. Most smallholders rely on other farmers and occasional visits from government or nonprofit extension staff for information. Although radio, television, short message service (SMS) texts, and video represent increasingly important media, they are not universally available, and the information provided may not be sufficient.

Mitigating strategy: In-depth market research carried out before program design and updated during implementation will help firms identify farmers' information gaps and respond to their needs. Farmer segmentation can help in targeting training for farmers.

Access to High-Quality Inputs

Few financial resources, poor technical knowledge, and physical distance combine to inhibit smallholders' ability to obtain and effectively use high-quality inputs. Many smallholders, particularly in Africa, do not have a well-stocked agro-retailer within a reasonable distance. Even when inputs are accessible, the widespread existence of counterfeit and poor-quality products reduces trust in the products' effectiveness.

Mitigating strategy: Outgrower schemes (contract farming) and other input delivery models can improve access to high-quality inputs. If side-selling is a risk, partnerships with input suppliers and financial institutions can reduce the off-taker risk (as further discussed in chapters 2 and 6).

Farm Records and Collateral

Many, perhaps most, smallholders do not keep written records, so their ability to robustly evaluate the benefits of new agricultural practices is reduced. Even if yields increase, many improved practices entail higher costs for inputs or labor. Without the ability to record and compare costs and revenues, farmers may not be able to confidently assess whether their profitability has increased. Without written records, farmers also face greater difficulty obtaining bank financing—a problem compounded by lack of land title or other collateral.

Mitigating strategy: Firms may include a farm management component, such as record keeping, within a larger training package. Firms also increasingly keep smallholder farm management records—a task assisted by new farm management applications. Chapter 6 discusses farm management training techniques.

Labor

Production area and intensity on small farms is highly dependent on the amount of family labor available. New practices to improve yields or sustainability often require more labor. If the new practices increase revenue, farmers can hire casual labor if it is available, cash-flow permitting, although this may give rise to an additional risk: that the farmer employs children.

Mitigating strategy: Careful analysis of increased labor needs can identify labor shortages. Solutions might entail shifts in household responsibilities or community labor-sharing arrangements (see chapter 7 on women's roles in agriculture).

Attitudes toward Risk

Smallholders may be unwilling to adopt new practices if the outcomes are uncertain or the benefits take time to manifest. Research in Uganda highlights the role of culture and group dynamics in attitudes toward risk, with implications for how to best address smallholder risk aversion (D'Exelle and Verschoor 2015; Wiggins 2016).

Risk aversion among smallholders makes sense: smallholders face the same risks as large farms—including crop diseases, inadequate rainfall, flooding, high input prices, and low crop prices—but these risks affect smallholders differently. Most smallholders lack risk mitigation mechanisms, such as crop insurance and hedging, though this is beginning to change. In addition, the consequences of failure are more severe for smallholders. In countries with limited social services, a reduction in farm income can lead to hunger or the inability to meet medical or education expenses. Risk taking has much greater consequences for smallholders lacking a financial or social safety net. New agricultural practices should be carefully tested before they are widely promoted. And firms should take care not to expose their suppliers or clients to excessive risks that could damage their livelihoods.

Mitigating strategy: Firms may encourage farmers to adopt new strategies on a portion of their land so they can test the practice before expanding to a larger area. Facilitating access to loans accompanied by crop insurance can also help ensure that farmers have a financial safety net in case crops fail. The tools and strategies identified in this handbook are intended to reduce risk for farmers and support their adoption of good practices.

Climate Change Adaptation

Low-income countries are more vulnerable to climate change because of poverty and dependence on agriculture. Climate change will affect every aspect of farming, and the smallholders' adoption of sustainable land, water, fishery, and forestry management practices will be crucial to efforts to adapt to climate change (FAO 2017).

Mitigating strategy: There is no simple fix. Firms, and their development partners, can link to the latest research results and help smallholders build resilience by prioritizing resilient agricultural practices (see chapters 6 and 10). Both firms and farmers have an important stake in climate change adaptation.

Attitudes toward Success

Intuitively, a successful demonstration by a lead farmer should encourage neighboring farmers to adopt new production techniques. In practice, however, cultural attitudes toward success vary. In some contexts, dramatic increases in production may provoke fatalism, envy, theft, or even accusations of sorcery. These dynamics may dissuade farmers from seeking higher yields.

Mitigating strategy: Careful partnerships with farmer leaders during implementation can highlight negative community reactions that might emerge as a result of program implementation. Chapter 5 offers insights into working with farmer leaders.

Attention to Detail

There is no "one size fits all" solution for strengthening smallholder supply chains. Different crops, origins, regions, producer group characteristics, supply chain structures, and retail market dynamics will all affect

FIGURE 1.2 Steps for Effective Program Design to Strengthen Smallholder Value Chains

PHASE 1: PLAN and DESIGN					
A. Perform a sector analysis ->	B. Segment farmers ->	C. Understand environmental and social risk	A. Prioritize goals and estimate timeframe ->	B. Analyze costs and benefits ->	C. Identify activities based on goals
STEP 1: COLLECT INFORMATION			STEP 2: ANALYZE AND DESIGN		

feasibility and effectiveness. Here, no less than in other business operations, careful planning and program design are needed and will help reduce risk.

For some firms that have not previously worked with smallholders, some of the specifics of the preparatory work required may be new, though there will certainly be analogous steps in the development of other supply chains. In essence, there's a need to collect information, analyze information, and use that result to inform program design (figure 1.2). Chapter 9 explores methods for data collection in more detail.

The following chapters explore smallholder-related topics in more detail, covering financing and partnerships as well as practical considerations of working with smallholders and options available to increase productivity.

Note

1. A frontier market is a developing country that is more developed than the least developing countries but too small to be considered an emerging market. The term "Frontier Market" was coined when IFC Emerging Markets Database (EMDB), led by Farida Khambata, began publishing data on smaller markets in 1992. Standard and Poor's bought EMDB from IFC in 1999.

References

AB InBev (Anheuser Busch-InBev). 2017. "Achieving More Together: Anheuser-Busch InBev Annual Report 2016." http://www.ab-inbev.com/content/dam /universaltemplate/ab-inbev/investors/reports-and-filings/annual-and-hy -reports/2017/03/ABI_AR16_ENG.pdf.

D'Exelle, B., and A. Verschoor. 2015. "Investment Behaviour, Risk Sharing and Social Distance." *Economic Journal* 125 (584): 777–802.

DutchNews.nl. 2013. "Animal Feed Withdrawn from Hundreds of Farms after Toxin Scare." *DutchNews.nl*, March 7. http://www.dutchnews.nl/news/archives/2013/03 /animal_feed_withdrawn_from_hun/.

Economist. 2017. "What's in a Name? Defining Emerging Markets: A Self-Fulfilling Prophecy." October 7. https://www.economist.com/news/special-report/21729866 -self-fulfilling-prophecy-defining-emerging-markets.

EcoVadis. n.d. "What Is Sustainable Sourcing?" EcoVadis web page, accessed April 10, 2017. http://www.ecovadis.com/sustainable-sourcing/.

Ecovia Intellligence. 2017. "Predictions for Sustainable Foods in 2017." Ecovia Intelligence (formerly known as Organic Monitor) web page, posted January 5, 2017. http://www.ecoviaint.com/r0401/.

FAO (Food and Agriculture Organization of the United Nations). 2017. *The Future of Food and Agriculture: Trends and Challenges.* Rome: FAO.

Fischer, T., D. Byerlee, and G. O. Edmeades. 2014. *Crop Yields and Global Food Security: Will Yield Increase Continue to Feed the World?* Canberra: Australian Centre for International Agricultural Research (ACIAR).

FSA UK (Food Standards Agency U.K.). 2014. "Okra and Curry Leaves from India under Regulation (EU) No 885/2014." Food Standards Agency web page, last updated September 12, 2014. https://www.food.gov.uk/business-industry/imports /banned_restricted/highrisknonpoao-885-2014.

Hystra. 2015. "Smallholder Farmers and Business: 15 Pioneering Collaborations for Improved Productivity and Sustainability." Research report, Hystra, Paris.

IFC (International Finance Corporation of the World Bank Group). 2017. "IFC Food Safety Toolkit." IFC, World Bank, Washington, DC.

Mondelez International. n.d. "Sustainable Resources and Agriculture." Mondelez International web page, accessed April 11 2017. http://www.mondelezinternational .com/well-being/sustainable-resources-and-agriculture.

Nestlé. 2017. "Nestlé in Society: Creating Shared Value and Meeting Our Commitments 2016." Summary report, Nestlé, Vevey, Switzerland.

Probst, C., H. Njapau, and P. J. Cotty. 2007. "Outbreak of Acute Aflatoxicosis in Kenya in 2004: Identification of the Causal Agent." *Applied and Environmental Microbiology* 73 (8): 2762–64.

Schraeder, C. 2016. "These 3 Consumer Trends Are Dominating the Food Industry. ForbesBrand*Voice* article, September 14. https://www.forbes.com/sites/cargill /2016/09/14/3-consumer-trends-dominating-food-industry/#71ec404e10c8.

WHO (World Health Organization). 2015. "Food Safety." Fact Sheet No. 399, reviewed October 2017. http://www.who.int/mediacentre/factsheets/fs399/en/.

Wiggins, S. 2016. "Risk Aversion among Smallholder Farmers in Uganda." Background paper for the "Behavioural Analysis of Agricultural Investment Decisions in Uganda" project of the U.K. Department of International Development (DFID) and Economic Social and Research Council (ESRC) Growth Research Programme (DEGRP).

World Bank. 2016a. *Doing Business 2017: Equal Opportunity for All.* Washington, DC: World Bank.

———. 2016b. *Enabling the Business of Agriculture 2016: Comparing Regulatory Good Practices.* Washington, DC: World Bank.

Additional Resources

Smallholder Farmers

CTA (Technical Center for Agricultural and Rural Cooperation). 2012. "Agriculture: Smallholder Value Chains." *This Is Africa: A Global Perspective Special Report* Dec/Jan 2012. https://slidex.tips/download/africa-this-is-agriculture-smallholder -value-chains-private-sector-commercialisi.

FAO (Food and Agriculture Organization of the United Nations). 2014. *The State of Food and Agriculture: Innovation in Family Farming.* Rome: FAO.

Pretty, J., W. J. Sutherland, J. Ashby, J. Auburn, D. Baulcombe, M. Bell, J. Bentley, et al. 2010. "The Top 100 Questions of Importance to the Future of Global Agriculture." *International Journal of Agricultural Sustainability* 8 (4): 219–36.

World Bank and UNCTAD (United Nations Conference on Trade and Development). 2017. "Outgrower Schemes: How to Increase the Chances of Success." Responsible Agricultural Investment (RAI) Knowledge into Action Note No. 4, World Bank, Washington, DC; UNCTAD, New York. http://documents.worldbank.org/curated /en/203541521090030245/pdf/124279-BRI-PUBLIC-KN04.pdf.

Investment Climate

Schwab, Klaus, ed. 2016. *The Global Competitiveness Report 2016–2017.* Geneva: World Economic Forum.

Transparency International. n.d. Website for information on corruption in more than 100 countries, TI, Brussels. https://www.transparency.org.

World Bank. 2017. *Doing Business 2018:* Reforming to Create Jobs. Washington, DC: World Bank.

———. 2017. *Enabling the Business of Agriculture 2017.* Washington, DC: World Bank.

———. n.d. World Bank Enterprise Surveys of firm-level data, accessed April 11, 2017. http://www.enterprisesurveys.org/.

World Bank and UNCTAD (United Nations Conference on Trade and Development). 2017. "Creating an Enabling Environment." Responsible Agricultural Investment (RAI) Knowledge into Action Note No. 5, World Bank, Washington, DC; UNCTAD, New York. http://documents.worldbank.org/curated/en/324441521090199064/pdf /124280-BRI-PUBLIC-KN05.pdf.

Tools for Data Collection and Planning

Christen, R. P., and J. Anderson. 2013. "Segmentation of Smallholder Households: Meeting the Range of Financial Needs in Agricultural Families." Focus Note No. 85, Consultative Group to Assist the Poor (CGAP), Washington, DC.

EMMA (Emergency Market Mapping and Analysis). n.d. "Emergency Market Mapping and Analysis Toolkit." Practical information and tools for mapping markets. http:// www.emma-toolkit.org/.

Hakemulder, Roel, et al. 2015. *Value Chain Development for Decent Work: How to Create Employment and Improve Working Conditions in Targeted Sectors.* 2nd ed. Geneva: International Labour Organization (ILO). [Includes a section on market systems research and analysis]

Market Systems and Value Chain Development

DFID (U.K. Department for International Development). 2014. "Agriculture and Private Sector." Agriculture and Growth evidence paper series, DFID, London.

Donovan, J., S. Franzel, M. Cunha, A. Gyau, and D. Mithöfer. 2015. "Guides for Value Chain Development: A Comparative Review." *Journal of Agribusiness in Developing and Emerging Economies* 5 (1): 2–23.

GTZ (German Agency for Technical Cooperation [Deutsche Gesellschaft für Internationale Zusammenarbeit]). 2007. *Value Links Manual: A Methodology for Value Chain Promotion.* Eschborn: GTZ.

Humphrey, J. 2014. "Market Systems Approaches: A Literature Review." Paper, BEAMExchange. https://beamexchange.org/uploads/filer_public/b2/3a/b23a3505 -e3f1-4f63-8c0c-aeb35a763f91/beamliteraturereview.pdf.

McVay, M., and A. Snelgrove. 2007. "Program Design for Value Chain Initiatives. Information to Action: A Toolkit Series for Market Development Practitioners." Toolkit, Mennonite Economic Development Associates, Lancaster, PA.

Neven, D. 2014. *Developing Sustainable Food Value Chains: Guiding Principles.* Rome: Food and Agricultural Organization of the United Nations.

Sopov, M., Y. Saavedra, W. Vellema, Y. Sertse, and H. Verjans. 2014. *Is Inclusive Business for You? Managing and Upscaling an Inclusive Company: Lessons from the Field.* Wageningen, Netherlands: Centre for Development Innovation, Wageningen UR.

The Springfield Centre. 2014. "The Operational Guide for the Making Markets Work for the Poor (M4P) Approach." 2nd ed. Guide prepared on behalf of the Swiss Agency for Development and Cooperation, Bern; and U.K. Department for International Development, London.

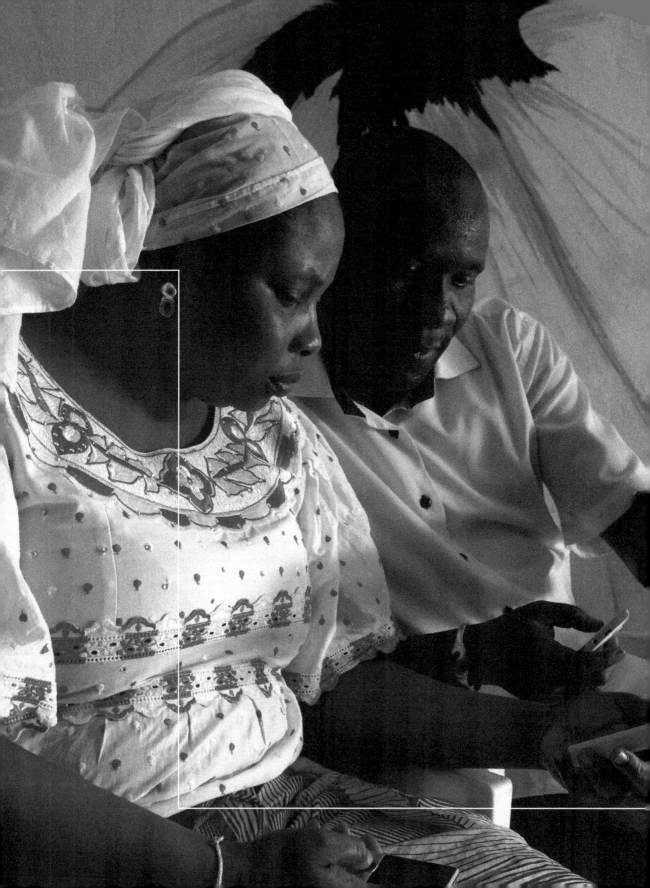

CHAPTER 2
AGRICULTURAL FINANCE AND AGRIBUSINESSES

KEY MESSAGES

➡ Finance is a useful tool for agribusiness companies to secure their business transactions with farmers.

➡ Business transactions backed by critical insights of farmers can reduce risks and costs in providing financial services.

➡ Financial services can be directly provided by the agribusiness companies and through financial institutions.

➡ Additional services such as insurance and digital payments can improve the efficiency and lower the risk of the transactions.

Making Finance Accessible to Smallholder Farmers: The Business Case

Access to finance for smallholder farmers can create a virtuous cycle: preharvest finance allows farmers to access high-quality inputs, which boost productivity and crop quality while helping ensure a more reliable supply chain for agribusiness companies. Postharvest finance is critical for cost-efficient aggregation of crops. Considering the numerous risks in dealing with smallholders, improving access to finance presents an opportunity to make agribusiness companies and their business operations more efficient and resilient.

A widely used definition of "agribusiness" includes all the businesses along the agriculture value chains, from provision of inputs to production, processing, trading, and retailing. In this chapter, agribusiness companies mainly refer to off-takers that buy agricultural products from farmers to process, trade, and so on.

Agribusiness companies that regularly contact smallholder suppliers know more about their suppliers than local banks do, and therefore have a strong advantage in providing or promoting financial services to smallholder farmers. The companies that procure crops from smallholder farmers often try to build a stable supply chain by promising the amount and price of the purchase and maintaining frequent contacts with the farmers (World Bank 2007). These transactions produce important insights about the farmers' creditworthiness that have been used to develop financial services, mainly credit for crop production. The transaction costs of these services can be minimized by bundling them with the procurement of the crops (Johnston and Meyer 2008).

There are two main ways to deliver such financial services:

- Direct lending by the agribusiness companies

- Lending through financial institutions (FIs) (Johnston and Meyer 2008; Miller and Jones 2010).

In both scenarios, other financial services, such as payments and insurance, are often included to make the business transactions more efficient by controlling transaction costs and managing risks. These delivery modalities are not mutually exclusive; rather, they often complement each other. Agribusiness companies tend to provide funds or inputs on credit for agriculture production to loyal and creditworthy ≈ farmers, leaving other farmers and other financial needs to be served by financial institutions.

The two financing models entail different sets of advantages and limitations, as summarized in table 2.1 and further discussed in this chapter.

TABLE 2.1 Advantages and Challenges for Agribusiness Firms of Smallholder Financing Models: Direct Financing versus Financing through FIs

Financing model	Advantages	Challenges
Both models	• Increased loyalty from suppliers and buyers	• Maintaining stable business transactions with farmers • Risk of side-selling (selling production to another agribusiness) by farmers who have received financing, particularly if loan repayment is through the agribusiness
Direct financing by agribusiness companies	• Easier to set up and control (no coordination required with financial institutions) • Allows strong control and connections with farmers	• Limited scope of the financial product along the business transactions • Much or most credit in the form of in-kind (inputs) • Opportunity costs and management of cash flow • Financing not a core business for the agribusiness • Limited to commercial farmers in tight value chains
Financing through FIs	• Enables scaling up of financing to farmers, while protecting own balance sheet • Enables focus on core business, leaving credit processes to financial partner • Broad range of financial products for farmers that support agriculture and nonagricultural activities and help cope with emergencies • Clarity in the terms of credit and other financial transactions • Loan repayment either directly to FI by the farmer or through the agribusinesses (when farmers deliver, agribusiness deducts the loan repayment for the FI)	• Possibility that FIs incur higher transaction costs and require collateral, increasing cost for farmers • FI loan processing requirements, including paperwork • Possible additional burden of coordination with FIs • Possibility that no local FIs are willing to partner with agribusiness companies

Note: FIs = financial institutions.

Overview

Relations between agricultural value chain actors—especially between agribusiness companies and farmers—are transforming from opportunistic relations to longer-term relations. Increased agricultural productivity, higher value added, and improved resilience to climate change require both longer-term and short-term investments. At the same time, improved logistics and consumers' increasing preference for specific quality and origin standards for produce bring the value chain actors closer to each other, especially to farmers (World Bank 2007).

In response, an increasing number of agribusiness companies in frontier and emerging markets have established formal and informal contract farming arrangements to secure a stable supply of crops. Integrating agricultural production into their businesses will minimize the operational risk of dealing with smallholder farmers for the agribusiness companies, but it is either too costly or not feasible, especially if the land is not easily available. However, ad hoc procurement transactions with farmers may pose unmanageable risks for agribusiness companies in exchange for operational flexibility. Thus, contract farming is an engagement model gaining popularity, among other options. Formal and informal contract farming has the following characteristics:

- *Formal and informal farming contracts* facilitate a stable supply of crops through predefined agreements covering important aspects such as product amount, quality, and price; transaction timing; and payment terms.

- *Contract contents and modalities* vary widely depending on the commodities, intensity of the buyer-seller relations, and characteristics of the farmers.

- *Formal contracts* can cover a wide range of aspects of the transactions.

- *Informal agreements* without legally binding documents are often used when contracting smallholder farmers.

Contract farming arrangements often contain mitigation mechanisms for certain risks that are associated with the involvement of smallholder farmers, such as side-selling. These built-in mechanisms in the formal and informal contracts reduce key risks for both the agribusiness companies (production risks) and the smallholder farmers (market risks).

The production risk is addressed through various services provided to the farmers, including agricultural inputs, technical assistance, technology transfer, market information, and quality control mechanisms. These additional services are provided to ensure the quality and quantity of the crops as well as to secure long-term relations with the farmers.

From the farmers' point of view, one of the biggest benefits is a guaranteed market, often with predefined price (or a predefined minimum price to reduce the risk of nondelivery when prices go up) and payment terms. Thus, market and price risks are minimized.

Further risk mitigation and cost optimization can be achieved by involving producer organizations in the value chains. Contracting numerous smallholder farmers is costly and difficult to manage. Thus, agribusiness companies often contract producer organizations to source crops in a cost-efficient manner. In the contracts, the organizations distribute inputs, disseminate technical knowledge, and aggregate the crops.

Although well-managed organizations could mitigate some risks at the individual farmers' level, their governance and management may become an additional risk for the transaction. Therefore, careful assessment is required to understand their strengths and cohesiveness. Assessment tools, such as those provided by SCOPEinsight, enable agribusinesses to identify reliable organizations and to design technical assistance tailored to their needs.[1]

Organizing farmers for a specific business transaction is an option but one that often requires considerable time and resources. Alternatively, some agribusiness companies choose to deal exclusively with lead farmers or nucleus farms, which handle relations with other smallholder farmers.

The links between the agribusiness companies and the farmers in value chains vary widely depending on the tightness or looseness of the chains (figure 2.1).

In addition to the commodities, the local or country context, including the regulatory framework, often influences the nature of the value chains. Between tight and loose value chains are many variations, and therefore, a specific analysis is required to understand the looseness or tightness of the chains (see table 2.2.).

Providing finance along value chains—typically by agribusiness companies and other value chain actors to farmers—further smooths the transactions and improves the efficiency of the value chains. The benefits are particularly significant when smallholder farmers face financial constraints. Indeed, this is one of the largest constraints of smallholder farming in low- and middle-income markets where most FIs are not

TABLE 2.2 **Product-Related Aspects of Tight and Loose Value Chains in Contract Farming**

Aspect	Tight value chains	Loose value chains
Characteristics	Reflect products that • Require centralized logistics and processing (for example, sugar, cotton, palm oil, and rubber) • Have certain qualities such as perishability (for example, fruits, dairy) • Aim for niche markets (such as fair trade products)	• Farmers could sell to multiple buyers • Several intermediaries involved • Often involve staple crops
How it works	Products flow through a "constriction" point, at which agribusinesses can offer finance and other services to the farmers supplying them	Products typically traded through spot markets or other informal arrangements
Overall impact	Long-term business relations between buyers and producers backed by formal contracts	• Difficulty of maintaining contracts between buyers and producers • Given risk of side-selling, contracts lack value-added services such as inputs, technical assistance, and finance

actively lending to the agriculture sector. Under such circumstance, value chains provide an effective platform for the provision of financial services for smallholder farmers.

Value chain actors such as large agribusinesses, local processors, traders, and input suppliers have always played a significant role in financing commercial farmers, especially in tight value chains. They supply about 40 percent and 13 percent of the short-term financing needs of commercial smallholder farmers in tight and loose value chains, respectively (Dalberg 2016). In both chains, value chain actors are the most important sources of short-term funds, followed by formal FIs (figure 2.1).

Direct Lending to Farmers by Agribusiness Companies

In lending to smallholder farmers, agribusiness companies possess critical advantages: existing business transactions that farmers value, records from past transactions, and often field presence from agents or staff of the agribusiness who can monitor the clients. Lending products typically build on these elements, which help manage risks and reduce transaction costs (Johnston and Meyer 2008).

FIGURE 2.1 Sources of Finance for Commercial Smallholder Farmers

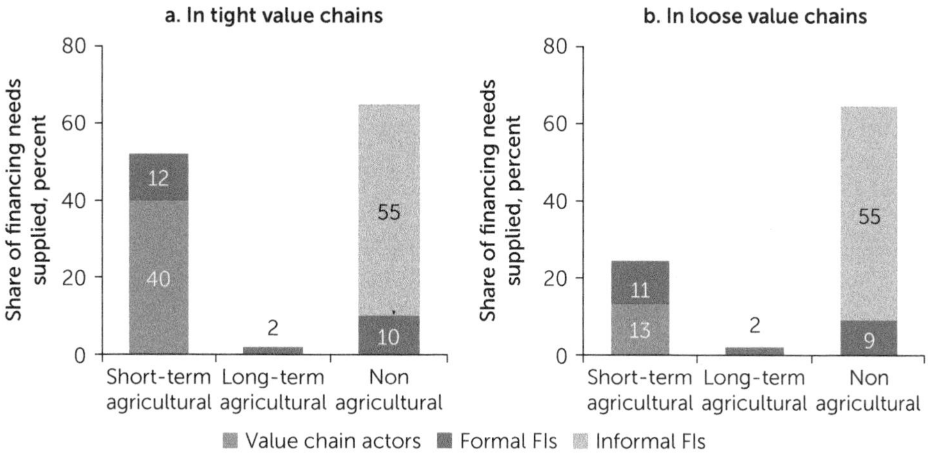

Source: Dalberg 2016.
Note: FIs = financial institutions. "Value chain actors" primarily refer to agribusinesses, processors, traders, or input suppliers.

Well-designed and executed business transactions with farmers contain incentive mechanisms to attract and retain farmers who can produce agricultural products in demand. The selected smallholder farmers often possess specific skills and adaptive capacity as well as innovative attitudes and values (Hernández 2017). In some cases, they are organized in producer organizations and closely monitored by the agribusiness companies through repeated business transactions. In this scenario, well-integrated farmers have proved their creditworthiness through past behavior in contracts. The additional transaction costs of the loans can be minimized by incorporating the lending operation into their normal business transactions.

These direct lending products should be designed based on a detailed knowledge of the value chain, including the actors, their functions, and the financial flows in the chain. A diagnostic analysis of the chain will help reveal interactions and relations between various value chain actors beyond the business relations of the agribusiness companies. The value chain actors usually include input suppliers, farmers, traders, processors, retailers and service providers such as extension services and financial institutions. In addition to the product flows in the chain, an analysis of financial flows will inform current financial transactions between value chain actors, representing critical financial arrangements made to produce, transport, and process crops (Miller and Jones 2010).

Combining the information from the analysis and insights of the agribusiness companies indicates potential entry points and key design features of the lending products.

Direct lending should ideally address critical financial requirements of the smallholder farmers that are necessary to fulfill the agreements with the agribusiness companies. Farmers face diverse financial requirements from their households and from both on- and off-farm business activities (Christen and Anderson 2013; Hazell and Rahman 2014). Some of these requirements are covered by financial services in and out of the value chains. For example, smallholder households often engage in various productive activities in addition to farming. Some farmers use income from these off-farm activities to finance agricultural production, but at the same time, they require savings and loan products to smooth their income and handle household expenses. Other farmers rely on external finance to produce crops. Agriculture loans for such farmers would need to allow repayments only after the harvest as opposed to frequent repayments in consumer loans.

Long-term finance for capital investments is critical for any farmer households to optimize and grow their productive activities. Farmers may also need other financial products for their household spending. However, non-agriculture funding needs are mostly covered by informal FIs at present, and long-term finance is often extremely limited (as shown in figure 2.2). The agribusiness companies should be aware of the diverse financial needs of the smallholder farmers in their value chains and the financial sources currently used.

Direct Lending Models and Incentive Mechanisms

Well-structured preharvest lending arrangements create incentives that increase the farmers' loyalty and reduce side-selling. Such lending mechanisms are embedded in the contract farming or informal agreements based on trust to mitigate risks and lower costs. Finance is typically provided as inputs on credit, in cash, or both. The debt is recovered directly, by deducting payments from the farmers at the point of output sale. Such lending models often include other products and services such as technical assistance to enhance farmer productivity and ensure repayment. This entails partnerships with other value chain actors such as input suppliers and technical assistance providers.

The contents of the package and engagement with partners vary widely depending on value chains and country context. In any case, agribusinesses that lend to smallholders would need systems like those of FIs to assess risks and monitor clients (Johnston and Meyer 2008). This structure can be applied to postharvest financing for aggregation where agribusiness companies advance finance to intermediaries (traders and producer organizations) to aggregate agricultural products. The repayments are made both in-kind and by subtracting from the sales when the crops are delivered. In many cases, agribusinesses engaged in direct lending could benefit from investing in credit processing systems and scorecards, similar to what an FI would have.

Value chain finance requires conducive enabling environments in both the financial and agriculture sectors. Because value chain financing models are dependent on the operating conditions and characteristics of the institutions in the chains, building an enabling environment is of critical importance. This is time-consuming work requiring coordination and involvement of various public and private institutions. Among other elements of a conducive business environment, safety and quality standards as well as contract enforcement often have a particular relevance in strengthening the chains and contracts (Miller and Jones 2010).

The cases presented in boxes 2.1, 2.2, and 2.3 describe typical value chain finance models for direct lending that have clear value propositions as well as limitations.

BOX 2.1

In Practice: The Ginger Value Chain in Vietnam

Background

Ginger production in Vietnam has been growing in response to strong global demand. Minh Be, a ginger trading company, took advantage of this market growth and successfully built solid business relations with ginger-growing smallholder farmers in the surrounding regions of the country.

Financing Model

Minh Be collects row ginger from farmers and cleans and packages it before selling it to the exporting company and retailers in Hanoi. In addition to providing seedlings and extension services, the

box continued

BOX 2.1

In Practice: The Ginger Value Chain in Vietnam *(Continued)*

company advances inputs such as seeds and fertilizers to a group of ginger growers with whom it has long-term business relations. This in-kind loan arrangement carries no interest but requires the borrowers to sell their ginger to the company at a discounted price and to repay the value of the inputs (at market value at the time of purchase) at the end of the harvest season. Working capital loans are also offered to purchase inputs and pay for on- and off-farm activities beyond ginger production.

The company provides loans flexibly by taking advantage of its long-term business relations: there are no predefined terms (usually up to 12 months) and no formal loan contracts. The agreement is made verbally and kept in a simple notebook. According to the company, there have been no defaulted loans. To finance its lending activities, the company borrows from better-off farmers, to whom it pays some interest.

Minh Be provides all these financial services primarily to maintain and improve its trade relations with the farmers. Although loans from public FIs are available, farmers prefer to borrow from the company because the loans are flexible and do not require any application forms, business plans, or collateral.

Beneficiaries

The farmers who have long-term business relations with Minh Be receive a complete package of support from the company including loans, inputs, and technical assistance. Some of the new growers became contracted suppliers through the matching-grant support of an International Fund for Agricultural Development (IFAD) project. The ginger production inputs were initially subsidized by the grant. These farmers may become eligible for loans in the future as they build trust through the business transactions.

Challenges

The growing demand for ginger offers greater business opportunities for the company, requiring additional investments such as equipment, warehouses, and capital to finance ginger growers. The limited access to formal finance of both Minh Be and the ginger growers poses a clear challenge for the future expansion.

Source: Hernández 2017.

BOX 2.2

In Practice: The Cotton Value Chain in Zambia

Background

Dunavant[a] and Cargill, the two largest cotton processors in Zambia, had a market share of around 90 percent and procured cotton from more than 160,000 farmers in 2006.

Financing Model

Both companies advanced high-quality inputs to cotton farmers, including seeds, fertilizer, and pesticide. After harvest, farmers brought the cotton to nearby buying points and received cash (the sales proceeds minus the cost of inputs) upon delivery based on the contracts. The transactions were based on trust and commercial incentive. The risk of side-selling was minimized through the monopolistic position of the companies and the attractive input packages.

The contracted farmers also received extensive training to ensure the stable supply of high-quality raw materials. For example, Dunavant partnered with the government of Zambia and donors to deliver tailored extension services to the cotton farmers.

The loan repayment rate remained consistently above 95 percent in the early 2000s although the companies had gone through a hike of defaults in the late 1990s, mainly because smaller processors entered the cotton market, which had induced side-selling.

Challenges

Side-selling increased in the past because of the changing competitive landscape, price fluctuations of the cotton market, and devaluation of the local currency, which discouraged some farmers and buyers from honoring contracts.

Sources: GPFI and IFC 2012; Tschirley and Kabwe 2009.
a. Dunavant was acquired by a South African company and became NWK Agri-Services in 2012.

BOX 2.3

In Practice: Coffee Value Chain Financing

Background

ECOM Agroindustrial Corp. Ltd. is a global commodity trading and processing company specializing in coffee, cotton, cocoa, and sugar globally. The company is one of the top coffee traders in the

box continued

BOX 2.3

In Practice: Coffee Value Chain Financing *(Continued)*

world and procures high-quality coffee beans from smallholder farmers for large buyers including Nestlé and Starbucks. In addition to finance, it provides technical assistance to farmers to increase production yields, improve quality, and promote certification of the products.

Financing Model

ECOM provides seasonal credits to coffee-producing farmers in countries including Costa Rica, Guatemala, Honduras, Mexico, and Nicaragua. The short- and mid-term finance is provided against future delivery of coffee for various farmers' financial needs throughout the production cycle, such as purchase of inputs, the maintenance of the coffee plants, and harvesting. The agronomists and credit officers of ECOM's local operating companies visit potential borrowing farms to determine their production capacity and validate their creditworthiness. Based on this assessment, the local credit officers decide the loan size, typically under $1,000, and manage the lending process from credit approval to monitoring.

Results

From 2007 to 2012, ECOM purchased more than 81,000 metric tons of certified coffee, representing $14.7 million in additional income for coffee farmers. Through these transactions, the support for farmers, including finance, increased farmers' productivity (in some cases by more than 40 percent) as well as their loyalty to ECOM, resulting in a more stable supply chain and increased trade volumes.

Source: IFC, https://www.ifc.org/wps/wcm/connect/90a79852-8b27-4810-a276-de17fa58d505/ECOM.pdf?MOD =AJPERES.

Limitations of Direct Lending

Although the direct lending model brings clear benefits for agribusiness companies, there are also important limitations:

- *Limited scope of the financial product:* The direct financial services tend to cover very specific financial needs of the farmers (for example, credit for crop production) along the business transactions (Miller and Jones 2010). Therefore, other critical financial constraints may remain unattended, and as a result, farmers may become incapable of supplying the crops in the long run.

- *Higher cost of lending:* Financing is not a core business of the agribusiness companies. Opportunity costs may become significant, especially when financial resources are limited and additional investments are required to grow their main business operations (Johnston and Meyer 2008; Milder 2008). Moreover, the companies need to allocate their resources to cover the operational costs and manage cash flow and risks related to lending. Such costs might be passed on to farmers in the form of the obligation to sell to the agribusiness at a discounted price that often reflects the costs of inputs provided. Farmers could possibly access cheaper funds than those from local FIs, thanks to the competitive financing that agribusinesses bring—meaning that some agribusinesses, mostly international companies, have access to cheaper funding in international markets, which they can use to finance their farmers.

- *Limited ability to scale up:* Agribusinesses' limited access to finance may be a challenge for the scaling up of direct lending.

- *Limited to commercial farmers in tight value chains:* As the three cases in boxes 2.1, 2.2, and 2.3 indicate, agribusiness companies typically establish long-term business relations with, and provide finance to, commercial farmers in tight value chains. Those farmers in loose value chains are difficult to finance, mainly for lack of formal contracting relations (an enforcement mechanism for repayment). The agribusiness companies in loose value chains would require additional risk management mechanisms, which often require coordination and collaboration with other stakeholders including FIs.

Attracting FIs Lending for Farmers Delivering to an Agribusiness or Off-Taker

Over the years, agribusiness companies have recognized the possibility of working with FIs to lend to smallholder farmers. Agribusiness companies lend to farmers usually in the absence of FIs lending to these farmers. Formal FIs, including banks and microfinance institutions (MFIs), may not be physically present in the rural areas. In addition, suitable financial products are not offered owing to lack of strategic interest in the sector or limited sector knowledge.

Although informal arrangements through local money lenders may be available, these arrangements may not serve the requirements of the agribusiness companies. As the previous section noted, borrowing funds to on-lend to farmers can become a burden on companies' balance sheets in terms of both cash flow and opportunity costs. Provision of financial services is usually not considered as a core competency or core business for agribusinesses. Their limitation in this respect could prevent agribusiness companies from growing and from engaging more smallholder farmers.

Benefits of FI Involvement

Involvement of FIs could strengthen the business transactions of the agribusiness companies and the value chains. Some formal FIs are attracted to the business opportunities in the agriculture sector and are exploring new business models in providing financial services (Milder 2008). A wider range of financial products from the FIs could increase the resilience of small farmers and, as a result, stabilize the business transactions in the value chains. For example, saving products and loans outside of the value chain transactions would enable farmers to cope with emergencies and diversify their income sources beyond the crops they produce for the agribusiness companies. The smallholder farmers may also be able to build credit records, thus gaining opportunities to access larger credit from FIs to expand their business activities. In addition, the increased flow of credit from FIs may allow the agribusiness companies to engage with a new set of small farmers as the business grows.

Financing from agribusiness companies and FIs are not mutually exclusive but could often complement each other. Agribusinesses tend to focus on loyal and medium-to-large farmers owing to the constraints mentioned earlier, such as limited funding and additional operational costs for financing. Thus, other farmers rely on different sources including self-financing and formal and informal finance providers. The focus of the financing could also vary. Funding from agribusinesses tends to exclusively cover short-term working capital requirements or in-kind input loans, while FIs can offer additional financial products such as personal and school fee loans as well as savings, insurance, payment services, and so on to meet the broader financial needs of agricultural households (Miller and Jones 2010).

There is a compelling business case for FIs—especially those already active in agriculture—to lend to smallholder farmers in agribusiness value chains. Through working with agribusiness companies, FIs could lend to low-risk farmers who have access to reliable markets, possibly with track records from past transactions (Milder 2008). In other words, FIs could reduce costs and risks by delegating the screening and monitoring of the borrowers to the agribusiness companies. The farmers may also have access to benefits that improve their productivity, such as technical assistance and high-value inputs. Provision of these services would further reduce their credit risk and increase cross-selling opportunities for the FIs. In addition, FIs could also reduce transactions costs by combining financial services and business transactions of agribusiness companies. For example, FIs often receive loan repayments from the agribusiness companies instead of a large number of farmers (borrowers). The agribusiness companies subtract loan principles and interests from the payments when they buy agricultural products from farmers.

FI Lending Models and Risk Mitigation Mechanisms

The numerous ways to bring in FIs to lend to the farmers in value chains fall into two broad subcategories. In the first, agribusiness companies provide some guarantees or share risks so that FIs could lend to the farmers. In the second model, FIs take the full risk in lending, but the transactions are often based on tripartite arrangements between FIs, agribusinesses, and farmers whereby the agribusiness commits to buy production from farmers.

In both models, the financial arrangements tend to be customized to the value chain and country context. Therefore, deep understanding of value chains and farmers is still indispensable, and the agribusiness companies normally contribute the private information on farmers (borrowers) gained through the business transactions. Additional risk mitigation mechanisms are often introduced regardless of the models above, typically structured by the development financial institutions, such as International Finance Corporation (IFC), that share risks with the participating FIs.

The two cases described in boxes 2.4 and 2.5 illustrate various arrangements whereby FIs provide financial services along the business transactions. In these cases, risk sharing between FIs and the agribusiness companies is combined with other risk-sharing mechanisms.

BOX 2.4

In Practice: Cargill and Société Ivoirienne de Banque:
Leasing in Côte d'Ivoire

Background

Cargill is one of the top cocoa exporters in Côte d'Ivoire, with a 15–16 percent market share. It sources cocoa from farmer cooperatives, but the cooperatives need trucks to reduce their operating costs and improve profitability.

Leasing and Services for Farmer Cooperatives

Cargill has partnered with Société Ivoirienne de Banque (SIB, or Ivorian Bank Corporation) to develop a five-year leasing program (called "doni doni" meaning little by little) to assist the cooperatives in acquiring trucks. From 2015 to 2017, approximately 60 cooperatives leased trucks worth a total of $4.3 million, with zero default after two years of implementation. In this model, once cooperatives deliver cocoa to Cargill, Cargill pays back debt service to SIB before it pays the farmers.

The leasing product was offered as part of a broader package of services including targeted training on business and finance.

Financing Model

In this example, the risk was shared among Cargill, SIB (50 percent), and other partners including the multilateral Global Agriculture and Food Security Program (GAFSP) and IFC (figure B2.4.1). The GAFSP Private Finance Window "targets countries with the highest rates of poverty and hunger. It provides long- and short-term loans, credit guarantees, and equity to support small-holders and small and medium enterprise (SME) farmers to help improve productivity growth, create and deepen links to markets, and increase capacity and technical skills" (IFC 2017).

Although that arrangement may have been needed to assuage concerns about risk, it has not been necessary to draw down on those guarantees so far. The costs of developing and implementing an innovative training program for cooperatives has, however, been supported in part by grant funding from donors.

Results

SIB has benefited from this experience with leasing to rural enterprise while the cooperatives were able to expand their businesses and improve their track records as bankable business partners.

box continued

BOX 2.4

In Practice: Cargill and Société Ivoirienne de Banque: Leasing in Côte d'Ivoire (Continued)

FIGURE B2.4.1 Financing Model for Farmer Cooperatives in Côte d'Ivoire

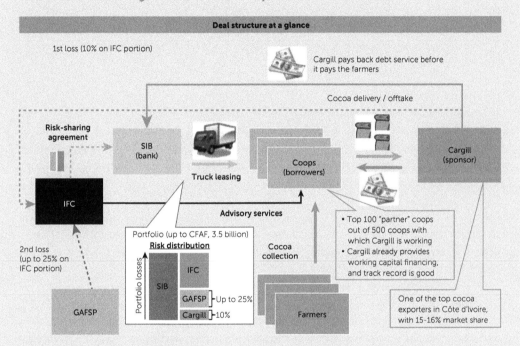

Source: IFC 2017, https://www.ifc.org/wps/wcm/connect/news_ext_content/ifc_external_corporate_site/news+and+events/news/impact-stories/affordable-credit-for-ivoirian-cocoa-co-ops.
Note: GAFSP = Global Agriculture and Food Security Program; IFC = International Finance Corporation; SIB = Société Ivoirienne de Banque (Ivorian Bank Corporation).

BOX 2.5

A Global Initiative: The Farm to Market Alliance

Background

The Farm to Market Alliance (FtMA) is a public and private initiative established by the United Nations World Food Programme (WFP) to create markets for smallholder farmers in emerging markets. It links farmer cooperatives with off-takers based on the partnership between farmer cooperatives;

box continued

BOX 2.5

A Global Initiative: The Farm to Market Alliance *(Continued)*

off-takers (such as WFP, ETG, local buyers); input providers (such as Yara, Syngenta, and Bayer CropScience); financial institutions as well as IFC and Rabobank; and support organizations such as the Alliance for a Green Revolution in Africa (AGRA).

The initiative has grown to 30 buyers and 200K farmers in Rwanda, Tanzania, Zambia and Tanzania. The overall goal of the alliance to sustainability link 1.5 million farmers to various service providers by 2022.

Financing Model

In Tanzania, CRDB Bank and National Microfinance Bank (NMB)—two leading commercial banks in agriculture finance—finance the farmer organizations contracted by the local and international off-takers. The risk exposure of the lending banks is limited to 40 percent of the loans, and the remaining risks are covered by the Danish-funded credit guarantee agency, The Private Agricultural Sector Support Trust (PASS); IFC; and the multilateral Global Agriculture Food Security Program (GAFSP). This risk-sharing arrangement reflects the high credit risk in food crop production, where formal contract arrangements are rarely available and the risk of side-selling is significant. In addition, most farmer organizations had never been contracted by the off-takers before the initiative, which increased the risk. The loans are further protected by the banks' collateral and deposit requirements.

The farmer organizations are expected to distribute inputs to their member farmers, aggregate the harvest, and sell it to the off-takers according to the contracts. The banks receive the sales proceeds from the off-takers, subtract the loan repayment, and transfer the remaining amount to the farmers. Among the residual risks in this scheme are natural disasters, and a yield index insurance will be designed and piloted in this initiative.

Beneficiaries

The farmer organizations are identified and technically supported by the WFP and AGRA. A related IFC advisory services project (funded via GAFSP) supports the assessment and capacity building of farmer organizations that have agreed to offtake contracts with FtMA buyers and who are potential borrowers from CRDB and NMB.

The provision of business management training to farmer coops helps them become professional independent businesses that are better able to manage loans and provide value-added services to their members. More than 45,000 farmers have received training in good agricultural practices and postharvest handling and storage. A custom-built mobile phone app is being used to collate input orders, substantially streamlining consolidation of the input needs of

box continued

Limitations of FI Involvement

These descriptions and cases demonstrate advantages of involving FIs in providing financial services. However, this model also has some critical limitations:

- *Limited availability or experience of FIs:* It is possible that no local FIs are willing to partner with agribusiness companies or that FIs are available but with limited experience in agriculture finance. A partnership with regional or international players could be an option, albeit with some additional costs and risks involved—such as coordination failure and foreign exchange issues. Upgrading the capacity of local FIs in agriculture finance requires external technical assistance and strategic commitment from the management of the FIs.

- *Transaction costs and collateral requirements:* FIs often require additional due diligence, which involves some paperwork for the farmers. This could become a deal breaker for farmers in view of the time and costs of collecting and filling out necessary documents. In addition, some FIs may require collateral, often in response to their loan appraisal rules or local regulations including loan loss provision requirements.

- *Coordination challenges:* Involving FIs often brings an additional burden of coordination. FIs have their own goals to achieve and procedures to follow. The time and resources for coordination may exceed the benefits. This is especially critical for crop financing where the timing of disbursement and repayment must be specific according to the crop calendar.

Other Financial Products and Services for Smallholder Farmers

Additional financial products and services are introduced in value chain finance arrangements to address residual risks in agriculture lending. Among them, agricultural insurance can help address production risks (such as rainfall deficit or flood) in value chains. Thanks to the advancement in digital financial services (DFS), mobile-based transactions are used to further reduce the transactions costs, increase security, and capture transaction records more systematically.

Role of Insurance

Agricultural insurance is a financial product that offers financial protection against agricultural risks. Such protection has a double objective: (a) reducing vulnerability ex post in case of shock by providing quick access to liquidity, and (b) increasing productivity ex ante by increasing incentives to invest in agriculture. Insurance overall enables repayment of credit in cases of loss of production and can increase both the demand and supply of credit.

Two main business models for agricultural insurance have been tested over the past decade: (1) the "micro-level" model, whereby each farmer gets his input loan insured, as in East Africa (box 2.6) and (2) the "meso-level" model, whereby an off-taker buys portfolio insurance to cope with the risk of shortage of supply (as in Bangladesh [box 2.7]).

Agricultural insurance faces a variety of challenges to effectively reduce risks along value chains, but new trends show promising opportunities to address these challenges. One of the key challenges concerns product quality: for example, basis risk may arise with index insurance, when farmers suffer losses but insurance payouts are not triggered. Other challenges are high costs, which remain a barrier to access, and limited voluntary take-up.

However, governments are increasingly fostering the development of insurance mechanisms through investments in data (such as weather and yield data), risk financing arrangements, premium subsidies, financial literacy and education, and an enabling legal and regulatory environment. In addition, new technology such as drones and satellite imagery

BOX 2.6

In Practice: Mandatory Micro-Level Index Insurance for Farmers with Offtake Agreements in East Africa

Background

Input costs for farmers who cultivate 0.5 to 5 hectares in East Africa are very high because of the use of irrigation and hired labor. In the past, a maize seed multiplier provided input loans to its contracted farmers but over time found its internal financing operation to be impractical and turned to local banks to provide financing. Initially, local banks offered farmers input loans of up to approximately $600 per hectare if they provided an offtake agreement with the seed multiplier as collateral, but loan performance was affected by production risks.

Mandatory Insurance with Input Credit

The maize seed multiplier worked with an East African advisory services firm, a local insurance company, and local banks to develop an index-based micro-level product for purchase by its contract farmers. Swiss Re provided reinsurance to the local insurance company. When the index insurance product became available in the market, the banks also began requiring that loan recipients purchase the products. Six banks and 700 farmers currently participate in the scheme.

Distribution Model

At the start of the season, the farmer registers with the insurance company and provides the bank with proof of registration as well as his or her offtake agreement with the seed multiplier. The bank provides the farmer with a loan for the cost of inputs and the cost of the insurance, then pays the insurance premium to the insurer on the farmer's behalf.

When the index triggers a payout for weather events during the season, the insurance company pays the bank the amount owed to the farmer. At the end of the season, the seed multiplier pays the bank the amount due to the farmer for his or her harvest delivery, less the payout amount provided by the insurance company (figure B2.6.1). The bank then deposits the total amount from the insurance company and the seed multiplier, less any remaining principal or interest from the original loan, into the farmer's bank account.

box continued

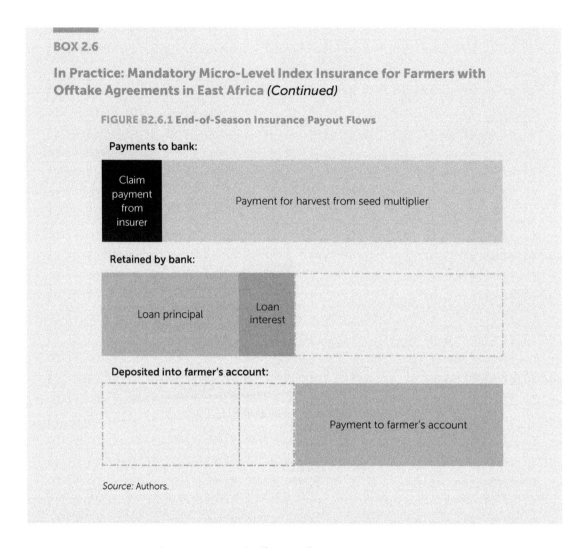

BOX 2.6

In Practice: Mandatory Micro-Level Index Insurance for Farmers with Offtake Agreements in East Africa *(Continued)*

FIGURE B2.6.1 End-of-Season Insurance Payout Flows

Payments to bank:

Claim payment from insurer

Payment for harvest from seed multiplier

Retained by bank:

Loan principal

Loan interest

Deposited into farmer's account:

Payment to farmer's account

Source: Authors.

(remote sensing) offer significant opportunities to reduce the cost of insurance and improve product quality.

Role of Digital Financial Services

DFS can play a key role in reducing transaction costs when it comes to financing value chain farmers. Distribution of funds and payments into digital accounts can offer effective solutions to reduce the need for human interface and increase security in the transactions. In addition, DFS create a record of transactions and big data upon which agribusiness companies and FIs could base development of digital scorecards

BOX 2.7

In Practice: Meso-Level Index Insurance as an Internal Risk Management Tool for Agriprocessors in Bangladesh

Background

Because cassava is not a traditional crop in Bangladesh, PRAN Foods, the country's largest agriculture processing firm, previously imported cassava from Africa for extracting glucose, which is used for manufacturing energy drinks. However, PRAN recently began developing a local supply of cassava by operating a contract farming scheme and employing small- and medium-scale farmers on a farm on leased land. The total cassava crop area associated with PRAN is now approximately 7,000 acres.

Insurance Product

PRAN Foods purchased a meso-level index insurance product from Green Delta Insurance Company covering the period from January to June 2016. IFC's Global Index Insurance Facility (GIIF) has supported Green Delta's development of the index-based product, which protects cassava crops from cold spells and excess rain at critical stages of the crop cycle.

For the first half of 2016, the product covered 60 farmers on 100 acres. PRAN purchased the insurance product to cover the value of the deliveries expected at harvest for the 100 acres selected for the pilot (approximately $130 per acre for a total of $13,000). PRAN is both the policyholder and the insured party. It paid the premium and will be the sole beneficiary of any payouts.

Advantage for PRAN and Farmers

The company anticipates using any payouts to help cover liquidity needs in the case of insufficient local supply due to a major weather shock. In the case of less-severe shocks that do not significantly threaten local supply, however, PRAN is considering providing the funds from any payout to farmers as a "bonus." PRAN would use these payouts to introduce farmers to the benefits of insurance as a first step in transitioning from meso-level coverage purchased by the company to micro-level coverage. The potential future micro-level coverage would have the individual farmer as the insured party and the company and farmer potentially sharing the cost of the insurance. PRAN believes that access to micro-level insurance would encourage more farmers to grow cassava (being that it is, as noted earlier, a relatively new crop in Bangladesh).

Source: The Practitioner Hub for Inclusive Business, http://www.inclusivebusinesshub.org/project/project-profile-pran-bangladesh/.

for credit decisions and also offer additional financial and nonfinancial products. Boxes 2.8 and 2.9 describe how digital payments transformed the transactions between agribusiness companies and large numbers of farmers in Côte d'Ivoire and Pakistan, respectively.

BOX 2.8

In Practice: Digitizing Payments to Cocoa Farmers in Côte d'Ivoire

Background

In Côte d'Ivoire, most agricultural payments to farmers are in cash, which is not only costly for agribusinesses but also creates safety issues. With the support of the Consultative Group to Assist the Poor (CGAP), Advans (a microfinance institution) approached cocoa traders and cooperatives with a proposal to channel their payments through an Advans savings account linked to an MTN Mobile Money wallet and accessible from any type of phone.

Payment Product

When farmers receive payment for their harvests, they can opt for a partial payment via an Advans digital savings account in partnership with MTN (one of East Africa's biggest mobile money operators) and the rest in cash. This flexibility gives farmers an opportunity to try out the system first, without committing their entire payment to a digital system.

As of October 2017, more than 14,000 cocoa farmers from 90 cooperatives had subscribed to the service and now have savings accounts with a formal financial institution (Advans). The total deposits in the accounts amounted to more than CFAF 300 million.

Advantages for Farmers, Agribusinesses, and FIs

- *For off-takers,* digitizing bulk payments helps cut costs, because cash payment processes are labor-intensive. It also helps deal with security issues associated with carrying large amounts of cash in rural areas. Giving the cocoa farmers access to financial services will increase traceability and the farmers' loyalty.
- *For farmers,* digital payments offer security as well as access to an interest-bearing savings account linked to their mobile wallet. They also offer a pathway for access to formal credit as a digital footprint is created. However, the value proposition of digital payments could be further improved for farmers, because digital money is not widely accepted for retail and other types of payments in Côte d'Ivoire and cash-out fees can be high.
- *For Financial Institutions (FIs)* the digitization of payments enables data collection on thin-file customers and can help the FIs to design a broader array of financial products suited to their needs. Advans Côte d'Ivoire has already launched (with CGAP support) a digital school loan based on savings and deliveries history for cocoa farmers.

Source: Mattern and Ramirez 2017.

BOX 2.9

Nestlé Payments to Dairy Farmers in Pakistan

Background

Nestlé works with around 150,000 dairy farmers In Pakistan, making annual payments totaling approximately $208 million for nearly 0.5 billion tons of milk. The payments are made to 2,500 milk collection centers, which then pay farmers via the banking system.

Payment Product

In April 2016, Telenor's Easypaisa mobile money service collaborated with Nestlé Pakistan to make these milk collection payments swift, easy, and transparent. Easypaisa registered mobile accounts for around 15,000 farmers for the weekly transfer of funds into their accounts. It expects to process payments totaling almost $10 million annually in the initial stage of partnership.

Advantages for Agribusinesses and Farmers

Transaction frequency makes this model attractive to Easypaisa. Many smallholders, each with just a few cows, deposit milk daily at collection centers. It was already processing more than 650,000 transactions daily for around 20 million registered customers, providing the business volume needed for a sustainable cash-in/cash-out agent network in rural areas.

Pakistan has several agricultural value chains that are suitable for digitization, notably wheat, grains, sugarcane, and cotton. Aside from the benefits it offers agribusiness firms and small-holder farmers, digitizing payments in these value chains offers potential to generate additional direct revenue for mobile money providers as well as increasing mobile use and financial inclusion in rural areas.

Source: Telenor 2016.

Conclusions and Recommendations

Strategies and Best Practices for Linking Smallholder Farmers with Finance

Agribusiness companies dealing with smallholder farmers in their businesses can facilitate finance for creditworthy farmers in a cost-effective manner. The chapter has mainly discussed the scenarios where the agribusiness companies procure crops from farmers based on formal and informal contracts in well-organized value chains. These arrangements have important prerequisites, including solid business transactions valued by the farmers, financial products addressing key constraints of the farmers in producing the crops, and an enabling environment.

Credit could be provided either by the agribusiness companies directly or by FIs. The two systems of direct credit by agribusiness and FIs could coexist: agribusinesses could finance certain clients (such as those who are more loyal or who are medium-size or larger) and for certain types of activities (such as inputs), leaving other clients and other activities to be served by FIs.

Despite the challenges in both models, practical experiences present some lessons learned and best practices, many of which are applicable to both direct financing and financing through FIs:

- *Include cash components in the lending arrangement* in addition to in-kind (inputs), recognizing the borrowers' various financial needs. This could enhance the resilience of the farmers, especially in the direct lending model by agribusinesses.

- *Address significant training needs for key players* including farmers, producer organizations, FIs, and input providers, particularly during the setup phase. Coordination among multiple actors is one of the key success factors of the financing arrangements. The parties involved should support weaker institutions to facilitate financial transactions in the value chain.

- *Invest in systems to evaluate and monitor credit.* These investments can have significant benefits if the agribusiness lends directly to farmers.

- *Consider areas of rapid change and the emerging opportunities* such as information and communication technology (ICT) and financial technology (fintech). Diffusion and innovation of technology are changing the financial sector and creating new opportunities in digitized payments, technical advice, traceability, record keeping, and so on. These changes could result in more cost-effective and low risk financial operations for the agribusiness companies and FIs.

- *Understand what leads farmers to default, and use well-chosen rewards and penalties* to improve farmer loyalty over time. Rewards are usually more important than penalties to gain farmers' trust. There are some best practices to ensure high levels of repayment while keeping the farmers engaged (Hystra 2015):
  ○ Tailor repayment schedule to a farmer's cash flow (for example, repayments according to the crop cycle).

- ○ Require a small prepayment before granting the loan to ensure strong commitment.

- ○ Offer farmers a wide range of benefits such as inputs, advice, and training as well as other services (for example, preventive health care and financial literacy) that could be provided by other parties and not necessarily the agribusiness.

- ○ Consider loyalty reward programs for farmers who deliver consistently.

- ○ Consider the possibility of group lending (with a coguarantee from group members) that provides extra incentives to repay.

- ○ Provide bundled insurance products as part of the package to deal with emergencies from both individual risks and systemic risks.

- *Address the smallholder's wider needs and constraints* in a design of the transactions to prevent business disruptions. For example, to the extent possible, encourage farmers to diversify their income sources and crops to increase their resilience.

- *Structure guarantees appropriately and use risk sharing facilities* to entice FIs to participate in the funding of farmers in well-organized value chains.

Note

1. For more information about the SCOPEinsight assessment tool, see http://www .scopeinsight.com/.

References

Christen, R. P., and J. Anderson. 2013. "Segmentation of Smallholder Households: Meeting the Range of Financial Needs in Agriculture Families." CGAP Focus Note 85. Washington, DC: World Bank Group. http://www.cgap.org/sites/default /files/Focus-Note-Segmentation-of-Smallholder-Households-April-2013.pdf.

Dalberg (Dalberg Development Advisors). 2016. "Inflection Point: Unlocking Growth in the Era of Farmer Finance." Report for The Initiative for Smallholder Finance and the Rural and Agricultural Finance Learning Lab, MasterCard Foundation, Toronto.

GPFI and IFC (Global Partnership for Financial Inclusion and International Finance Corporation of the World Bank Group). 2012. "Innovative Agricultural SME Finance Models." Report, IFC, Washington, DC.

Hazell, P., and A. Rahman, ed. 2014. *New Directions for Smallholder Agriculture.* Oxford, UK: Oxford University Press.

Hernández, Emilio, ed. 2017. *Innovative Risk Management Strategies in Rural and Agriculture Finance: The Asian Experience.* Rome: Food and Agriculture Organization of the United Nations (FAO).

Hystra. 2015. "Smallholder Farmers and Business: 15 Pioneering Collaborations for Improved Productivity and Sustainability." Research report, Hystra, Paris.

IFC (International Finance Corporation of the World Bank Group). 2017. "Blended Finance at IFC." Factsheet, IFC, Washington, DC. https://www.ifc.org/wps/wcm/connect/ff942a004d332e698961cdf81ee631cc/Ecom.pdf?MOD=AJPERES.

Johnston, C. and R. L. Meyer. 2008. "Value Chain Governance and Access to Finance: Maize, Sugar Cane and Sunflower Oil in Uganda." *Enterprise Development & Microfinance* 19 (4): 281–300.

Mattern, M., and R. Ramirez. 2017. "Digitizing Value Chain Finance for Smallholder Farmers." Focus Note 106, Consultative Group to Assist the Poor, Washington, DC.

Milder, B. 2008. "Closing the Gap: Reaching the Missing Middle and Rural Poor through Value Chain Finance." *Enterprise Development & Microfinance* 19 (4): 301–16.

Miller, C., and L. Jones. 2010. *Agricultural Value Chain Finance: Tools and Lessons.* Warwickshire, UK: Food and Agriculture Organization and Practical Action Publishing.

Telenor. 2016. "Easypaisa Empowers Nestlé Dairy Farmers with Smart Milk Payments Mechanism." Press release, April 11. https://www.telenor.com.pk/about/about-telenor-pakistan/our-history.

Tschirley, D., and S. Kabwe. 2009. "The Cotton Sector of Zambia." Africa Region Working Paper Series No. 124, World Bank, Washington, DC.

World Bank. 2007. *Agriculture for Development: World Development Report, 2008.* New York: Oxford University Press.

Additional Resources

Cuevas, C., and M. Pagura. 2016. "Agricultural Value Chain Finance: A Guide for Bankers." Guide, Agriculture Finance Support Facility (AgriFin), World Bank, Washington, DC.

Dugger, C., and R. Sberro-Kessler. 2016. "Developments in Distribution for Index Insurance: Micro- and Meso-Level Approaches." Agrifinance Flash Note 2016, World Bank, Washington, DC. https://blog.private-sector-and-development.com/2016/11/07/experiences-in-index-based-insurance-for-farmers-lessons-learnt-from-senegal-and-bangladesh.

FAO (Food and Agriculture Organization of the United Nations). 2013. "Contract Farming for Inclusive Market Access." http://www.fao.org/3/a-i3526e.pdf.

Mensink, M., and J. de la Rive. 2011. "How to Support Value Chain Finance in a Smart Way?" Policy Statement of the European Microfinance Platform, Rural Outreach & Innovation Action Group, e-MFP, Luxembourg.

USAID (United States Agency for International Development). 2011. "Rural and Agricultural Finance: Taking Stock of Five Years of Innovations." Micro report 181. USAID, Washington, DC.

CHAPTER 3
AGGREGATION AND WORKING COST-EFFECTIVELY AT SCALE

KEY MESSAGES

➡ Working with smallholders requires aggregation mechanisms to deliver output at volume and provide cost-effective channels for inputs and training.

➡ Producer organizations can be important in frontier and emerging markets, but contract farming, agro-retailers and collectors can also help aggregate farmers.

➡ Aggregation choices may be affected by type of crop or product (food or cash, export or domestic market).

➡ Agribusiness is the lead sector globally in terms of numbers of cooperatives.

➡ Financial literacy and business management are often weak in small agribusinesses, but recent work on assessment, training, and accreditation is addressing this gap.

➡ Loans can help upgrade capacity of aggregating organizations or businesses.

Introduction

It is unrealistic for agribusiness firms to directly source from multiple small farms, so the firms need mechanisms for accessing the aggregated supply of small producers—whether through contract farmer schemes, producer organizations (POs), market intermediaries, or other channels. POs are member-based organizations that provide an opportunity for agribusiness companies to efficiently market inputs, procure supply, and convey information between firms and smallholders. As global firms increasingly turn to smallholders as a key part of their procurement and input marketing strategies, the interest in and need to work with well-run POs is unprecedented.

Recent developments in the assessment and development of small-scale agribusinesses, including POs, allow firms to steadily grow a responsible and business-minded smallholder supplier base. Meanwhile, the emerging experience with innovative partnerships shows how roles and risks can be shared during setup and early stages. As a model, working with member-based organizations is win-win—offering benefits to firms and farmers alike—and promoted in the development community as an important component and vehicle to achieve the Sustainable Development Goals for 2030 (FAO and AgriCord 2016).

This chapter explores the potential for working with aggregators as follows:

- Aggregation Options for Reaching and Integrating Smallholders

- Food Crops and Domestic Markets: Implications for Aggregation

- The Business Case for Working with Producer Organizations

- Producer Organizations Help Expand the Market Pie

- Assessing Aggregators' Capabilities

- Strategies and Best Practices for Aggregation and Effective Supply Chains.

Subsequent sections of the handbook build on this chapter, as they incorporate group-based approaches into discussions of, for example, standards and certification, inputs, and training.

Aggregation Options for Reaching and Integrating Smallholders

The very nature of smallholder farming means that a single producer can only supply relatively small amounts of any given crop, and that each individual producer has modest input needs. Larger volumes, if to be sourced from smallholders, must necessarily come from multiple dispersed producers, most probably growing their crops in slightly different ways, with considerable varietal variation as well. At a minimum, aggregating or assembling that crop entails several tasks:

· Identifying producers

· Securing access to their crop: communicating and making timely purchases and payments)

· Instigating some form of quality control or standards for purchase

· Handling, storage, and transport.

Any attempt to increase yields; improve quality or consistency; introduce traceability and certification; or add value through grading, sorting, drying, fermenting, or bagging in standardized bags will need improved smallholder access to inputs, extension, finance, management systems—or all of those resources combined—and necessitate a much wider array of tasks.

Companies wishing to source *in volume* from smallholders have several options:

1. Purchasing from wholesalers

2. Purchasing via established local traders active in rural areas, possibly facilitating this by advancing funds

3. Purchasing via a lead farmer or agricultural small and medium enterprises (SMEs), such as agro-input dealers, who collect and purchase crops from other smallholder farmers to generate sufficient volume to be attractive to commercial buyers—the firm possibly advancing funds to the farmer or entrepreneur

4. Employing their own field agents to take on the same roles as the trader

5. Sourcing crops via contract farming—defined, at a minimum, as a promise of resources such as money, inputs, or services in return for crops to be supplied at a specified time, quantity, and quality (World Bank 2014)—for which there are various models:

   · Options 2, 3, and 4 could be forms of contract farming if there is at least a prior agreement to purchase a crop from the farmer (subject to certain conditions).

- Other, more interventionist variants include

  ○ Farmers receiving an advance of inputs from the buyer, which they repay at harvest time, when they sell their crop;

  ○ Schemes that involve more partners (such as financial institutions, nongovernmental organizations [NGOs], traders, or input distributors), typically including a third party able to communicate more effectively with farmers and/or credit risk being shared among more partners; and

  ○ The nucleus estate (with surrounding outgrowers); smallholders who farm in a contiguous area (for example, in a land development or land reclamation scheme); or ingrower schemes, which provide farmers with services such as irrigation or spraying.

6. Purchasing crops from POs.

These options overlap (one possibly including elements of another), and several could be pursued in tandem. Business-minded POs are in SMEs and thus could be included in option 3. There is also potential for shifts between each "level" as contract farmers, for example, may transform themselves into a PO—or behave like one.

Input and other service providers face similar tasks and options, in tapping into the potential of smallholder markets—for example, operating via wholesalers or established local traders, employing their own field agents, working with contract farming schemes in collaboration with the off-taker, or reaching smallholders via POs. So-called "last mile retailers" (small agri-SMEs, accessible to smallholder farmers) can also fill an aggregation role by selling inputs to multiple smallholders.

Note that despite the reference to *contract* farming, in practice companies have (nonbinding) basic agreements with farmers. Enforcing contracts in this context is generally difficult but, if based on trust and mutual gain, these agreements can be somewhat effective. Agreements that specify, for example, the crop volume that a PO is expected to supply can help provide clarity and an indication of expectations for both parties.

In selecting one or more aggregation strategies, a firm might weigh the balance of options of two dimensions: (1) the extent of "hands-on" firm involvement required and (2) the strategy's scope to influence supply chain development and market growth.

Firm involvement. Although any of these strategies allow off-taker or input companies to reach smallholders, they have quite different implications for the role of the firm (being more or less "hands-on") and may be more or less suitable, depending on company objectives and local circumstances. For instance, if companies are sourcing food crops where side-selling can be an important problem, integrating potentially competitive traders into the supply chain may be an effective strategy to reduce side-selling (for more discussion of this, see chapter 6).

Many companies may pursue more than one aggregation strategy in tandem to reduce dependence on a single source or as part of a phased intervention strategy. In all cases, companies will need to develop their own capacity to work with smallholders. Investments in the development of structured procurement networks to support their smallholder sourcing and marketing activities will be needed, taking up to three years before generating a positive cash flow. A prior gap analysis—to assess the capabilities of the PO or other aggregator—is also important in planning the steps to effectively integrate smallholders, including realistic assumptions about the time required.

Scope to influence supply chain and market. The aggregation strategies outlined above also differ in their scope for supply chain development and market growth through, for example, the following:

- *Integration* of other products and services, such as training

- *Influence* over how inputs are used and hence the quantity and quality of the crop produced

- *Value addition* via certification and traceability

- *Expansion* of smallholder opportunity and the promotion of farmer loyalty over the long-term.

Figure 3.1 indicates how each strategy compares with respect to firm involvement and scope to engage farmers in the value chain. Working with POs seems to offer the most cost-effective long-run strategy to expand the market because as the PO develops into a more professional and commercial operation, it helps to promote and manage that growth while also gradually being able to take over more of the roles that the firm may play initially. For a global company, this could be more attractive than operating a relatively interventionist contract farming scheme (for example, buying crops but also ensuring training and input supply, and hence exerting considerable influence or control) because growth via contract farming is more likely to depend on the ongoing, expanded involvement of the firm itself. However, working with agro-retailers or lead farmers could also be an attractive option—certainly requiring training, coordination, and

FIGURE 3.1 Strategies to Reach Smallholder Supplies: Relative Scope for Market Growth versus Extent of Hands-On Firm Involvement

Scope to influence supply chain and market growth

follow-up—but less interventionist than some other options, with the potential to nonetheless leverage large numbers of farmers. Circumstances will vary, however, and as noted earlier, contract farmer schemes may sometimes transform into POs.

The merits of each strategy differ depending on several considerations and contexts, including the firm's strategic goals (and especially, its planning horizon), whether its business is procurement or input sales, as well as the amount of upfront investment and involvement it is willing to make, and for procurement, which types of crops (and hence scope for side-selling) it is targeting.

Food Crops and Domestic Markets: Implications for Aggregation

Population growth and urbanization means that future market growth in low- and middle-income countries will be an important driver of agribusiness investment (external or indigenous) in the coming years. As covered in the Introduction, urban growth particularly will expand market opportunities for high-value products, affordable traditional food products, and animal source foods as well as markets for feed and biofuels.

These different products have different implications for aggregation and for the diversified or phased strategies that companies might use to aggregate smallholder supplies. An important consideration is that the food crop and domestic markets tend to be less organized, with less aggregation and multiple buyers, than other product markets and export markets; there are exceptions and varying degrees to which this is true, but this generalization is widely observed.[1] There is also more scope for household consumption of food crops, and extreme price volatility may result from either very good or very poor harvests (including possible government intervention or the effects of events in countries in the region that may also trigger relief purchases). These factors, combined with weak scope for contract enforcement, create conditions where side-selling is a major risk. This, in turn, affects ability to advance credit, which affects the scope to upgrade farming practices. Price volatility will also affect farmer willingness to adopt new technology. The yield gaps underline significant potential to increase yields for the benefit of farmers, consumers, and agribusiness. For companies to work effectively and grow their businesses under these conditions, they must have robust strategies to manage these risks.

For animal source foods (particularly more-perishable products) and feed, there is more scope for aggregation points nearer the farm—and to connect farmers with the handling or processing unit—possibly making for somewhat easier conditions for extending input credit. The other consideration is the extent to which these markets overlap, which again might favor side-selling (for example, when feed is also food or when milk products are easily traded in local informal markets). Clearly, there are numerous context-specific considerations.

In the short to medium term, companies may be reliant on existing aggregation points (existing warehousing, for example). They may choose to work with local traders instead of being in direct competition with them. Equally, companies may choose to work with multiple aggregation mechanisms to spread risk and to source more product (as illustrated by the Heineken case study, box 3.1).

However, if farmers are to be encouraged to produce more and to improve quality, some form of credit will be needed. In this case, it will be necessary to tackle side-selling, which may require a concerted and enduring effort to build farmer loyalty. Under these circumstances, working with POs may be the most effective long-term vehicle to grow the supply base. See the recommended practices on credit and reduced

---

BOX 3.1

In Practice: Food Security Contributions by Heineken in Ethiopia

Heineken entered the Ethiopian brewery industry in 2011, when it acquired two state-owned breweries, and, in 2015, it opened a new brewery in Addis Ababa. With the Ethiopian formal beer market growing at 10–15 percent per year, the market consumption of malt reached 120,000 metric tons in 2016 and is expected to reach 200,000 metric tons by 2020.

With limited local malting capacity (52,000 metric tons per year), Heineken imported 30,000 metric tons of malt in 2016. Recognizing this, in line with its local sourcing strategy, Heineken initiated a public-private partnership in 2013 and, jointly with the Dutch government, financed a project aiming to improve local barley production and to procure from smallholder farmers. Ethiopian government policy encourages companies to partner with farmer organizations.

Heineken now works with a total of 90 aggregators, engaging 24,836 smallholder farmers who grow malt barley on almost 21,000 hectares. International Finance Corporation (IFC) is a partner in Phase 2 of the project, which involves tailored support in farming skills, business management, access to finance for selected aggregators, and strengthening multistakeholder platforms to connect producers to the brewing industry.

During Phase 1 of the project, in addition to the effects on the brewery industry supply chain, the project also contributed to food security. The new Heineken varieties (Traveller and Grace) were found to be compatible with local tastes. For example, it was also discovered that the new barley varieties combine well with local teff grain in the preparation of good-quality *injera*, the traditional Ethiopian flatbread pancake that is a popular staple food. Furthermore, the fact that teff prices are high and increasing caused an unexpected and significant rise in the use of malt barley for food. The Phase 1 project indicates that farm households consumed close to 80 percent of the total production of malt barley (51,374 metric tons) in the form of food products in 2016.

Although the project planned to make an additional 5,000 metric tons of barley available for household consumption by December 2017, the actual outcome was 10 times greater than the planned amount. It now looks as if future phases of the project will contribute further to food security (about 84,000 metric tons by 2019), as well as to development of the malt barley supply chain for the beer industry.

side-selling highlighted in chapter 6 (on yield gaps), noting particularly the importance of the following:

- Making it convenient for farmers to sell to the company—for example, providing bags, having a frequent and timely presence at harvest time, and making timely payments

- Having a value proposition that really does respond to farmer needs

- Using an appropriate mix of rewards and penalties

- Using POs for procurement and to benefit from peer pressure to limit side-selling

- Taking a long view to develop the right strategy and build farmer loyalty.

In short, companies procuring food crops or other domestic market crops may find that initially they have to work with multiple aggregation mechanisms. This may continue over time, but in the long run, developing the capacity of POs to provide at least part of their procurement needs is likely to be an effective strategy to reliably source more product.

Table 3.1 summarizes the factors that differentiate food markets from more traditional or high-value export market chains—and what these factors mean for agribusiness firms' strategies to engage smallholders and increase aggregation.

TABLE 3.1 Food Crops for Local Markets: Implications for Agribusiness Firms' Smallholder Engagement Strategies

Key factor	How this differs from cash crops	Implications for company's smallholder engagement strategy
Market structure and scope for side-selling	More buyers or more outlets for food crops—and more household consumption	• For food crops, harder to get loan repayment; need strong focus on reducing side-selling (see chapter 6) • Less aggregation (and to the extent it exists, it is nearer the consumer), so less chance of using it as channel for input credit and improved productivity • Engage existing traders to reduce competition for farmer output
Quality	More tolerance of range of quality	May be hard to improve quality as market accepts lower quality
Market opportunity	Rapid growth in local urban markets in the following: • Affordable traditional food products • Small but growing market for higher-value, better-quality, and convenience foods • Animal source food • Feed	• International markets well understood by global companies • Price competition and increasing competition on sustainability factors • Structure and players in local markets likely to be unstable as these shift and the market response develops • Attractive market opportunities but caution or flexibility probably needed in developing operations

table continued

TABLE 3.1 **Food Crops for Local Markets: Implications for Agribusiness Firms' Smallholder Engagement Strategies** *(Continued)*

Key factor	How this differs from cash crops	Implications for company's smallholder engagement strategy
Reputational risks	• Less predictable reputational risks and vulnerability to politicization in local markets, including international spillover if, for example, food crop operations perceived to have adverse effect on food security and vulnerable groups • Harsher local and international judgment of international companies (for example, on food safety breaches)	• Key issue in international markets, where it is relatively well understood by global companies • Need for agribusinesses to adopt risk avoidance strategies in local markets, where possible—and to develop partnerships and engage key players to help manage such risks
Availability of finance from banks	• More limited than with cash crops because of side-selling potential • Local banks may be less convinced of local market potential and hence the likelihood of repayments	Difficult to assess effect, which will vary by country; government or donor support for food crops may be available
Price risk	• More price volatility locally depending on production volumes and unexpected presence of large-scale buyers such as relief agencies • Likelier to be subject to politically motivated price intervention that might be sudden	• Probable need to adopt cautious, flexible strategies while engaging with the policy process, even if indirectly, to minimize adverse effects • Financial buffer needed against this sort of risk
Adoption of technology and scope to upgrade	Harder because of lack of finance, potential side-selling, and availability of markets for poorer-quality produce	Easier in tight supply chains with value chain finance; need concerted effort to reduce side-selling
Contract enforcement	Probably weaker contract enforcement, exposing company to more risk (affecting entire value chain, not only a part)	See price risk section

The case study about Heineken's sourcing of malt barley in Ethiopia (box 3.1) not only illustrates the aggregation strategy's benefits to farmers, consumers, and the Heineken business, but also highlights many of the points made above:

- Rapid growth in the domestic market for malt barley for brewing

- Even faster market growth because of apparently unexpected acceptance of malt barley as food (to combine with teff)

- Diversion of malt barley (to food markets and household consumption) amid rising prices

- Heineken's ability to adapt by planning for the additional food barley needs of farmers (part of its value proposition to growers).

The Business Case for Working with Producer Organizations

POs provide an opportunity for economies of scale in integrating small-holders into global agribusiness value chains, such as in relation to the following:

- *Collecting and disseminating information* for firms seeking certified crops or increased supplier productivity

- *Strengthening logistics*, with added potential for improvements in quality premiums associated with timely and localized sorting, drying, rebagging in standard-weight sacks, and storage

- *Marketing, processing, distribution, lending, and other services*, for firms targeting inputs or financial services to smallholders (noting that working with groups helps reduce side-selling and ensure loan repayment).

These advantages help explain why the global agriculture and food sector makes prominent use of cooperatives as a business structure. Globally, agriculture and food is the lead sector in numbers of cooperatives and second (to insurance) in cooperative business turnover (COOP and Euricse 2016). Many household names have their roots in agribusiness cooperatives (for example, Credit Agricole, Rabobank, FrieslandCampina, Land o' Lakes, Arla Foods, Sunkist, Ocean Spray, and Blue Diamond).

In low- and middle-income countries, despite some notable exceptions (such as China and India), the cooperative sector is generally less prominent. Less than 3 percent of the population in Sub-Saharan Africa are cooperative members, compared with approximately 13 percent in Asia overall and in the Caribbean, and 8 percent in Latin America (COOP and Euricse 2016; Dave Grace and Associates 2014; Mayo 2012).

In these places, although producers are somewhat organized, much of the amalgamation is informal as well as highly diverse—of varying size, focus, and capabilities. Examples include farmer field schools, extension groups, rotating savings and credit associations, farmers' associations, clubs, and community groups that share labor for large tasks (such as clearing land). Although less common, examples of more-formalized organizations include the International Family Forestry Alliance, which advocates for policies that are supportive of family forestry, providing a voice for 25 million forest owners through its global network of member organizations (FAO and AgriCord 2016). Box 3.2. describes different types of producer organizations.

Class C

Class C POs are often informal farmer groups or assemblies that have basic capacity to manage information. Examples include a farmers group that attends regular training sessions on certification or improving productivity; dairy farmers who sell their milk at a central point, which also

---

BOX 3.2

Producer Organizations Help Expand the Market Pie

When farmers join producer organizations (POs), their ability to negotiate better terms with buyers is enhanced because they control larger volumes of crops. Some firms may view this as a disadvantage. However, this is shortsighted for four reasons:

- *Increased margins for POs often come from middlemen*, whose services are not needed when farmers themselves aggregate crops.

- *Aggregation presents opportunities to improve quality* during marketing and through cleaning and sorting, which can justify higher prices.

- *Farmer organizations are best placed to undertake some key tasks* (such as loan recovery or ensuring timely planting) when it is in their interests to do so.

- *When farmers receive fair prices, they are more likely to invest in their farms* (if they own their land). This investment raises productivity, which benefits both farmer and firm, helping create sustainable enterprises over the short and long term, giving the next generation of smallholders an incentive to continue farming.

POs are most useful to firms when they buy inputs and sell crops in large volumes, whether for their own members or for other farmers.

Source: IFC 2014.

serves as a hub for training and information; and long-established traditional groups formed to manage community access to scarce natural resources like water. Depending on the group's focus, there may not be much trust among members.

These organizations can assist firms principally by providing an initial building block, permitting

· A means to reach a group of farmers for information exchange;

· An entry point from which to build and strengthen supplier loyalty; and

· A way to identify farmer leaders to support future interventions.

Class B

Class B POs operate as small enterprises, collectively managing group resources such as inputs, crops, savings, land, or water for a membership of perhaps 20 to 30 farmers, often from a single village. They gain some benefits from being organized, but from a company's perspective, even their combined production may be uneconomical to collect directly.

Such groups may be formally registered with a bank account or have legal tenure over a plot of land. Collective management of resources requires trust in the group's leadership and in one another, as well as a shared vision of the group's plan and overall purpose. Such cohesion, which is critically important if the group is to develop further, usually develops through either traditional leadership structures or democratic processes (figure 3.2).

FIGURE 3.2 Group Cohesion Development in Producer Organizations

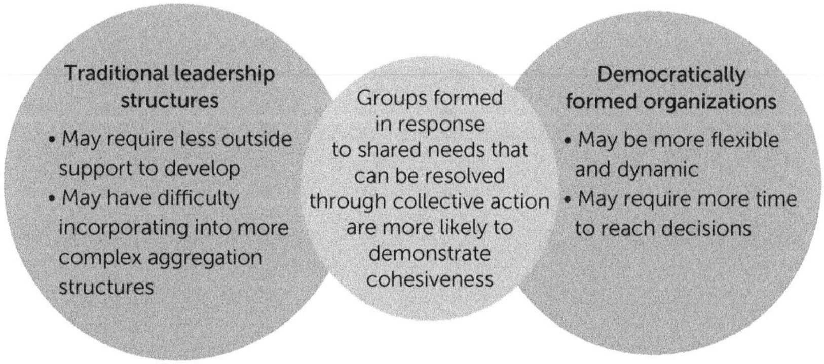

Traditional leadership structures
· May require less outside support to develop
· May have difficulty incorporating into more complex aggregation structures

Groups formed in response to shared needs that can be resolved through collective action are more likely to demonstrate cohesiveness

Democratically formed organizations
· May be more flexible and dynamic
· May require more time to reach decisions

Class B POs are useful to firms because they present the same opportunities as Class C organizations, as well as the following advantages:

- *Scope for aggregated input sales and crop purchases*, reducing transport and marketing costs

- *Potential for sharing labor* to grow crops on individual or communal land

- *Group savings opportunities*, paving the way for their own seasonal financing, larger investments, and access to other sources of finance

- *A mechanism to manage and allocate shared resources*, for example, irrigation water.

Class A

Class A POs can support supply chain efficiency and reduce the costs of marketing inputs and purchasing crops. They do so in part by managing external resources and coordinating farmer members throughout the production process. Operating like a middleman in some ways, they too can earn a margin from assembling crops to sell-on or distributing inputs or services. Sometimes, multiple grassroots POs may join (in what are sometimes called "depots" or "fora") to increase input and crop volumes. Or individual POs or groups of POs receive loans from financial institutions or advances from off-takers for crop purchases.[2]

Although they are probably formally registered and active in markets, Class A organizations often still have some business development needs. As in the Class B groups, cohesion is important here: trust in leaders, trust in other members, and a shared purpose. In addition, such groups need systems for managing cash, crops, and inventory—and they need time to develop those systems, establish a track record, and build trust with outside parties.

Their added value to a firm, over and above the advantages offered by Class B and C organizations, is their ability to do the following:

- Assemble crops from a larger geographic area

- Manage loans to purchase inputs to be resold to other farmers

- Manage loans to purchase crops from members and nonmembers

- Coordinate postharvest processing, drying, storage, and transport

- Improve traceability among smallholder farms and support certification

- Reduce side-selling through group cohesion
- Act as a vehicle for fair trade certification, which requires that crops be purchased via formal POs.

All three classes of organization are linked in various ways. Class A organizations may buy farmer output from Class B organizations and from members of Class C organizations. Class C organizations may struggle to formalize and grow their operations, whereas Class B, with formal capacities, may be able to move up the pyramid. However, it is unlikely that many organizations will develop without assistance.

A new development (described in the "Assessing Aggregators' Capabilities" section) is the objective assessment of PO business management capacity and tailored capacity development to address areas of weakness, promoting graduation to a higher class.

Widespread Community Benefits from POs

PO members, for their part, benefit from access to information and higher prices due to increased volume, value-added processing, and brand development (figure 3.3). POs can also earn margins by procuring crops from nonmembers and reselling them. When POs procure crops

FIGURE 3.3 Sample PO Classification System, by Off-Taker Needs

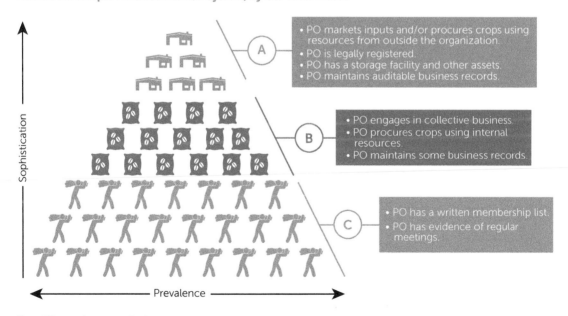

- A
  - PO markets inputs and/or procures crops using resources from outside the organization.
  - PO is legally registered.
  - PO has a storage facility and other assets.
  - PO maintains auditable business records.

- B
  - PO engages in collective business.
  - PO procures crops using internal resources.
  - PO maintains some business records.

- C
  - PO has a written membership list.
  - PO has evidence of regular meetings.

Sophistication → Prevalence

Note: PO = producer organization.

from nonmembers, the nonmembers benefit from increased market access. However, prices tend to be competitive for the area, reflecting the margin earned by the PO.

POs may also provide social services, such as road repair or construction of health clinics, that benefit the wider community. Cooperatives that are certified by fair trade organizations receive social premiums, which are used to fund community initiatives.

Assessing Aggregators' Capabilities

The many different types of POs are formed for a wide variety of reasons and often in response to an external incentive, for example, access to training and subsidized inputs, or as a requirement to obtain a loan. Clearly, their capabilities vary enormously and may strengthen or weaken.

As with small businesses in general, many POs fail in the first few years, particularly if they were formed mainly to access short-lived development project assistance. Problems with governance (such as nepotism, corruption, and other forms of mismanagement) are not unusual. A prior gap analysis—to assess capabilities—is extremely useful for a company planning to work with a PO or other small agribusiness.

SCOPEinsight—a Dutch company founded in 2010 to develop "tools that measure farmer professionalism in emerging markets"—has developed an independent quantitative assessment system for PO capacity (box 3.3).[3] Training and coaching are linked to these assessments to

---

BOX 3.3

SCOPEinsight's PO Assessment Tool

SCOPEinsight provides business intelligence to create opportunities in agriculture by measuring the level of professionalism of farmers and their organizations. The aim of the SCOPEinsight assessment tool is to develop a universally applicable and standardized assessment methodology focused on the business capacities of professional producer organizations (POs). This methodology can be administered at reasonable cost and yields results that highlight specific training needs.

SCOPEinsight's flagship assessment tool, SCOPE Basic®, targets "emerging farmer organizations that need targeted capacity building services or stronger supply chain links."[a] It requires a four- to

box continued

SCOPEinsight's PO Assessment Tool *(Continued)*

FIGURE B3.3.1 Eight Dimensions of SCOPE Basic® Assessment

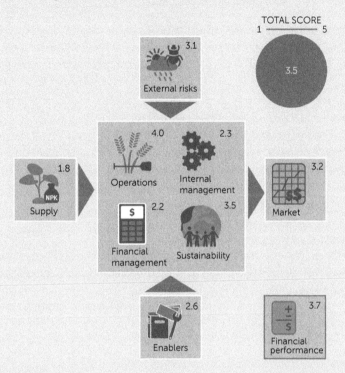

Source: ©SCOPEinsight. Reproduced, with permission, from SCOPEinsight; further permission required for reuse.

six-hour field visit, a questionnaire, and moderate data and document collection. It focuses on eight key dimensions (figure B3.3.1).

As of 2018, 537 assessors had been trained and more than 2,700 assessments conducted in 39 countries and 26 agricultural sectors, reaching 7 million farmers.

a. "SCOPE Basic" (accessed March 22, 2018), http://www.scopeinsight.com/assessments/scope-basic/.

support the development of cooperatives, lead farmers and small rural entrepreneurs, in areas of financial literacy and business management. The Olam case study illustrates experience with this approach with farmers' groups in Côte d'Ivoire (box 3.4). (See also the discussion of IFC's Agribusiness Leadership Program in chapter 5.)

BOX 3.4

In Practice: Olam: Building the Capacity of Farmers' Groups in Côte d'Ivoire

To bolster the business capacity of cooperative leaders and members, Olam International, a leading agribusiness, in collaboration with IFC, provides a program of evaluation, training, and coaching to groups in its cocoa and cotton supply chains in Côte d'Ivoire. Cooperatives first undergo a baseline evaluation using SCOPEinsight tools that measure and assess nine different dimensions of agribusiness capacity. The numerical scores provide a transparent guide to the level of professionalism of farmer groups. Cooperative leaders then receive training on best practices and work with a coach for the next 12 months, focusing on areas that need improvement, until undergoing a second evaluation to understand their progress. These evaluations provide valuable information for Olam and its cooperative partners as well as for other parties that do business with these groups (suppliers, banks, and others), acting as a useful risk management and mitigation tool.

The training builds sustainability and a knowledge-based multiplier effect: IFC provides training of trainers to a core group of Olam's cooperative specialists, who then train and coach cooperative leaders. Once cooperative leaders are trained, they share their know-how with the cooperative members, who in turn share their newfound knowledge with their dependents. To ensure that the training is pitched at the right level, the program uses two curricula: one for advanced cooperatives and another for cooperatives that need training on the fundamentals of cooperative management. The latter is highly innovative, providing a picture-based training curriculum suitable for those who may not know how to read.

Over three years, Olam plans to reach at least 275 cooperatives and 62,000 farmers in the cocoa and cotton sectors. Almost one year into the program that started in 2016, 35 cooperatives and 871 cocoa farmers were evaluated, trained, and coached. As a result of the evaluation and coaching, nearly 50 percent of the initial 35 cooperatives has decided to hire a professionally trained accountant, and 17 percent has been able to acquire equipment since training started.

Similar initiatives are happening with other companies in value chains across Côte d'Ivoire. Long-term success will require the harmonization of metrics and the active—and open-minded—participation of the many stakeholders involved.

Strategies and Best Practices for Aggregation and Effective Supply Chains

Building the capacity of small agribusinesses and POs to be useful partners to companies is an investment. If the aggregator is only needed as an information channel, such as for advice on agronomy or certification requirements, the existing capacity may suffice. However, if the small business or PO is to manage advances or to aggregate or process crops, additional capacity may be needed. Even something relatively straightforward, such as making a payment to a group, may be difficult if the partner does not have a bank account.

Gaps in the geographical coverage of POs, or PO membership restrictions to concentrate margins among fewer farmer members, may mean that the farmers who are "left out" sell their crop to collectors, taking the product out of the supply chain and impeding certification efforts.

To mitigate the risks and ensure a good return on capacity-building investments in POs and other types of small aggregators, several elements are critical: suitable partnerships, trust between the partners, use of best practices in crop procurement, adequate financing (such as loans) to upgrade capacity, clear planning of the POs' roles and responsibilities, and periodic assessment of the POs' performance.

Develop Partnerships to Establish and Build PO Capacity

Developing PO business skills will likely require training and mentoring over at least two or three production and marketing cycles—a cost that firms may consider prohibitive, especially if they are already stretched by other activities. Finding the right partners, so each can focus on what it does best, is critical. For example, government extension workers or a firm's own field staff are likely to be more familiar with farmer training, crop purchase, and certification requirements (areas in which agricultural specialists all have had some exposure) than in providing business development training. Yet certain organizations such as specialist NGOs or private training providers also work in these areas and might be suitable partners. An example of such an organization is the Agribusiness Market Ecosystem Alliance (AMEA), which is a foundation registered in the Netherlands. It has the objective to improve the professionalism of POs. AMEA has a multistakeholder membership and curates best practices in PO assessments, PO leadership training, and coaching methodologies.[4]

International organizations or NGOs using donor funds can complement a firm's efforts to build the capacity of a PO, and good examples abound of such collaboration. The case study on Yara's work with maize farmers in northern Ghana illustrates this partnership approach to developing PO capacity (box 3.5). Different types of partnerships have different advantages and disadvantages (figure 3.4), as chapter 8 covers in more detail. Box 3.7 provides an overview of Solidaridad's experience in training POs.

BOX 3.5

In Practice: Yara in Ghana: Building Producer Organization Capacity via Training as Well as Inputs and Market Access in Ghana

Ghana's Breadbasket Initiative aims to transform northern Ghana into a more stable and prosperous area, with a focus on smallholder production of staple grains and legumes, particularly maize, rice, and soybeans. About one-fourth of Ghana's maize production comes from northern Ghana—despite poor soil fertility. Government and donors support the initiative with agricultural subsidies and social programs.

To improve the efficiency of the maize value chain in northern Ghana, Yara, a leading global fertilizer company, together with the local inputs provider Wienco, initiated the Ghana Grains Partnership (GGP) in 2008. They joined forces with the Africa Enterprise Challenge Fund; the farmers and farmers' associations initially in Wienco's outgrower scheme in the northern region; the Ministry of Food and Agriculture; commercial banks; TechnoServe, an international NGO specializing in private sector development; and output buyers (including processors) and traders.

The partners helped set up a farmers' association: the Masara N'Arziki ("Maize for Prosperity" in the local Hausa language). Acting on behalf of its members, Masara purchases inputs and sells the crops, while the GGP provides seeds and fertilizers on affordable credit terms, as well as storage and transport facilities—helping to reduce losses and increase profits.

Through the initiative, smallholders are supported by the following:

- Technical advice and training on improved agricultural practices to increase yield and quality via farmer crop clinics, farmer forums, and educative radio

- Access to credit

- Guidance on good land use and management practices

- Business management training

- Storage capacity

- Guaranteed price for the produce

- Access to a sustainable market.

By 2013/14, Mazara N'Arziki comprised 10,500 farmers. In 2011, farmer yields were an estimated 4.5 metric tons per hectare compared with the national average of 1.8 metric tons. Maize production profitability, however, is critically dependent on the input package used, including the use of high-yielding varieties (Ragasa and Lambrecht 2018). To produce and supply fertilizer at lower prices, Yara Ghana Ltd. plans to establish a fertilizer plant in Ghana within the next five years (Kwofi 2017).

Sources: Fintrac 2012; Grow Africa 2013; Guyver and MacCarthy 2011; Kwofi 2017; Ragasa and Lambrecht 2018.

FIGURE 3.4 Advantages and Disadvantages of Third-Party Partnerships to Build PO Capacity

EXISTING NGOs	NEW NGO	GOVERNMENT EXTENSION STAFF	PRIVATE PROVIDERS OF TRAINING SERVICES
(+) Expertise in PO development	(+) Goals of organization can be aligned with firm	(+) Linkage to national agriculture development program	(+) Expertise in PO development
(+) Training materials already developed	(−) Lack of track record can make fund-raising difficult	(−) Staff may lack capacity in PO development	(+) Training materials already developed
(−) May not share firm's priorities		(−) Government development of cooperatives has a poor history	(+) Focus can be tailored to the company's priorities
(−) Firm has no control over NGO funding			(−) Costs of training may be higher than other options

Note: NGO = nongovernmental organization; PO = producer organization.

Best practices for partnerships among firms, farmers, and other service providers include the following:

- Develop a memorandum of understanding, and clarify roles and responsibilities before starting.

- Agree on common policies on critical issues; for example, discuss the sanctions for side-selling and loan defaults before entering into any agreement.

- Agree on a uniform scale for benchmarking PO capacities.

- Base performance benchmarks on realistic assumptions about future performance and justifiable reasoning linked to the firm's needs.

- Determine the PO's performance benchmarks together before the program starts.

Farmer Training and PO Capacity Building: Similar Investments

The organizational development needs of POs are part of a spectrum of training needs in smallholder agriculture, though traditionally more attention has probably been given to other, more *agricultural* topics. In both areas, firms must identify and manage extension agents (or other trainers), work with farmer leaders, and leverage print and information and communication technology (ICT) media to disseminate a message. The development of more capable POs can strengthen the impact of messaging to farmers.

Given the overlapping training structures and outcomes, firms may choose to develop the capacity of farmers and farmer groups simultaneously. Chapter 5 explores farmer training and other communication channels in more detail.

See box 3.6 for an example of successful partnership between off-takers and a service provider to deliver training to POs.

Importance of Building Trust

It takes time to build trust between partners with clear, sequential steps that develop the relationship (figure 3.5). Operational strategies can increase efficiency, reduce costs, and build long-term relationships that benefit the firm, partner NGOs, and smallholders.

Trust between firms and POs allows partners to reassess the level of risk and hence to assume more risk to jointly advance their shared enterprise. A long-term perspective—demonstrating commitment—also helps build trust. (For an example, see box 3.7 about Cooperative Business International's joint venture with coffee and spice cooperatives in Southeast Asia.)

Best Practices in Crop Procurement

In working with POs to procure crops, experience has yielded many best-practice recommendations: Start with groups that have already conducted business activities together, such as crop assembly and onward sale.

FIGURE 3.5 Phases of Trust and Risk in Partnerships between POs and Agribusiness Firms

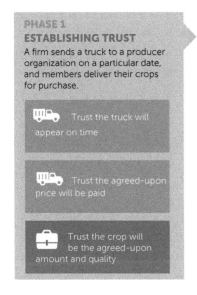

PHASE 1
ESTABLISHING TRUST

A firm sends a truck to a producer organization on a particular date, and members deliver their crops for purchase.

- Trust the truck will appear on time
- Trust the agreed-upon price will be paid
- Trust the crop will be the agreed-upon amount and quality

PHASE 2
ASSUMING RISK

Producer organization uses its own capital to buy member and nonmember crops.

Producer organization obtains bank loan to buy member and nonmember crops.

Firms advance funds to producer organizations to purchase farmers' crops at agreed prices.

- Risk that firm will not buy at agreed-upon price or quantity
- Risk of decapitalization
- Risk that the organization can't get another loan or loses its collateral
- Risk that the producer organization will not meet the terms of the agreement for volume or quality

PHASE 3
SHARING INCENTIVES

Firm and producer organization share the margin between the commodity's price at farm gate and export. More traceability and higher quality can increase export prices and the margins accruing to firm and producer organization.

 Producer organizations

 Firms

Note: POs = producer organizations.

BOX 3.7

In Practice: A Firm's Long-Term Perspective Develops Supplier Loyalty

In Southeast Asia, Cooperative Business International (CBI) has formed joint venture companies with cooperatives for the procurement and export of coffee and spices. These cooperatives have approximately 500,000 smallholder members.

At the start of the process, CBI provided resources to create joint ventures, including working capital, logistics, and processing facilities, and usually owns a minimum of 51 percent of the joint

box continued

BOX 3.7

In Practice: A Firm's Long-Term Perspective Develops Supplier Loyalty
(Continued)

venture shares. Over a number of years, the cooperatives purchased shares, eventually reaching 49 percent.

   During this process, CBI and its sister organization, the not-for-profit National Cooperative Business Association, provided mentoring and technical assistance to the cooperative and joint venture staffs. This approach has increased productivity, built supplier loyalty, and curbed side-selling.

- Work with organizations that have secure storage space.

- Use both traditional and democratically organized groups, which can be effective at the village level.

- Establish written agreements with POs specifying crop quality and price (or premium above prevailing market price, depending on the value added by the PO)—keeping in mind the difficulty of enforcing contracts specifying, for example, volume to be supplied by the PO. Formal agreements nonetheless help emphasize the company's supply requirements.

- Keep agreements clear and basic, because the level of literacy in the PO may be limited.

- Establish a dispute resolution process and clear consequences for not honoring agreements.

- Encourage POs to keep written records so annual profit-and-loss statements can be prepared.

- Use automated systems such as Frontline SMS, Esoko, and FarmForce to collect and disseminate information about prices and crop volumes.

- Encourage financial institutions to provide loans or basic supplies and equipment that enhance PO ability to procure and process crops. These supplies may include empty grain bags, weighing scales, moisture meters, crop fumigants, and cement to seal the floors of traditional warehouses. Donor or government funds may be available to construct or improve rural crop storage facilities, and firms may assist POs to apply for these resources. Providing empty grain bags with the company name helps reduce side-selling.

Loans to Help POs and Other Aggregators Upgrade Capacity

POs may be good customers for loans if they are legally registered, have written records, and can demonstrate strong relationships with input firms or buyers. These may be seasonal loans to individual members for crop production or shorter-term loans to the group for crop marketing. In the case of individual loans, the business plan might require a guarantee in the event of default.

POs that work with livestock may also be good customers for loans. Heifer Project International has developed a successful methodology in which loans of goats, cattle, and other livestock are repaid with offspring, which are passed to other members of the group to continue the cycle. Another successful model involves loans of young cows, which are fattened by group members and then sold by the group, with the increased value shared between the farmers and the PO. For dairy POs, loans to construct milk-collection and chilling facilities can improve quality by reducing transport time and cooling the fresh milk more quickly.

When group loans are extended to POs, it is a good practice to require an up-front cash contribution, usually 10 percent of the loan amount. Typically, these funds come from previous business activities or members' savings. It represents evidence of prior achievement as a group—and provides a coguarantee against the risk of side-selling or default.

When PO members receive production loans, good practice includes providing a combination of cash and inputs to ensure that the correct inputs are used and to cover expenses during the growing season. Loans should follow standard good practices for microfinance, such as using a smaller peer group to validate the need for the inputs or loans and to ensure they are used as intended. Group guarantees of member loans can provide peer pressure to insure repayment.

Blended finance—where more than one party shares the loan risk—may be available, particularly for longer-term investments (as in the truck leasing example discussed in chapter 2, box 2.4). That such guarantees exist can be sufficient to allay a partner's concerns, even if there is no need to draw-down on the guarantee.

Planning PO Tasks and Performance Assessment

Depending on the firm's presence in a region, the sector in which it works, and its quality requirements, firms may wish to work more or less closely with smallholder suppliers. A supply chain analysis may point to POs as a way to reduce costs and provide other benefits. If so, a more detailed review and planning will help determine which capacities are needed and help the firm identify suitable organizations.

For example, analysis of an Indonesian cocoa supply chain revealed that low productivity was due to limited and incorrect fertilizer use. To resolve these problems, a cocoa exporter partnered with a bank and a fertilizer manufacturer to raise cocoa farmer productivity. The program design meant that all of the tasks required of the POs could be met from Class B and C POs (though there was no restriction on participation by the more-able Class A POs). Table 3.2 provides an example of which tasks can be performed by which class of PO.

TABLE 3.2 Sample Cocoa Outgrower Scheme Using POs, by PO Class

PO class	Fertilizer manufacturer	Financial institution	Cocoa exporter
ABC	—	• Hold meetings for Good Agricultural Practices training.	• Hold monthly meetings on financial literacy. • Hold meetings for certification.
AB	• Distribute fertilizer to members from a central point.	• Do not sell to other buyers.	• Receive payment as a group. • Deliver cocoa to buying unit. • Do not sell to other buyers. • Grade cocoa before sale.
A	—	—	—

Note: POs = producer organizations. "A," "B," and "C" designate classes of POs, which are defined and discussed in detail earlier in this chapter. The top row of the table represents the agribusiness firm's requirements that any class of PO (A, B, or C) can satisfy because they involve only information collection and dissemination. The middle row represents activities that would pertain only to PO classes A or B because they involve group management of cash, fertilizer, and cocoa, which requires the group cohesion and trust of a Class B PO or above. The bottom row displays no additional requirements for a Class A PO beyond those for a Class B PO. — = no additional requirements.

TABLE 3.3 Sample Sesame Procurement Scheme Using POs, by PO Class

PO class	Financial institution	Noncertified sesame exporter	Certified sesame importer
ABC	• Develop business plans and loan applications. • Be legally registered and open bank account. • Hold meetings to understand loan provisions.	• Determine locations of sesame to purchase.	• Obtain and hold fair trade and organic certification. • Hold meetings on certification requirements.
AB	• Provide 10 percent loan guarantee.	• Receive payment as a group. • Grade and bag sesame.	• Receive second payment after delivery. • Grade and bag sesame. • Hire a manager for logistics and export.
A	• Manage loans of up to $5,000 for crop purchases.	• Manage cash advances to purchase sesame from farmers outside group.	–

Source: IFC 2014.
Note: POs = producer organizations. "A," "B," and "C" designate classes of POs, which are defined and discussed in detail earlier in this chapter. The top row of the table represents the agribusiness firm's requirements for any of the PO classes (A, B, or C), although they require a minimal level of sophistication regarding bank loans and crop advances. The middle row represents activities that would pertain only to PO classes A or B, requiring greater levels of group cohesion and trust. The bottom row outlines needs that only Class A POs can fulfill.

A second example shows the requirements of three firms in two sesame supply chains in Mozambique (table 3.3). One supply chain is for certified sesame, and the other is for noncertified sesame. In this case, all of the selected POs needed to be more sophisticated because they would be managing bank loans and advances for crop purchases—and certain tasks can be undertaken only by the more-capable Class A POs.

In the following chapters, group-based approaches are further explored focusing on their role in standards and certification, training, inputs, and farm management.

Notes

1. See, for example, Dalberg (2012) and Kelly, Vergara, and Bammann (2015).
2. Reference is sometimes made to "second-tier" organizations, a term used to describe networks of cooperatives or associations.

3. "About SCOPEinsight" (accessed March 22, 2018), http://www.scopeinsight.com
/who-we-are/.
4. See http://www.ameaglobal.org.

References

COOP and Euricse (International Co-operative Alliance and European Research
Initiative on Cooperative and Social Enterprises). 2016. "World Co-operative
Monitor. Exploring the Cooperative Economy: Report 2016." Annual data report,
COOP, Brussels.
Dalberg (Dalberg Global Development Advisors). 2012. "Catalyzing Smallholder
Agricultural Finance." Research report, Dalberg Global Development Advisors,
New York.
Dave Grace and Associates. 2014. "Measuring the Size and Scope of the Cooperative
Economy: Results of the 2014 Global Census on Co-operatives." Report for the
United Nations Department of Economic and Social Affairs (UN DESA), New
York.
FAO (Food and Agriculture Organization of the United Nations) and AgriCord. 2016.
*Forest and Farm Producer Organisations—Operating Systems for the SDGs: Strength in
Numbers*. Rome: FAO and AgriCord.
Fintrac Inc. 2012. "The Market for Maize, Rice, Soy, and Warehousing in Northern
Ghana." Market assessment report for the Enabling Agricultural Trade (EAT)
project of the U.S. Agency for International Development, Washington, DC.
Grow Africa. 2013. "Investing in the Future of African Agriculture: 1st Annual
Report on Private Sector Investment in Support of Country-Led
Transformations in African Agriculture." Annual report, Grow Africa
Secretariat, Johannesburg.
Guyver, P., and M. MacCarthy. 2011. "The Ghana Grains Partnership." *International
Journal of Agricultural Sustainability* 9 (1): 35–41.
IFC (International Finance Corporation). 2014. "Working with Smallholders: A
Handbook for Firms Building Sustainable Supply Chains." IFC, Washington,
DC.
Kelly, S., N. Vergara, and H. Bammann. 2015. *Inclusive Business Models: Guidelines for
Improving Linkages between Producer Groups and Buyers of Agricultural Produce*. Rome:
Food and Agriculture Organization of the United Nations (FAO).
Kwofi, M. 2017. "Yara Ghana to Establish Fertiliser Plant." *Graphic Online*, September 18,
https://www.graphic.com.gh/news/general-news/yara-ghana-to-establish
-fertiliser-plant.html.
Mayo, E. 2012. "Global Business Ownership 2012: Members and Shareholders across
the World." *New Insight 9* report, Co-operatives UK, Manchester.
Ragasa, C., and I. Lambrecht. 2018. "Options for Reducing Poverty in Remote Areas of
Northern Ghana: Can Maize Contract Farming Help?" IFPRI Research Blog,
International Food Policy Research Institute (IFPRI), January 18. http://www.ifpri
.org/blog/options-reducing-poverty-remote-areas-northern-ghana-can-maize
-contract-farming-schemes-help.
World Bank. 2014. "An Analytical Toolkit for Support to Contract Farming." Working
paper, Report No. 88181, World Bank, Washington, DC.

Additional Resources

Producer Organizations

AMEA (Agribusiness Market Ecosystem Alliance). https://www.ameaglobal.org/.

ACDI/VOCA (merger of the former Agricultural Cooperative Development International and Volunteers in Overseas Cooperative Assistance). http://www.acdivoca.org.

Agriterra. http://www.agriterra.org/en.

CLARITY (Cooperative Law & Regulation Initiative). 2006. "Enabling Cooperative Development: Principles for Legal Reform." First-year report of CLARITY, an initiative of the Overseas Cooperative Development Council (OCDC), http://www.clarity.coop/pdf/PUB_Clarity_one.pdf.

FAO (Food and Agriculture Organization of the United Nations). http://www.fao.org. [Information on producer organizations]

———. 2011. "2010 Annual Report on FAO Activities in Support of Producers' Organizations and Agricultural Cooperatives." Report of the FAO Inter Departmental Committee and Inter Departmental Working Group on Institution Building for Agriculture and Rural Development, FAO, Rome.

FOSCA (Farmer Organization Support Center for Africa). http://www.agra-alliance.org/section/work/fosca.

GFRAS (Global Forum for Rural Advisory Services). http://www.g-fras.org/en. [Source of expertise on producer organization training]

Grow Africa SWG (Smallholder Working Group). 2015. "How Do Off-Takers and Smallholder Farmers Use Aggregation Models to Grow Their Business?" Strategic Note, Grow Africa SWG for IDH The Sustainable Trade Initiative, Utrecht, Netherlands; and Grow Africa, Johannesburg.

Hystra. 2015. "Smallholder Farmers and Business: 15 Pioneering Collaborations for Improved Productivity and Sustainability." Research report, Hystra, Paris.

IFAD (International Fund for Agricultural Development). 2010. "IFAD and Farmers' Organizations. Partnership in Progress: 2008–2009." Report to the global meeting of the Farmers' Forum in conjunction with the Thirty-Third Session of the Governing Council of IFAD, Rome, February 15–16.

IFPRI (International Food Policy Research Institute). http://www.ifpri.org. [Economic and technical research on producer organizations]

Inades-Formation. 2016. "Our Intervention Approach." http://www.inadesformation.net/en/instutional/our-intervention-approach/. [Organization active with producer organizations in West Africa]

Land O'Lakes International Development. http://www.idd.landolakes.com/. [Technical expertise with dairy producer organizations]

NCBA CLUSA (National Cooperative Business Association and Cooperative League of USA). http://ncba.coop/.

OCDC (U.S. Overseas Cooperative Development Council). 2007. "Cooperatives: Pathways to Economic, Democratic and Social Development in the Global Economy." Report, OCDC, Arlington, VA.

———. 2009. "Measuring Cooperative Success: New Challenges and Opportunities in Low- and Middle-Income Countries. Measurements for Tracking Indicators of Cooperative Success (METRICS)." Report of the METRICS initiative, OCDC, Falls Church, VA.

SCOPEinsight. http://www.scopeinsight.com/.

Contract Farming

Contract Farming Resource Center. [FAO-sponsored source of information on contract farming]. http://www.fao.org/in-action/contract-farming/en.

Minot, N., and L. Ronchi. 2014. "Contract Farming: Risks and Benefits of Partnership between Farmers and Firms." *Viewpoint: Public Policy for the Private Sector* No. 344, International Food Policy Research Institute, Washington, DC.

Torero, M., R. Hill, and A. Viceisza. 2010. "Contracting Out of Poverty: Experimental Approaches to Innovation in Agricultural Markets with Small Farmers." Project Note, International Food Policy and Research Institute, Washington, DC. http://www.ifpri.org/sites/default/files/publications/mtidspotlight_contracting.pdf.

World Bank and UNCTAD (United Nations Conference on Trade and Development). 2017a. "Choosing Appropriate Business Models." Responsible Agricultural Investment (RAI) Knowledge into Action Note No. 3, World Bank, Washington, DC; UNCTAD, New York. http://documents.worldbank.org/curated/en/174811521089712683/pdf/124278-BRI-PUBLIC-KN03.pdf.

———. 2017b. "Outgrower Schemes: How to Increase the Chances of Success." Responsible Agricultural Investment (RAI) Knowledge into Action Note No. 4, World Bank, Washington, DC; UNCTAD, New York. http://documents.worldbank.org/curated/en/203541521090030245/pdf/124279-BRI-PUBLIC-KN04.pdf.

Tools for Communication with Farmers

CCI (Communications Cooperative International). http://www.cci.coop/home.html. [Expertise in communication with producer organizations]

Esoko. https://www.esoko.com/. [Tools for communicating with producer organizations, such as scouting polling via SMS]

FAO (Food and Agriculture Organization of the United Nations). 2011. *Building Networks for Market Access: Lessons Learned from the Rural Knowledge Network (RKN) Pilot Project for East Africa (Uganda, Kenya and Tanzania)*. Rome: FAO.

Frontline SMS. http://www.frontlinesms.com/.

Other Relevant Resources

Collion, Marie-Hélène, and Pierre Rondot. 2001. "Investing in Rural Producer Organizations for Sustainable Agriculture." Good Practice Note, Report No. 22386, World Bank, Washington, DC.

Lundy, M., G. Becx, N. Zamierowski, A. Amrein, J. J. Hurtado, E. E. Mosquera, and F. Rodríguez. 2012. *LINK Methodology: A Participatory Guide to Business Models that Link Smallholders to Markets*. Cali, Colombia: International Center for Tropical Agriculture (CIAT).

McGregor, A., and K. Stice. 2014. "Agricultural Value Chain Guide for the Pacific Islands: Making Value Chain Analysis a Useful Tool in the Hands of Farmers, Traders and Policy Makers." Technical Centre for Agricultural and Rural Cooperation (CTA), Wageningen, Netherlands.

McVay, M., and A. Snelgrove. 2007. "Program Design for Value Chain Initiatives. Information to Action: A Toolkit Series for Market Development Practitioners." Toolkit, Mennonite Economic Development Associates (MEDA), Lancaster, PA.

Mercoiret, Marie-Rose, Denis Pesche, and Pierre Marie Bosc. 2006. "Rural Producer Organizations (RPOs) for Pro-Poor Sustainable Development." Report of World Bank workshop on RPOs for *World Development Report 2008: Agriculture for Development*, Paris, October 30–31.

Oiko Credit. http://oikocreditusa.org/. [Financial institution providing "patient capital"]

Oxfam International. https://www.oxfam.org/. [Organization providing producer organization training]

ResponsAbility. https://www.responsability.com/en. [Financial institution providing credit to producer organizations]

Root Capital. https://rootcapital.org/. [Financial institution providing credit to producer organizations]

Shared Interest. http://www.sharedinterest.org/. [Financial institution providing credit to producer organizations]

Solidaridad. https://www.solidaridadnetwork.org/. [Dutch organization and network providing producer organization training]

The Springfield Centre. 2008. "A Synthesis of the Making Markets Work for the Poor (M4P) Approach." Guide prepared on behalf of the Swiss Agency for Development and Cooperation (SDC), Bern; and U.K. Department for International Development (DFID), London.

Triodos. http://www.triodos.com. [Financial institution providing credit to producer organizations and intermediaries]

Vermeulen, S., J. Woodhill, F. Proctor, and R. Delnoye. 2008. *Chain-Wide Learning for Inclusive Agrifood Market Development: A Guide to Multi-Stakeholder Processes for Linking Small-Scale Producers to Modern Markets*. London: International Institute for Environment and Development (IIED); Wageningen, Netherlands: Wageningen University and Research Centre.

Wiggins, S., and S. Keats. 2013. "Leaping and Learning: Linking Smallholders to Markets in Africa." London: Agriculture for Impact, Imperial College and Overseas Development Institute.

World Bank. 2007. "Supporting Smallholder Competitiveness through Institutional Innovations." In *World Development Report 2008: Agriculture for Development*, 138–57. Washington, DC: World Bank.

CHAPTER 4
STANDARDS FOR SUSTAINABILITY
AND QUALITY

KEY MESSAGES

⇒ There is an increasing focus on standards that promote improved agricultural practices.

⇒ Agribusiness companies are increasingly making prominent public commitments on their social and environmental positions.

⇒ These trends are driven by environmental and climate change concerns, consumer demands, food safety compliance, and the wish to avoid reputational damage.

⇒ Sustainable sourcing is increasing, including certified areas of key crops, which more than tripled between 2010 and 2015.

⇒ Compliance can expand market access but may not deliver higher prices.

⇒ Overall production costs can be recouped through productivity gains and efficiency.

⇒ New information and communication technology capability has facilitated the emergence of systems for tracking smallholder compliance with standards.

Introduction

Standards help firms ensure good agricultural and forestry practices and avoid potential negative social and environmental impacts. Any agribusiness firm considering whether to adopt voluntary sustainability standards along its smallholder supply chain must weigh expected benefits against the costs of meeting the requirements and verifying compliance, including the costs of possibly excluding large numbers of smallholders.

Standards benefit firms that source from smallholders by the following:

· Identifying and managing social and environmental impacts

· Improving productivity, efficiency, and security of supply

· Expanding market access through certification.

Standards can highlight potential problems in smallholder supply chains, such as transparency in pricing, land rights, soil fertility, erosion and degradation, water quality, pests and disease management, and health and safety. Firms that source directly from farmers or from local intermediaries can use standards as a framework for diagnosing which components of a supply chain need targeted capacity building and resources.

Certification is a communication tool that can increase access to markets that demand verification of a firm's good practices. (For definitions of standards, certification, and verification, see box 4.1.) If the market doesn't demand compliance with standards, firms may find that implementation of standards is cost-effective but that certification of standards is not (figure 4.1). In Thailand, however, certification in palm oil mitigated smallholder costs through the additional income from increased productivity (box 4.2).

Types of Standards for Agribusiness Supply Chains

Social and Environmental Practices

For primary production, some standards focus on social and environmental practices, including the following, by product type (all of which typically include traceability and control systems for the supply chain):

· *Forestry:* Forest Stewardship Council Principles and Criteria

· *Soy:* Roundtable on Responsible Soy Standard and the Proterra Standard

---

BOX 4.1

Standards, Certification, and Verification Defined

Definitions

- *Standards:* Norms or requirements that establish thresholds of good practice developed under various processes, from internal company protocols to multistakeholder established processes
- *Certification:* The mechanism for communicating that a firm has verified compliance with an established standard
- *Verification:* The process for confirming compliance with a standard

Types of Verification

- *First party:* A firm verifies compliance with standards using in-house staff.
- *Second party:* Buyers or other interested parties conduct verification of standards.
- *Third party:* An external, independent auditor checks compliance.

FIGURE 4.1 Costs and Benefits of Agricultural Standards and Certification

STANDARDS	CERTIFICATION
(+) Lower costs due to being internal process	(−) Higher costs due to external certifiers
(+) Productivity improvement	(−) Not all certification focuses on productivity improvement
(+) Reduction of inefficiencies	(+) Independent verification of supply chain practices
(−) Limited ability to make credible sustainability claims (greenwashing potential)	(+) Market access enabled or increased
(+) Potential to support better business practices	(+) Improved transparency in market claims
(+) Increased sustainability	(−) Only some production aspects may be covered, leading to problems such as "certifying poverty"
(+) Help in management and reduction of potential exposure to supply chain challenges	(−) Costs may exceed benefits
	(+) Setup for explanation of supply chain management challenges

- *Oil palm:* Roundtable on Sustainable Palm Oil

- *Coffee, cocoa, bananas, flowers, pineapple, and tea:* Sustainable Agriculture Network (SAN) Standard

- *Coffee, cocoa, and tea:* Rainforest Alliance Standard (which, as of 2017, combines elements of the SAN and former UTZ standards).

Good Agricultural Practices

Primary producers may also apply standards that focus on good agricultural practices (GAP) and traceability. GAP standards are particularly relevant to products directly consumed, in which case such standards are legally required for market access.

   These standards may also include elements of food safety. For example, GLOBALG.A.P. standards are applied to fruits and vegetables, combinable crops, coffee, tea, flowers, and ornamental plants.[1]

Jurisdictional or Landscape Standards

There is also growing interest in jurisdictional or landscape standards, to help address critical environmental issues, such as deforestation, on a larger scale. These standards could target a single commodity or multiple commodities, with boundaries defined to cover the production area or to include adjacent forests as well or an entire watershed. Pilot approaches are being developed in, for example, Southeast Asia for palm oil and Brazil for soy.

Among the incentives driving these holistic approaches is a search for tools that can help mitigate risks from sustainability threats in their supply chains, as a recent ISEAL Alliance report points out: "Companies like Unilever and Marks and Spencer are taking the next step by committing to source only from responsibly-managed jurisdictions" (Mallet et al. 2016, ii). Rapid developments in mapping and real-time surveillance are helping make these approaches more feasible.

Organic Certification

Organic certification, also used in primary production, includes avoidance the following:

- Synthetic chemical inputs not on the National List of Allowed and Prohibited Substances (covering fertilizer, pesticides, antibiotics, and food additives)

- Genetically modified organisms (GMOs)

- Irradiation

- Use of sewage sludge.

The International Federation of Organic Agriculture Movements unites more than 1,000 affiliates in more than 120 countries. Non-GMO standards are also available, including the Non-GMO Project Standard (Non-GMO Project 2017).

Other Standards

Additional key standards include the following:

- *Food safety standards* include Safe Quality Food, British Retail Consortium, International Food Safety, and Food Safety System Certification 22000. These include practices in the supply chain and traceability back to source. The Global Food Safety Initiative (GFSI) acts as an umbrella initiative supporting the uptake of food safety standards.

- *Fair trade standards* aim to ensure that producers are paid fairly. Twenty national fair trade organizations and three producer networks are members of Fairtrade International. These organizations use a standard that requires buyers to pay producers a price that aims to cover the costs of sustainable production and to pay an additional sum that producers can invest in development. Advance payments and signed contracts are also included in the approach. The World Fair Trade Organization, the Network of European Worldshops, and the European Fair Trade Association are other examples.

- *Management system standards* provide a framework for setting policy and developing and implementing policy and procedures but do not define what these should be. For example, the International Organization for Standardization's (ISO) 9000 series is for quality management, and ISO 14000 series is for environmental management.

The Business Case for Standards in Smallholder Supply Chains

Improving Productivity, Efficiency, and Security of Supply

Implementing standards may require training of smallholder suppliers in practices that improve farm productivity and quality. These improved practices have the potential to increase farm income and to channel additional supply to sourcing firms. Better farmer organization, leveraged through group certification, can also help establish shared labor pools, microcredit unions, and other economies of scale. Investing in farmers in the context of implementing a standard can increase farmer loyalty to a firm.

Firms and farmers can gain advantage from the adoption of standards or better management practices. For example, many companies are using GLOBALG.A.P. standards to define their approach to working with smallholders (box 4.3).

Another example is the standards system developed by the Better Cotton Initiative (BCI). To receive a BCI license, farmers must achieve a set of minimum requirements to ensure that their production meets clearly defined standards for pesticide use, water management, decent work, record keeping, training, and other factors. Thereafter, farmers are encouraged to keep making improvements, against which they are further assessed—and those with the strongest performance are rewarded with extended license periods. Member ginners note that meeting the BCI standard entailed some up-front training costs, but they were able to secure their supply and their markets, while farmers increased their net revenues per hectare—results that BCI hails as "a win-win business for both us and the farmer."[2]

Compliance with standards may also indirectly affect firms', or farmers', access to finance. Via funding windows and programs reserved for inclusive or eco-friendly supply chain development,

---

BOX 4.3

In Practice: GLOBALG.A.P. Certification for Smallholder Mango Growers in West Africa

Large-scale retailers, particularly in Europe and the Middle East, increasingly require the produce they sell to be GLOBALG.A.P. certified. Available for three scopes of production—crops, livestock, or aquaculture—the core GLOBALG.A.P. Certification covers the following:
• Food safety and traceability
• Environment (including biodiversity)
• Workers' health, safety, and welfare
• Animal welfare.

It also includes integrated crop management, integrated pest control, a quality management system (QMS), and Hazard Analysis and Critical Control Points (HACCP).

GlobalG.A.P.-compliant smallholders can be certified as members of a producer group ("Option 2 Producer Group Certification"). More than two-thirds of the GLOBALG.A.P.-certified producers are organized in producer groups. Certification requires the implementation of an approved QMS covering specified aspects of the production system, internal inspections for all members, and a group management representative with ultimate responsibility. The certification body then assesses whether the group's internal controls are appropriate and inspects a sample of the group members' farm operations.

With support from a U.S. Agency for International Development (USAID)-funded regional project (the West Africa Trade & Investment Hub), mango farmers' groups in Burkina Faso, Ghana, and Senegal have acquired GLOBALG.A.P. certification. In Ghana, the Yilo Krobo Mango Farmers' Association received training and assistance with both internal inspections and recruitment of an accredited certification body for external audits. Consequently, its members have higher incomes resulting from access to export markets in the European Union and the Middle East.

Sources: "Cultivating the Future of the Planet," GLOBALG.A.P. Certification (accessed March 23, 2018), https://www.globalgap.org/uk_en/what-we-do/globalg.a.p.-certification/globalg.a.p./; USAID 2016.

---

firms may find that they can access finance and technical assistance to implement standards with smallholders. Smallholders may gain access to finance because of compliance or certification. (For a case in which group certification facilitated bank access for Filipino banana farmers, see box 4.4.)

BOX 4.4

In Practice: Certification of Smallholder Banana Farmers in the Philippines

For a standards initiative in Mindanao, Philippines, International Finance Corporation (IFC) worked with Unifrutti Traders Ltd., the Rainforest Alliance, and farmers' cooperatives starting in 2008 to achieve two goals: (1) certify banana growers so their production could reach high-value markets in Japan, and (2) establish a local capacity for third-party inspection and certification.

Because of the program, the Rainforest Alliance-certified banana farmers improved their social and environmental practices and increased their revenue by more than $300 per hectare, while reducing their costs by $50 per hectare. In addition, the certified farmers found it easier to access bank financing and, because of the business training, felt more confident to engage with banks. Since the end of the IFC program in December 2010, the presence of three local inspectors has benefited firms and farmers in other sectors to obtain Rainforest Alliance certification.

Source: Macawaris, Taylor, and Zamora-Galinato 2011.

Meeting Growing Market Expectations on Sustainability

Sustainable sourcing—"the integration of social, ethical, and environmental performance factors into the process of selecting suppliers"[3]—has become a key concern for global agribusiness companies.

As companies extend their value chains into frontier and emerging markets in pursuit of lower costs, greater production capacity, and new markets, they are also exposed to a widening array of risks. Companies must meet the growing expectations of stakeholders (including customers, shareholders, employees, nongovernmental organizations [NGOs], trade associations, labor unions, and government observers) to take responsibility for their suppliers' environmental, social, and ethical practices.[4]

As a result, global brands are increasingly making public commitments about sustainability—especially in relation to labor standards and the environment—and this is driving the way they work with smallholders and the partnerships they form. Their statements have a lot in common: Many position their arguments in relation to growing global food needs. All the companies emphasize responsible sourcing, environmental management, and food safety. Many have partnerships with NGOs and researchers. All make clear sustainability commitments. Many refer to the development of indexes, assessment tools, and other methodologies.

In sum, the clear message is that these are key issues that concern consumers and shareholders, which no major company can now afford to ignore (Gordon and Woodhill 2011).

As a result, large agricultural commodity buyers—such as branded manufacturers, retailers, national governments, traders, and downstream industries—increasingly require evidence of good social and environmental practices in primary production. As discussed throughout this chapter, several organizations issue such standards and certify compliance. As this trend gains ground, so too are companies beginning to develop their own standards. Banks, too, may require borrowers to demonstrate compliance with guidelines on social and environmental issues, including community consultation, indigenous peoples, and labor standards. Overall, these trends toward sustainable sourcing—and accountability for it—are driven by consumer demands, food safety concerns, pressure for climate change mitigation, and companies' desire to avoid reputational risk.

Selected Products, Selected Markets: Growing Demand for Sustainable Sourcing

Environmental and social sustainability standards, being mostly voluntary and market-driven, are therefore not regulated (with food safety and environmental health standards being significant exceptions). Consequently, sustainable sourcing derives from companies setting their own standards as well as from third-party standards and certification schemes. Within each category are myriad standard-setting schemes—more than 400 in all (Von Hagen, Manning, and Reinecke 2010)—each with slight differences in reach and requirements. (The International Trade Centre has developed a "Sustainability Map" tool to help companies find the best fit for their needs.[5])

Interest in sustainable sourcing became evident in the 1970s and has gradually gained momentum since then. The certified acreage for selected crops nearly doubled between 2008 and 2010, again by 2011, and again between 2011 and 2015. Notably, certified cocoa, coffee, and tea command production shares of 20–30 percent globally, while production of certified cotton, soy, palm oil, vanilla, and sugar is also increasing. For many other products, sustainably sourced crops remain a niche market.

Geographically, interest is most notable in North America and Europe: the market share for organic food, a specific category of sustainably sourced product, is 7–10 percent in several European countries, and the North American organic market is worth more than $50 billion.[6] As the market responds to stronger consumer awareness of sustainability, the potential for certification (and for commanding premiums) is greater in higher-income markets (with some exceptions, such as Japan, where interest has been slower to emerge [USDA FAS 2013]), including among higher-income groups in poorer countries as well as for products that reach consumers directly (such as beverage crops) rather than intermediate products (such as soy).

As the trend toward sustainable sourcing matures, several developments are evident:

- In some markets (for example, coffee in Europe), sustainable sourcing is almost becoming a requirement but does not necessarily confer premium prices to suppliers (as further discussed in the "Price Premiums" section below).

- At present, some of the certified product is sold in conventional markets, and supply exceeds demand, such as for coffee and cocoa (CBI 2017; Potts et al. 2014).

- Companies are increasingly defining their own standards. Examples include the following:

  ○ *Starbucks C.A.F.E.* (coffee and farmer equity) practices

  ○ *The Olam Livelihood Charter* (eight principles to tackle economic, environmental, and social challenges including business management, empowering women, reducing child labor, and building resilience to climate change)

  ○ *Mondelēz International*, through its Cocoa Life program, which promotes positive lasting change for cocoa communities.

- Companies and farmers are seeing the benefits of implementing standards in increased productivity and farmer loyalty—irrespective of market demand and price premiums.

- The traceability of a product's origin becomes increasingly important. Box 4.5 reviews the pros and cons of traceability and its certification.

Sustainable Sourcing Standards, by Type

International Finance Corporation Performance Standards

A credible standard has the following attributes:

- Is objective and achievable

- Is founded on a multistakeholder consultative process

BOX 4.5

Traceability and Certification

Traceability—the ability to identify a product's origin and subsequent movements throughout a supply chain—is important in the food and agribusiness sector because it helps companies manage risk, particularly in relation to food safety, labor, and environmental practices.

If the production base is fragmented—with individual farmers providing small quantities of produce—full traceability can be particularly challenging and costly to establish. Smallholder pro- duce is often subject to "mixage," that is, produce from multiple producers being combined shortly after harvest, at the level of the cooperative or trader (ITC 2015).

By guaranteeing the manner of production and by attributing that production to a particular (certified) source—encompassing multiple producers in the case of smallholder production— certification obviates the need for any additional tracking system at the producer level. (In practice, producer-level tracking is handled by the group or company seeking certification.) Certification enables the seller to communicate a large quantity of information about good practices in a simple way to buyers, but it also makes significant demands on the management capacity of the producer organization (or the body seeking certification). Improved market access may partially offset costs (but see the caveats discussed below about market access and premiums).

Both traceability and certification entail costs, significantly weighted to the initial setup of the system, but certification also requires periodic costs to maintain certification. (Most certification schemes use third-party verification.) However, growth in the availability of suitable digital tools can potentially dramatically reduce costs for both processes. A review of five widely used systems for supply chain management found they all offered the following:

- Data collection, data analysis, and reporting
- Photo tagging and geocoding of farms
- Voice- and text-based messages between field staff and management
- Selling and payment transactions
- Tracing the crop as it is cultivated, sold, and stored in a warehouse.

· Encourages stepwise and continual improvements

· Provides for independent verification or certification through appropriate accredited bodies for such standards.

International Finance Corporation's (IFC) Sustainability Framework articulates its strategic commitment to sustainable development. In the case of its direct investments, clients must apply Performance Standards to manage environmental and social risks and impacts so that development opportunities are enhanced. The Performance Standards cover eight areas:

1. Assessment and Management of Environmental and Social Risks and Impacts
2. Labor and Working Conditions
3. Resource Efficiency and Pollution Prevention
4. Community Health, Safety, and Security
5. Land Acquisition and Involuntary Resettlement
6. Biodiversity Conservation and Sustainable Management of Living Natural Resources
7. Indigenous Peoples
8. Cultural Heritage

Some of IFC's Performance Standards on Environmental and Social Sustainability provide good examples of sustainability standards applied in agribusiness supply chains, particularly the following (IFC 2012):

- *Performance Standard (PS) 1* requires that companies have social and environmental assessment and management systems. In many cases, industry-led or third-party standards, such as the Roundtable for Sustainable Palm Oil (RSPO), are aligned with PS 1.

- *PS 2* relates to labor and working conditions. For smallholder supply chains, the most relevant aspects are a prohibition on child, slave, or forced labor. Many companies in the cocoa sector have pledged to eliminate child labor in their smallholder supply chains. Reducing the risk of child labor could involve changing agricultural practices or increasing access to education.

- *PS 6* requires conservation of biodiversity and sustainable use of natural resources. Meeting this standard in smallholder supply chains could include monitoring land use change and introducing agricultural practices that increase productivity per unit of land area. Paragraphs 26–30 refer to the use of credible globally, regionally, or nationally recognized standards for clients' own operations and their primary suppliers.

The Equator Principles

The Equator Principles are based on IFC's Performance Standards and serve as guidance for financial institutions to determine, assess, and manage environmental and social risk in projects (EP Association 2013). These principles provide a basis standard for due diligence and monitoring to support responsible decision making concerning risk.

The Equator Principles apply globally to all industry sectors and determine eligibility for four financial products:

- Project finance advisory services

- Project finance

- Project-related corporate loans

- Bridge loans.

Food Safety Standards

Food safety standards tend to be regulated in both international and domestic markets—and as such, differ from many of the other voluntary standards discussed here. Traceability (discussed below) is important in isolating the cause of food safety problems.

Although many food standards require relatively straightforward adherence to widely accepted food safety practices (which nonetheless may be challenging to implement in some contexts), others are quite complex. One example is aflatoxin, a carcinogen produced by mold that grows on improperly dried or handled crops (box 4.6).

Expansion of Market Access

Verifying compliance with standards and communicating compliance through certification is important for market access. In European markets and increasingly in U.S. markets, consumers have a significant expectation that the goods they purchase have been produced using good social, environmental, and agricultural practices. Large buyers are increasingly requiring their suppliers to meet labor and environmental standards—making compliance a necessity to meet minimum entry requirements or simply maintain market share.

Meeting standards for sustainable sourcing does not always increase market access, however. There may not be clear market direction—perhaps because the firm is a first mover or is getting mixed market signals—but there may be other benefits, including less risk and more efficiency.

A careful assessment of the available standards will identify the set of standards that best meets a firm's needs. Firms may find it helpful to participate in sector or industry roundtable discussions to understand and

---

BOX 4.6

In Practice: Managing Aflatoxin in Maize in Rwanda

Aflatoxin is a serious and complex problem for Rwanda maize growers, as the following facts illustrate:

- The problem stems principally from two fungi, especially *Aspergillus flavus*.
- *A. flavus* affects 42 crops, of which maize and groundnuts are most important in Sub-Saharan Africa.
- Prevalence of *A. flavus* is expanding in space and time.
- Not all strains of suspect fungi generate aflatoxins; toxigenic strains are unpredictable.
- In maize, *A. flavus* is both a field and a storage fungus; it is pervasive, systemic, and hard to control.
- *A. flavus* is not evenly distributed; there are hot spots of contamination determined by the geographical agronomical and trade practices.
- *A. flavus* is stimulated by the right conditions of temperature and relative humidity, especially when a plant is stressed by drought, pests, disease, or otherwise damaged.
- The current situation stems not only from growing conditions but also from maize shortage practices, high prices, lack of familiarity with the issue, and lack of incentives to take measures to address the problem.

Because the geographical source of aflatoxin is not known, maize production is widespread, and the recommended biocontrol agent (Aflasafe) is not available in Rwanda, current recommendations focus on multiple critical steps in harvesting, drying, and storage. However, to focus on immediate sourcing issues, it is also important to dedicate efforts to sourcing, awareness raising, testing, and making strategic decisions regarding tolerance levels (as different levels are set for different end uses).

The main point is that such issues are important and not easily solved. Adopting food safety standards to address the issue is part of the solution but may not be sufficient to address the issue fully. Leadership on this must come from the companies affected and at risk, as well as from governments, which in turn would need to (a) source appropriate expertise; (b) build their own capacity to recognize, test for, and implement control strategies; and (c) require suitable control measures from their farmer suppliers.

---

anticipate what will be required and to share best practices and lessons learned with others.

Price Premiums from Standards: The Exception, Not the Rule

Firms and farmers who comply with standards may increase their market access but do not necessarily earn price premiums. In complex supply chains, premiums paid by the consumer may be absorbed by downstream retailers, manufacturers, and other intermediaries.

In other cases, retailers may determine that the market does not allow for price premiums for any of several reasons:

- Large retailers in Europe and the United States, for example, now offer an expanded range of certified products, but they are unwilling to pay premium prices that would have to be passed on to their customers.

- Many consumers are willing to pay a premium for certified products, but the additional amount they are willing to pay is relatively little (as further discussed in box 4.7).

- In markets where certification has moved from the exception to an expectation, the increased supply of certified product may dilute past price premiums or eliminate them altogether.

BOX 4.7

Sustainable Sourcing: Mixed Consumer Messages on Price Premiums

Surveys consistently show that most consumers state a preference for sustainably sourced products— and many state a willingness to pay premiums for those products (see, for example, WBCSD [2008] and the Nielson consumer studies).[a] However, the relatively few studies of *observed* purchasing behavior often indicate less willingness to pay than claimed. Some exceptions include a premium of 11 percent for "green labeled" coffee in the United Kingdom (Galarraga and Markandya 2004) and a premium of 12–52 percent for organic baby food in the United States (Smith, Huang, and Lin 2009).

Several studies indicate that consumers choose "eco-labeled" products over other products and choose brands with a good reputation for responsible business practices. An analysis of results from 80 studies found that almost 60 percent of consumers are willing to pay a premium of some kind for socially responsible products and that such products, on average, command a 16.8 percent premium over similar but less overtly "responsible" products (Tully and Winer 2014). A particularly robust finding was greater willingness to pay for attributes that benefit people directly (such as labor standards) than for environmental benefits.

This is still an underresearched area—particularly the understanding of how consumers respond to the set of "signals" about a product (brand, labeling, other product information, pricing, and other factors) and how this response may change over time. Nonetheless, it seems that sustainable sourcing, where apparent and without a higher price tag, will certainly command a growing market share or be important in maintaining market share.

a. For Nielsen consumer studies on willingness to pay for products certified as sustainably sourced, see the Nielsen, http://www.nielsen.com/us/en.html.

Costs of Implementing Standards

As with any supply chain investment, the expected benefits of compliance with standards must be weighed against the costs. The net value will vary depending on multiple considerations (as summarized earlier in figure 4.1). In general, the costs of compliance, certification, and cost mitigation for producers should all be considered, including the following:

- *Compliance costs* are affected by factors including the following:
  - Baseline practices of smallholder suppliers
  - Existing degree of smallholder organization
  - Number of smallholders supplying the firm
  - Country in which the smallholders operate
  - Market demands
  - Level of performance required by the standard.

- *Certification costs* include third-party verification, as well as fees for membership in the standards body.

- *Cost mitigation for suppliers*—that is, the net value for smallholders—should also be considered. Extra costs, such as additional labor or working hours, must be understood and included in the cost-benefit analysis for farmers.

As the focus on sustainable sourcing has gained ground, the development of this trend has been characterized (Dalberg 2012) as follows:

- *An initially defensive strategy* (companies having corporate social responsibility positions and policies), which developed further into

- *Sustainable branding* to meet market demands, which grew into

- *Protecting and building the core business*—becoming almost "mainstream" (especially in high-income markets).

Sustainable and responsible operations have become a way of doing business, which also helps companies manage risk (particularly reputational risk). Standards may facilitate market access (by meeting consumer expectations or because of legislated or required standards for, for example, food safety)—but they are also becoming an important tool for raising productivity (that is, improving yields and quality).

Deforestation and Modern Slavery: Major Concerns for Agribusinesses

Supply chains involving smallholders have a fragmented supply base that is challenging to monitor. Consumers, shareholders, NGOs, and governments nonetheless call for transparency on standards relating to, for example, labor and environmental issues. Companies are acutely aware of the potential reputational risk if their actions are perceived to have harmful social and environmental impacts (see the description of Performance Standard 2 earlier in this chapter).

Modern Slavery

A documentary on modern slavery in cocoa plantations in West Africa caused outrage when broadcast on the United Kingdom's Channel 4 in 2000 (Woods and Blewett 2000). Apparently catching the chocolate industry unawares, several companies rapidly commissioned work to probe the extent of slavery in their supply chains.

In 2015, the United Kingdom passed the Modern Slavery Act (modeled partly on California's 2010 "Transparency in Supply Chains" Act). Any business, or part of a business, that has a global turnover of £36 million or more and supplies goods or services in the United Kingdom must produce and publish an annual slavery and trafficking statement, setting out the steps it has taken to ensure there is no slavery in any part of its business, including its supply chains. In 2017, France passed a law that requires companies with more than 10,000 employees worldwide to develop plans for rooting out human rights abuses, while the Dutch parliament adopted a law to prevent child labor. Australia is considering a Modern Slavery Act like the one in Britain (Fortado 2017).

Deforestation

Deforestation is another area of concern. Many companies now have "zero deforestation" policies that commonly commit to the following (Lake and Baer 2015):

- No clearing on carbon-rich peat lands
- No use of fires for clearing
- No clearing on High Conservation Value areas
- No clearance on High Carbon Stock areas
- Respect for indigenous land rights
- Obtaining free, prior, and informed consent from local communities

- Production only on legal lands

- No use of forced or slave labor

- A commitment to transparency regarding their production practices.

These issues call for a high level of vigilance and proactiveness on the part of companies. Many companies now make a point of negotiating and maintaining a social license to operate from communities around their sites of operation as well as from society more widely (in the form of local service provision, employment, and tax payments).

There is growing interest in the multilateral Principles for Responsible Agricultural Investment (PRAI),[7] and companies are increasingly developing their own codes that establish standards that their suppliers must meet and help formalize the relationship between companies and smallholders.

Initiatives that promote change across the sector through joint action are also being used to tackle key areas of concern that are widespread. For example, the International Cocoa Initiative, whose industry partners include major cocoa traders and chocolate manufacturers, works with stakeholders in cocoa-producing countries to ensure a better future for children and contribute to the elimination of child labor.[8]

Strategies and Best Practices for Implementing Standards

Firms interested in adopting standards along smallholder supply chains may follow several strategies:

- Leveraging existing structures and relationships

- Taking a stepwise approach

- Using standards to improve productivity, benefiting farmers and firms alike

- Using group certification.

Leveraging Existing Structures and Relationships

Firms adopting good practices in their smallholder supply chains will benefit from integrating them into their core business activities. As much as possible, firms should build on existing systems and programs. Among those are traceability systems that are used for food safety, monitoring of farmer productivity, quality assurance programs, and payment systems—all of which can be extended to include additional social and environmental verification elements. Supply chains rely on several types of chain-of-custody systems:

- *Book and claim.* In these systems, the producing company receives a certificate for each unit of the certified commodity. These certificates can then be sold or traded to manufacturers or retailers. There is no physical traceability of the commodity. GreenPalm provides this kind of supply chain model for certified sustainable palm oil.[9]

- *Mass balance.* In these systems, a measured amount of the commodity leaves the producer, and the manufacturer records the same amount entering its processing facility. This provides partial traceability of the commodity. Because certified and uncertified product can be mixed, manufacturers must state that the final product "may contain" certified material. The Roundtable for Sustainable Palm Oil (RSPO) provides one example of a mass balance system.[10]

- *Segregation.* In segregated systems, the certified crop is physically separated from uncertified product. Bar codes or other physical identifiers accompany each bag or container as it is transported. However, the product is not physically traceable upstream from the exporter. Rainforest Alliance certification is an example of a segregated system.[11]

- *Identity preserved.* In these systems, the identity of the product is preserved through the entire supply chain. Radio Frequency ID (RFID) tags or bar codes are attached to each unit of production, so that they can be tracked at each step. For example, the Brazilian Specialty Coffee Association offers a Safe Trace system that allows consumers to trace their roasted coffee back to its producer.[12] Sophisticated beef-producing countries, such as Uruguay, have systems that can trace the meat coming from individual animals for phytosanitary control. Existing management systems, such as the Environmental and Social Management System, the International Organization for Standardization (ISO 14001 and ISO 2200), and Hazard Analysis and Critical Control Points (HACCP) can be valuable platforms for implementation.

Building on existing external programs and groups that smallholders may be involved in is another efficient pathway for implementation. Existing farmer field schools and other farmer development programs operated by governments, development agencies, or other NGOs may provide useful synergies and partnerships. Building on existing farmer organizations can save time and money. Firms should also look beyond the more traditional, farmer-based groups to villages, families and clans, schools, churches, and even sports groups to leverage existing relationships and trust between farmers. Working with these groups may require building capacity to implement traceability or to oversee group certification programs, which is discussed further below.

It can be useful for firms to engage with others in the sector as partners for implementation, particularly in cases of potentially precompetitive challenges, such as child labor, that would benefit from sectorwide or national approaches. Partnerships and pooling of resources may be valuable when firms have limited leverage, such when smallholders have the flexibility of selling to multiple firms (as further discussed in chapter 8 on partnerships).

Taking a Stepwise Approach to Implementation of Standards

When production standards among smallholder farmers are significantly *noncompliant* with the preferred standard scheme, a stepwise approach may be a cost-effective strategy to address buyers' demands for good environmental and social practices. This can lay out a road map for firms, farmers, and buyers. Firms will need to plan the investment costs and time such an approach will require—and they may have to negotiate with buyers on the compliance time frame.

The first step should be the development of a baseline, indicating the smallholders' status regarding performance against the standard and the organizational status of farmers. The biggest challenges for compliance should be identified and the end goal defined (for example, third-party certification of 100 percent of the smallholder supply base or measured improvements in specific smallholder practices).

Interim goals could include setting up an internal control system (ICS) for the smallholder suppliers and annual targets for the number of farmers receiving training or being included in the verification program. Other interim steps may be to benchmark continuous improvement and set targets for closing out noncompliance.

Implementation could start with a handful of farmer groups, with wider rollout over time. (For an example, see box 4.8.) This way, firms may meet compliance or certification requirements earlier with a smaller portion of supply. Alternatively, firms may stagger the rollout of their smallholder program based on key issues. For example, training and verification may focus first on easy wins and proceed to more challenging implementation topics later.

BOX 4.8

In Practice: A Stepwise Approach to Standards Compliance in India

India is one of the largest and lowest-cost producers of fruits and vegetables, but little of that production reaches global markets because supply chains fail to comply with stringent food-safety standards demanded by major importing countries. Indian firm Jain Irrigation Systems Ltd. (JISL) is the largest mango puree producer in the world and the second largest dehydrated onion producer. It wanted to provide buyers with assurances on the use of good agricultural practices at the farm level, specifically around pesticide use and worker health and safety, without significantly increasing costs to farmers or the firm.

With support from IFC, JISL developed and piloted a private "Jain GAP" standard for farmers in its supply chain. The Jain GAP standard is a modified and simplified version of the GLOBALG.A.P. standards to bring some measure of food-safety and GAP standards to the JISL supply base while minimizing the costs of compliance to both farmers and JISL. The Jain GAP standard comprises 74 compliance criteria of GLOBALG.A.P.'s total 256 criteria.

The firm trained 79 JISL extensionists on the standard, who subsequently supported 1,340 farmers to achieve compliance, bringing 5,573 acres of land under the Jain GAP system. JISL is now scaling up the standard to the rest of its direct farm suppliers.

In addition to the direct impacts of Jain GAP, the project had sector-level impacts. GLOBALG.A.P. recognizes the Jain GAP standard as a "Primary Farm Assurance" standard. A basic requirement IndiaGAP standard was developed based on the Jain GAP standard with significant input from IFC. Farmers now have a two-step approach for compliance with IndiaGAP.

Source: IFC 2014.

Using Standards to Improve Productivity

Much of the focus here has been on the adoption of standards and certification in response to market demands. However, those standards do not necessarily deliver farm-level benefits. A recent study found that the impact of certification on yields was mixed and that income from sale of certified products was "slightly higher overall," with considerable variation between schemes (3ie 2017). In some schemes, higher prices failed to sufficiently compensate for lower yields. Moreover, average household incomes and ownership of assets did not increase.

However, farming practice standards that deliver productivity benefits are becoming an increasing focus for firms—and this is particularly relevant to smallholder farming, where the yield gap between farmer yield and potential yield is significant (more than 40 percent of current farm yield) (Fischer, Byerlee, and Edmeades 2014). Standards that improve farming practices, generate farm-level cost savings, and deliver higher yields or better-quality produce are win-win propositions for both farmers and firms—helping firms secure their supply base and improving farmer rewards. In some cases, the benefit is becoming the main driver for farmers to adopt standards. The costs of compliance with those standards are covered by the productivity or efficiency gains rather than any market premium. This strategy may also be useful in emerging or intermediate markets where certification is less important.

Using Group Certification

Group certification models issue one certificate to multiple small-holders who are complying with a standard. Depending on the buying relationship between the firm and the smallholders and the capacity of the producer organization (PO), either the firm or the PO maintains an ICS that manages compliance with the standard and facilitates certification.

The ICS documents each farmer in the group and coordinates an internal verification program (first- or second-party) that measures each farmer's performance. The system also tracks noncompliance and remedial actions taken in response. In doing so, an ICS provides full traceability of suppliers to the PO. Some systems include mechanisms to exclude nonperforming farmers or farmer groups. Third-party verifiers inspect the functioning of the system and spot-check the practices of a sample of individual farmers (box 4.8).

If smallholders sell to multiple firms or have a strong existing group organization, it may be more appropriate for the group to maintain and manage an ICS for group verification. However, if the smallholders are effectively tied to the firm because of geography, land-lease and input agreements, or other contracts, it may be more appropriate for the firm to manage certification initially and build the group capacity to deploy some of the elements of the system.

The ICS may be tiered, in which groups of farmers are trained and verified, feeding results into a central system (much like a plantation might manage blocks or a large farm manages fields), or the results for all farmers can be fed directly into a single ICS. For large numbers of smallholders, a subgroup approach is recommended. In many cases, standards systems require homogeneity of members in terms of geographical location, production system, size of holding, and common marketing systems.

In sum, group certification generally requires the following:

- A central body such as a PO
- A defined group of smallholders
- Records on all members
- At least annual internal inspection
- Set procedures and sanctions to address noncompliance.

Considerations When Deciding on Engagement Strategies

Identify the Resources Needed for Implementation

When considering the approach to standards and certification, agribusiness firms should budget for the costs of compliance, certification, and mitigation of producer costs.

Firms must also plan for the time needed to manage implementation. Responsibility for this may rest with, for example, a quality manager or a smallholder sourcing manager, but it is important to include additional staff time for planning and monitoring implementation, in addition to field activities. These tasks will include the following:

- Strengthening farmer organization
- Conducting a gap assessment of current smallholder practices
- Providing training and other materials and resources to improve practice
- Conducting ongoing first-party verification of smallholders.

If a firm is investing in strengthening smallholder supply chains, these costs might not be exclusive to standards implementation. However, new digital systems and applications are making it much easier for firms to manage smallholder supply chains, including compliance with standards.

In addition, firms should budget for audits when third-party verification is used as part of a certification system. Full audits are typically undertaken every three to five years, with annual surveillance visits. Certification may include membership fees for the firm to join the national or global organization that administers the standards system and may also include a certification fee levied by the auditor. Budgeting for certification is straightforward: firms can either obtain quotes from the certification bodies or, using the guidance provided by the standards systems on auditing, they can calculate the number of days it will take to audit their smallholder operators and estimate a day rate for auditing.

Even in situations where certification is not sought, it can be useful to use third parties to provide an independent assessment of compliance as both a tool for internal program management and for risk management. Third parties may also be used for pre-assessment, before the certification audit, to identify any final outstanding issues.

Ensure the Approach Is Sustainable for Smallholders

As with any smallholder investment, it is important to ensure that smallholders' incentives are aligned with the firm's incentives when implementing a standards system. When determining an engagement strategy for standards and certification of smallholders, firms should consider the costs and benefits not only to their own organization but also to the smallholders themselves. If farmers do not perceive benefits from changing their practices or are asked to incur additional costs—or additional labor (as the example in box 4.9 explains)—they may be unwilling to adopt and implement the practices required to comply with the standard.

For example, yields tend to be lower from organic systems than from those using chemical fertilizer. Farmers who are certified organic may lose income if there is no price premium or if the premium does not recover the productivity loss. In certification programs like Rainforest Alliance Certified™, which permits judicious use of agricultural chemicals, farmers must purchase protective gear for spraying and construct

---

BOX 4.9

Labor Implications of Improved Agricultural Practices

Pruning tree crops increases yields but also requires labor, pruning saws, or other equipment as well as the technical knowledge and skills to prune effectively. When pruning has been neglected for a long time, the amount of labor needed may be beyond the capacity of farming households.

Farmers can control weeds at the base of tree crops with herbicides such as paraquat, motorized weed trimmers, or through hand cutting. However, because many certification programs ban paraquat, and smallholders might lack access to motorized weed trimmers, the farmers often use machetes to hand cut weeds—a labor-intensive and arduous task.

secure storage for the chemicals. If these additional costs are more than the premium farmers receive from certification, they will likely discontinue the practices, and the firm will lose on the investment. Some firms purchase these additional items for farmers to mitigate farmers' costs. In other cases, training to farmers on health benefits and groundwater protection may help farmers appreciate these nonfinancial benefits.

Even if the firm is proposing to pay a higher price, the firm needs to check that the result for the farmer will be positive after meeting any additional costs (including, for example, additional record keeping and maintaining an ICS with first-party verification). If the benefits are too small or accrued only in the long run, firms may propose a cost-sharing mechanism with farmers during the first few years of the program. Firms should ensure that smallholders and groups of smallholders know how to calculate cost and benefits for themselves and also encourage smallholders to consider other benefits, such as health, drinking water, and other ecosystem values.

Finally, certification may exclude large numbers of smallholders—a social cost that may conflict with government policy or expectations.

Taking care to make sure that farmers understand the standards and their implications—and timely sharing of information from periodic reviews, with clear links to remedial actions—is important. Strategies for effective training and communication are explored in the next chapter.

Notes

1. GLOBALG.A.P., the world's leading farm assurance program, translates consumer requirements into good agricultural practices in more than 125 countries. For more information, see the GLOBALG.A.P. https://www.globalgap.org.
2. "Stories from the Supply Chain," About Better Cotton, Better Cotton Initiative (accessed March 23, 2017), http://bettercotton.org/about-better-cotton/stories -supply-chain-2/.
3. "What Is Sustainable Sourcing?" EcoVadis (accessed April 10, 2017), http://www .ecovadis.com/sustainable-sourcing/.
4. "What Is Sustainable Sourcing?" EcoVadis (accessed April 10, 2017), http://www .ecovadis.com/sustainable-sourcing/.
5. See ITC Sustainability Map version 4.016 (accessed March 22, 2018), http://www .standardsmap.org/.
6. "Predictions for Sustainable Foods in 2017," Ecovia Intelligence (formerly known as Organic Monitor), (posted January 5, 2017), http://www.ecoviaint.com/r0401/.
7. The Principles for Responsible Agricultural Investment (PRAI) were jointly developed by the United Nations Conference on Trade and Development (UNCTAD), the Food and Agriculture Organization of the United Nations (FAO),

the International Fund for Agricultural Development (IFAD), and the World Bank. For details, see the UNCTAD PRAI: http://unctad.org/en/Pages/DIAE/G-20/PRAI .aspx.

8. For more information about the International Cocoa Initiative, see the https:// www.endslaverynow.org/international-cocoa-initiative.

9. For more information about GreenPalm, see the http://greenpalm.org.

10. For more information about RSPO support of all four types of chain-of-custody systems, see https://rspo.org/certification/supply-chains.

11. For more information about the merged Rainforest Alliance–UTZ certification program and chain-of-custody systems, see https://www.rainforest-alliance.org /business/agriculture/certification/coc.

12. For more information about the Safe Trace identity preserved chain-of-custody system, see http://bsca.com.br/index/home.

References

CBI (Centre for Promotion of Exports). 2017. "Exporting Sustainable Coffee to Europe." Research report, CBI, Netherlands Ministry of Foreign Affairs, The Hague.

Dalberg (Dalberg Global Development Advisors). 2012. "Catalyzing Smallholder Agricultural Finance." Research report, Dalberg Global Development Advisors, New York.

EP Association (The Equator Principles Association). 2013. "The Equator Principles June 2013: A Financial Industry Benchmark for Determining, Assessing and Managing Environmental and Social Risk in Projects." Risk management framework document, EP Association Secretariat, Sussex, U.K.

Fischer, T., D. Byerlee, and G. O. Edmeades. 2014. *Crop Yields and Global Food Security: Will Yield Increase Continue to Feed the World?* Canberra: Australian Centre for International Agricultural Research (ACIAR).

Fortado, L. 2017. "Slavery Is the Weak Link in Corporate Supply Chains." *Financial Times*, June 22.

Galarraga, I., and A. Markandya. 2004. "Economic Techniques to Estimate the Demand for Sustainable Products: A Case Study for Fair Trade and Organic Coffee in the United Kingdom." *Agricultural and Resource Economics* 4 (7): 109–34.

Gordon, A., and J. Woodhill. 2011. "Raising the Bar: What Is Global Food and Agri-Business Saying about Their Sustainability Goals?" Discussion paper, Centre for Development Innovation, Wageningen University, Netherlands.

IFC (International Finance Corporation of the World Bank Group). 2012. "IFC Performance Standards on Environmental and Social Responsibility." IFC, Washington, DC. https://www.ifc.org/wps/wcm/connect/c8f524004a73daeca09 afdf998895a12/IFC_Performance_Standards.pdf?MOD=AJPERES.

———. 2014. "Addressing Food Safety and Traceability in India." Fact sheet, IFC, Washington, DC.

ITC (International Trade Centre). 2015. "Traceability in Food and Agricultural Products." Bulletin No. 91/2015, ITC, Geneva.

Lake, S., and E. Baer. 2015. "What Does It Really Mean When a Company Commits to 'Zero Deforestation'?" *Insights* (blog), World Resources Institute, May 4.

http://www.wri.org/blog/2015/05/what-does-it-really-mean-when-company-commits-%E2%80%9Czero-deforestation%E2%80%9D.

Macawaris, N., C. Taylor, and C. Zamora-Galinato. 2011. "Sowing the Seeds of Sustainability: A Case Project with Unifrutti, IFC, and Smallholder Banana Farmers in the Philippines." SmartLessons brief, International Finance Corporation of the World Bank Group (IFC), Washington, DC.

Mallet, P., M. Maireles, E. Kennedy, and M. Devisscher. 2016. "How Sustainability Standards Can Contribute to Landscape Approaches and Zero Deforestation Commitments." Study report, ISEAL Alliance, London.

Non-GMO Project. 2017. "Non-GMO Project Standard." Version 14.2. Consensus standard document, Non-GMO Project, Bellingham, WA.

Potts, J., M. Lynch, A. Wilkings, G. Huppé, M. Cunningham, and V. Voora. 2014. *The State of Sustainability Initiatives Review 2014: Standards and the Green Economy.* Winnipeg: International Institute for Sustainable Development (IISD); London: International Institute for Environment and Development (IIED).

Smith, T. A., C. L. Huang, and B.-H. Lin. 2009. "How Much Are Consumers Paying for Organic Baby Food?" Paper presented at the Southern Agricultural Economics Association Annual Meeting, Atlanta, January 31–February 3.

3ie (International Initiative for Impact Evaluation). 2017. "Does Agricultural Certification Improve Well-Being?" Systematic Review Brief, Agriculture, 3ie, New Delhi.

Tully, S. M., and R. S. Winer. 2014. "The Role of the Beneficiary in Willingness to Pay for Socially Responsible Products: A Meta-Analysis." *Journal of Retailing* 90 (2): 255–74.

USAID (U.S. Agency for International Development). 2016. "Ghanaian Mango Producers' Association First in Country to Acquire New GlobalG.A.P. Certification for Export to EU and Middle East." *West Africa Trade & Investment Hub* (blog), July 26. https://www.watradehub.com/en/ghanaian-mango-producers-association-first-country-acquire-new-global-g-p-certification-export-eu-middle-east/.

USDA FAS (Foreign Agricultural Service, U.S. Department of Agriculture). 2013. "Japanese Organic Market." Global Agricultural Information Network (GAIN) Report No. JA3705, USDA FAS, Washington, DC.

Von Hagen, O., S. Manning, and J. Reinecke. 2010. "Sustainable Sourcing in the Food Industry: Global Challenges and Practices." *Moderne Ernährung Heute* 4: 1–9.

WBCSD (World Business Council for Sustainable Development). 2008. "Sustainable Consumption: Facts and Trends from a Business Perspective." Report, WBCSD, Geneva.

Woods, B., and K. Blewett. 2000. *Slavery: A Global Investigation.* Documentary film, produced by True Vision of London.

Additional Resources

Managing Environmental and Social Risk

IFC (International Finance Corporation of the World Bank Group). 2017. "Global Map of Environmental and Social Risks in Agro-Commodity Production (GMAP) Pilot." http://www.ifc.org/wps/wcm/connect/topics_ext_content/ifc_external_corporate_site/sustainability-at-ifc/company-resources/gmap.

Marks and Spencer. 2016. "M&S Modern Slavery Statement 2015/16." https://corpo
rate.marksandspencer.com/documents/plan-a-our-approach/mns-modern
-slavery-statement-june2016.pdf. [Example of anti-slavery statement]
——. 2017. "Our Approach to Human Rights: M&S Human Rights Report 2017."
https://corporate.marksandspencer.com/documents/plan-a-our-approach/mns-
human-rights-report-june2017.pdf. [Example of human rights statement]
Nestlé. 2013. "The Nestlé Supplier Code." https://www.nestle.com/asset-library/doc
uments/library/documents/suppliers/supplier-code-english.pdf.
Olam International. 2014. "Olam Supplier Code." http://olamgroup.com/wp-content
/uploads/2015/07/16507-Olam-Supplier-Code_v2_web.pdf.
World Bank and UNCTAD (United Nations Conference on Trade and Development).
2018. "Community Development Agreements." Responsible Agricultural
Investment (RAI) Knowledge into Action Note No. 18, World Bank, Washington,
DC; UNCTAD, New York. https://openknowledge.worldbank.org/bitstream
/handle/10986/29467/124293-BRI-PUBLIC-KN18.pdf?sequence=1&isAllowed=y.
——. 2018. "Community Engagement Strategies." Responsible Agricultural
Investment (RAI) Knowledge into Action Note No. 15, World Bank, Washington,
DC; UNCTAD, New York. https://openknowledge.worldbank.org/bitstream/hand
le/10986/29473/124290-BRI-PUBLIC-KN15.pdf?sequence=1&isAllowed=y.
——. 2018. "Environmental and Social Impact Assessments." Responsible Agricultural
Investment (RAI) Knowledge into Action Note No. 14, World Bank, Washington,
DC; UNCTAD, New York. https://openknowledge.worldbank.org/bitstream/hand
le/10986/29477/124289-BRI-PUBLIC-KN14.pdf?sequence=1&isAllowed=y.
——. 2018. "Respecting Land Rights and Averting Land Disputes." Responsible
Agricultural Investment (RAI) Knowledge into Action Note No. 11, World Bank,
Washington, DC; UNCTAD, New York. https://openknowledge.worldbank.org
/bitstream/handle/10986/29470/124286-BRI-PUBLIC-KN11.pdf?sequence
=1&isAllowed=y.

Standards and Certification

AMEA (Agribusiness Market Ecosystem Alliance) and SCOPEinsight. https://www
.ameaglobal.org/, http://www.scopeinsight.com/. [Standards for professionalism
in producer organizations and small agribusinesses]
COSA (Committee on Sustainability Assessment). http://www.thecosa.org. [Organization
that fosters effective ways to measure and understand sustainability in the agri-food
sector]
Giovannucci, D., S. Scherr, D. Nierenberg, C. Hebebrand, J. Shapiro, J. Milder,
and K. Wheeler. 2012. "Food and Agriculture: The Future of Sustainability."
A strategic input to the Sustainable Development in the 21st Century (SD21)
project, United Nations Department of Economic and Social Affairs (UN
DESA), New York.
ISEAL Alliance. http://www.isealalliance.org. [Represents the global movement of
sustainability standards; mission to strengthen sustainability standards for the
benefit of people and the environment]
WWF (World Wildlife Fund). 2010. "Certification and Roundtables: Do They Work?"
WWF Review of Multi-Stakeholder Sustainability Initiatives, WWF, Gland,
Switzerland.

Oil Palm Smallholder Certification

POPSI (Palm Oil Producer Support Initiative). https://www.solidaridadnetwork.org
/supply-chains/palm-oil.
RSPO (Roundtable on Sustainable Palm Oil). 2013. "Principles and Criteria for the
Production of Sustainable Palm Oil." Guidance document, RSPO, Geneva.

Soy Smallholder Certification

RTRS (Roundtable on Sustainable Soy Association). http://www.responsiblesoy
.org/?lang=en. [International multistakeholder initiative founded in 2006 that
promotes the use and growth of responsible production of soy; has developed a
global standard for responsible soy production]
SOYPSI (Soy Producer Support Initiative). http://solidaridadnetwork.org/soy-produ
cer-support-initiative. [Helps owners of small- and medium-size farms improve
production and prepare for RTRS certification. In 2011, more than 20,000 smallholders in Brazil, Bolivia, and India participated in SOYPSI projects, with thou-
sands more smallholders in Brazil, Bolivia, China, and India projected to become
certified.]

Agriculture Smallholder Certification

FLO (Fairtrade International), Fairtrade Foundation, and Fairtrade Federation. http://
www.fairtrade.net, http://www.fairtradefederation.org. [Organizations that support
and certify improved terms of trade between producers and consumers, each focusing on consumers in a different part of the world and with varying standards and
certification processes]
4C Association for Coffee. http://www.4c-coffeeassociation.org/. [Multistakeholder
organization committed to addressing the sustainability issues of the coffee sector
in a precompetitive manner; defines and maintains the 4C Code of Conduct, the
baseline standard for sustainability in the coffee sector]
FSC (Forestry Stewardship Council). http://www.fsc-uk.org/. [Global forest
certification]
FSC. Smallholders Portal. https://ic.fsc.org/smallholder-support.152.htm. [Provides
guidance, resources, and communications directly from FSC on small, low-
intensity, and community certificate holders]
GlobalG.A.P. http://www.globalgap.org. [Smallholder implementation guidelines,
practical tools, and global best practice guidelines to facilitate implementation of
the standard by smallholders worldwide]
IFOAM (International Federation of Organic Agriculture Movements). www.ifoam
.org. [For resources on organic certification, see https://www.ifoam.bio/en/gener
al-information-organic-standards-and-certification]
PEFC (Programme for the Endorsement of Forest Certification). http://www.pefc
.org. [Group Forest Management Certification (PEFC ST 1002:2010) technical
documentation: http://www.pefc.org/standards/]
Rainforest Alliance. www.rainforest-alliance.org. [Develops social and environmental
standards in a variety of fields, with the auditing division, RA-Cert, providing
independent verification services based on these standards]

SAN (Sustainable Agriculture Network). http://sanstandards.org/. [Standard and
    policy for group certification]
Smithsonian Bird Friendly Certification. https://nationalzoo.si.edu/migratory-birds
    /bird-friendly-coffee. [Program implemented by the Smithsonian Migratory Bird
    Center certifies coffee production that preserves bird habitats]

CHAPTER 5
TRAINING AND COMMUNICATION

KEY MESSAGES

➡ Training is an essential component in any productivity-enhancing strategy, and agribusiness companies sometimes play a significant role in smallholder training.

➡ The content of training programs and management of field staff are being transformed by new information and communication technology (ICT) potentiality, including affordable use of smartphones, Global Positioning Systems (GPS), and tablet computers.

➡ Farmer-level volunteers, supported by appropriate incentives, are a cost-effective way to expand extension reach.

➡ Producer organizations, as well as agro-retailers and output collectors, are potential conduits for farmer training.

➡ International Finance Corporation's (IFC) Agribusiness Leadership Program targets farmer organizations, agro-retailers, and collectors to improve financial literacy and business management skills.

➡ It is important to include women (who have a significant presence in farming but often achieve lower yields) with proactive tailored approaches to training.

The Business Case for Farmer Training and Improved Communication

If agribusiness firms are to integrate smallholder farmers directly into global value chains, they need effective ways to communicate with one another. This facilitates the smooth development and operation of the supply chain in several ways:

- *Building capacity and changing farmer behavior* (via knowledge about technology, management, and business) to meet the needs of global markets and to interact with the relevant stakeholders

- *Encouraging loyalty* to reduce side-selling and build a long-term partnership between the firm and farmers

- *Enabling the development of joint solutions* to overcome inefficiencies or challenges

- *Creating the conditions for adaptation and innovation* in the supply chain

- *Fostering competitive advantage* beyond output and quality effects, such as through (1) transfer of selected roles from firm to smallholders, and (2) using communication channels for multiple functions, including traceability

- *Providing an early warning system* whereby farmers can notify the firm in advance of any emerging problems (and vice versa).

Traditional extension approaches focused on *technology transfer*, as part of a top-down *teaching* process, usually provided by government. Now, there is much more emphasis on training for *learning* and *changin behavior*, with more diverse providers: public; private (farmer-led, nongovernmental organization [NGO], or commercial); and public-private.

Several studies that have analyzed the impact of agricultural extension indicate high returns on investment, in the range of 33–57 percent (Fischer, Byerlee, and Edmeades 2014, 1–26). Despite such returns, many governments in low- and middle-income countries have reduced expenditures on extension services over the past 20–30 years as they have sought to control public spending. This has happened even as new challenges and needs are emerging that require stronger, more flexible communication channels in relation to, for example, climate change adaptation and participation in fast-moving global agribusiness value chains. This need is leading to the development of new training and communication approaches.

A recent study of experience with *private extension* providers highlighted the following findings (Babu and Zhou 2016):

- The creation of shared value—among farmers, input suppliers, and aggregators—is crucial to the sustainability of the approach.

- The provision of integrated services is important to success, especially in combining extension messages with input supply.

- Private extension leads to better links between research and extension.

- The provision of extension to improve quality gives farmers an assured market and stronger market connections.

- Integral links to the market mean that farmers face less price uncertainty.

- The interaction between supply chain actors fosters inclusive technological and institutional innovation.

- The private extension approach assists in product differentiation (for example, via quality improvements) and hence with marketing—an aspect not usually covered by public agencies.

- Private extension services contribute to farmer cohesiveness, amplifying their voice in dealing with firms.

- Extension costs are recovered, essentially by being internalized within the marketing chain.

- Private extension is a partially demand-driven approach, focusing on market needs (although not necessarily addressing farmers' wider needs).

- There are spillover effects as farmers apply enhanced skills to the other crops they grow.

There are, of course, many ways to approach training and communication, including still-emerging and transformative ICT systems. This chapter explores these approaches, highlighting what they offer and where and when they are most appropriate.

A related point on training should not be overlooked: agribusiness companies must build their own capacities to work with smallholders. Although they may do this in partnership with other organizations (as further discussed in chapter 8), they will certainly need in-house expertise, too. An interesting and logical development seen increasingly in the past 10 to 15 years is the recruitment and rotation of staff with relevant smallholder experience between NGOs, research organizations, development organizations, certification programs, government extension agencies, and agribusiness companies. This interchange makes a helpful contribution to reducing the cultural, language, and understanding gaps between these "sectors."

Farmer Training: Strategies and Best Practices

Training Entry Points: Beyond Traditional Extension Workers

Agriculture value chains offer several potential entry points for providing training to farmers:

- *Traditional channels* via extension workers (government, NGO, or firm) or agricultural training establishments with their own teams of agricultural trainers (training centers, farmer field schools, and so on)

- *Producer organizations,* which can be both targets of training and enlisted to provide training to their memberships

- *Lead farmers* or small-scale traders buying local crops

- *Local businesses*, particularly small agro-retailers, which have strong business incentives to expand their reach in ways that complement their core business (training and inputs).

At any of these entry points, cost-effective strategies will involve training of trainers so that messages can be cascaded to a wider group.

Traditionally, farmer training tends to focus on technology and management of field and postharvest operations, but an increasing number of initiatives now also address business, marketing, and other aspects of farmer "professionalism." Equally important is providing trainers with training in facilitation skills and training methodology—emphasizing the approaches that are suitable for smallholder farmers with little formal education. If farmers are to be reached in part through computer-assisted technology, then it is important to match the medium with the technology that farmers have. (For example, in rural Africa, although the use of mobile phones is widespread, penetration of smartphones is still quite limited.)

Field Staff: Effective but Costly

Agricultural extension workers, or field staff, are often the first channel that firms think of for a farmer training or outreach program. Although this may permit comprehensive and detailed messaging to farmers, it is also costly—typically $50 to $200 per farmer per year (table 5.1) (Fischer 2014). Various factors influence the cost, such as salaries, farmer density, number of interactions per year, whether training materials are developed or adapted, and to what extent administrative and managerial overheads are included. Written materials and ICT use can reduce the need for extension agents, complement their input, and, in some cases, replace them altogether.

Companies may be able to share training costs—or access donor funds to cover these costs—via public-private partnerships and other multipartner value chain initiatives (see chapter 8 on partnerships). Alternatively, it may sometimes be possible to factor training costs into the farmer crop purchase prices while still allowing increased income to farmers and companies because of improvements in farmer productivity.

TABLE 5.1 Cost Benchmarks for Farmer Training Using Extension Field Staff, Selected African and Asian Countries, 2014

Metric	Benchmark	Notes
Reach	2,500–100,000 farmers	Private extension programs typically have a reach of 2,500–25,000 farmers (sometimes more), while NGO or donor programs are often larger (50,000–100,000).
Duration	160–320 hours	Shorter programs typically seek to change specific agricultural practices over one cropping cycle; longer programs often address additional topics (such as financial literacy) and extend over several cropping cycles.
Cost per farmer	$52–$206	Variation in training duration makes this less meaningful than cost per hour per farmer.
Cost per hour per farmer	$0.24–$0.99	Systems with large reach have lower per capita costs; systems with paid staff (not volunteers) have higher costs.
Farmer benefits	Annual increase in income of $50–$443	Variation is due to magnitude of productivity gains and farmgate price of the crop.

Note: Benchmarks reflect preliminary results from an International Finance Corporation inquiry into extension costs, representing data from 10 extension programs in eight African and Asian countries. NGO = nongovernmental organization.

Hiring Field Staff

Firms employ field staff with a range of profiles and experience: from university-trained agronomists (more competent and costlier) to people with some practical experience but no formal schooling in agriculture (including farmers and staff of agricultural input distributors who are trained to provide advice on selected topics). Banks that have agricultural loan officers, although not trainers, often employ agriculture graduates because these staff need to be able to understand a farm enterprise and communicate with farmers. If it is important to reach female farmers, the team may need to proactively hire female extension team members.

Useful skill sets for extension workers include the following:

- A degree or diploma in agronomy, if possible (less likely in some regions, including Africa), enhancing potential for recruitment via agricultural schools and internships

- Practical experience with target crops

- Work experience on a smallholder farm

- Ability to speak the native language or dialect of targeted farmers

- Dynamic personality with a positive attitude

- Willingness to live and work in rural areas.

The various roles allotted to field staff (figure 5.1) may entail complementary tasks, but managers can improve staff members' effectiveness by carefully reviewing logistics, time requirements, and staff training schedules.

Deploying Field Staff

To deploy field staff, firms have generally followed one or a combination of two models: training farmers at a central location or sending staff members out to farms. Each model has its advantages and disadvantages.

Model 1: training at a central location. In this model, the farmers come to a depot, crop buying station, farmer training center, or (in the case of input firms) agro-retailer.

Establishing decentralized buying stations shortens the chain between farmers and off-takers and enables communication between the two. Farmers bring their crops directly to the station, where field staff conduct simple quality tests, including moisture and defect testing. The test

FIGURE 5.1 Roles of Field Staff in Agricultural Firms

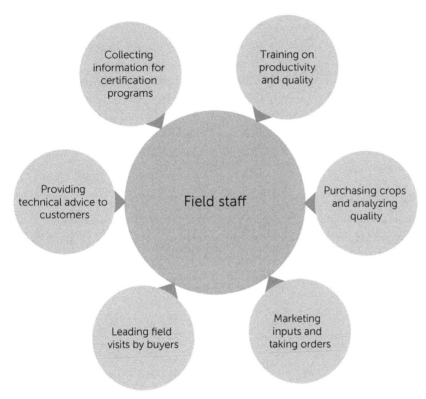

results determine the price paid to farmers, creating incentives for farmers to improve crop quality. Training on quality and other topics can be held at the station to reinforce key messaging. Since the firm is directly involved at the point of crop purchase, field staff can track and sort products by quality.

Although buying stations can improve crop quality, they have limited ability to improve traceability because interactions with farmers occur at the stations rather than at the farms. Furthermore, for most certification programs, firms must collect information on field locations and agricultural practices with farmers at their farms. Field staff placed at farm training centers and agro-retailers have limited influence because they do not regularly visit farms to provide on-site coaching directly to farmers.

Model 2: sending staff to farms. This traditional extension model is more expensive because the field staff are required to travel.

When field staff work with farmers directly, or through a network of farmers, training can take place in farmers' own fields and address their specific concerns. This model is especially useful for building trust and goodwill among farmers, which can in turn reduce side-selling. Disputes between farmers and the firm can be resolved quickly.

Combination model: In other cases, a hybrid strategy makes sense. For example, a farmer training center could have fixed trainers for farmers attending center-based sessions, but it could also serve as a base for mobile staff. For input suppliers, staff based at agro-retailers could visit customers to diagnose problems and explain products to farmers who visit the shop.

Managing Field Staff

Management planning. Managing field staff, and their multiple roles, cost-effectively is critical for a program's success. Clear messaging to staff on expectations, schedules, and responsibilities can increase their effectiveness. Developing a management plan *before* hiring staff is critical (figure 5.2), and firms may consider piloting the approach initially.

FIGURE 5.2 Stages of Field Staff Management Planning

Develop the outreach plan and determine the number of staff needed
An experienced labor lawyer can help design employment policies and staff contracts. Minimum wages, probationary periods, disciplinary action, performance evaluation, and retirement payments should be considered.

Evaluate and train field staff
Training will increase staff confidence and help ensure that they can respond accurately and appropriately to farmers' questions. Training should cover agronomy for the crop in question, including the "why" behind the message. In addition, training in communication skills and meeting facilitation are very useful.

Provide ongoing performance supports
Coaching and mentoring will build confidence among staff and help them vary their teaching methodologies. Opportunities for advancement encourage staff retention and succession strategies when staff leave.

Advertise for and hire field staff
Extension staff with a mix of technical knowledge, teaching skills, and an understanding of the local farming context will be able to respond to farmers' questions and relate to farmers' concerns.

Send staff to the field
Establish clear workplans and supervision.

Request farmer feedback on staff performance
Identify high and low performers among staff and underscore the farmers' role as a stakeholder in the program's success.

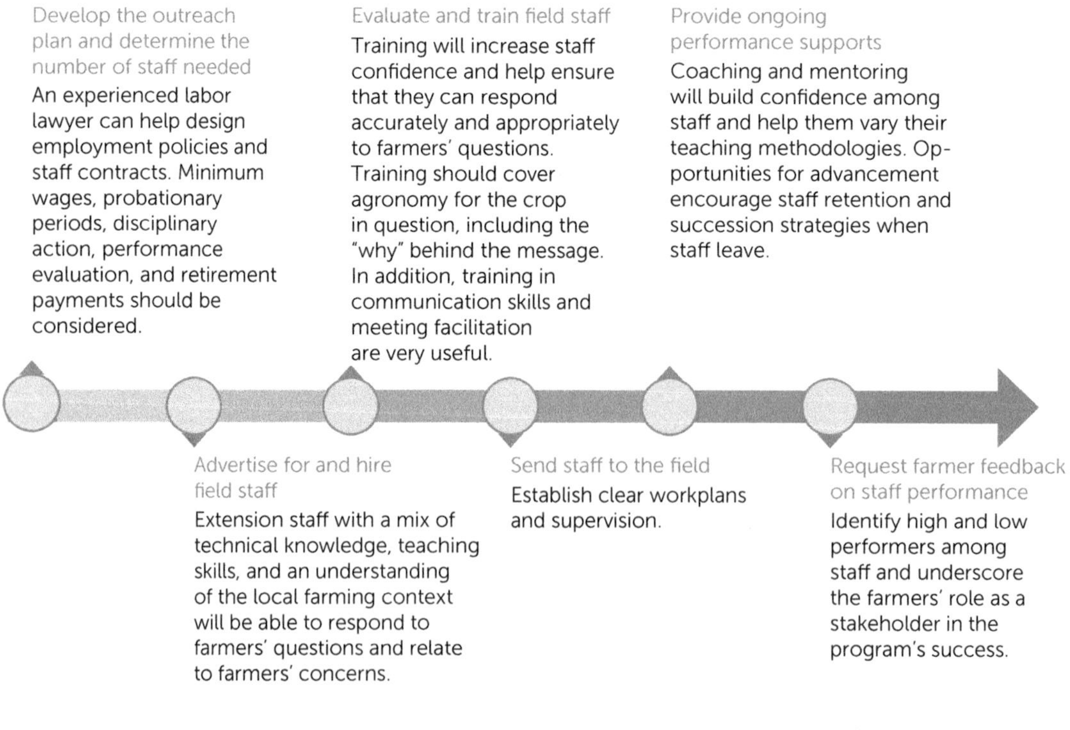

BOX 5.1

ICT Systems for Supervision and Management of Field Staff

Information and communication technology (ICT) is transforming agricultural extension—potentially reducing costs while increasing its power and efficiency. ICT solutions can help address the following challenges arising in smallholder supply chains:

- Supply chain management and traceability
- Supervision and management of field staff
- Extension content and delivery
- Supplier aggregation and benchmarking
- Precision agriculture.

All five areas are relevant to field staff, and some of the supply chain management and traceability systems also have specific functions that facilitate better supervision of field staff. Three systems for the supervision and management of field staff were reviewed: TaroWorks, Farmbook Suite (Catholic Relief Services), and extensionWorker (MSSB Consulting).

All systems provide a solution for supervision activities in the field. Field agents who give advice to smallholders and provide training usually work in remote areas with no internet connection. Managing complex field campaigns digitally is the solution offered by extensionWorker, TaroWorks, and Farmbook Suite. All systems are designed to be able to collect data with mobile devices in the field and to synchronize data with the system (when there is network coverage) with features for field monitoring. All of these digital solutions have similar core functionalities:

- Data collection, data analysis, and reporting
- Communication between field agent and farmer and between system and farmer
- Mapping projects and field agent activities.

Sources: "extensionWorker for Conservation Agriculture Field Workers," MSSB Consulting (accessed December 8, 2017), http://mssbconsulting.com/extensionWorker.html; "Farmbook Suite," Our Work Overseas, Programming Areas—Agriculture (accessed March 26, 2018), https://www.crs.org/our-work-overseas/program-areas/agriculture/farmbook-suite; "TaroWorks" (accessed December 8, 2017), http://www.taroworks.org.

Using ICT systems. New developments in ICT are also transforming agricultural extension (box 5.1). These include systems for the supervision and management of field staff as well as supply-chain management systems and electronic media for extension that affect how field staff work and the real-time field information available to their managers.

Using female extension staff. Female field staff tend to increase the number of female farmers and leads in the program. Women are significant contributors to smallholder agriculture, but the yield gap between men and women averages 20–30 percent. Closing that gap would increase

agricultural output in frontier and emerging markets by 2.5–4 percent
(see chapter 7 on increasing women's participation in the supply chain).
In certain communities, female field staff may need additional training
to perform traditionally male tasks. Box 5.2 discusses approaches to
reaching women farmers.

Best practices. Good performance depends on effective logistics and
strong monitoring. Strategic scheduling, transportation, and staff management increase the effectiveness of an extension program. Best practices include the following:

· *Locate field staff as close to farmers as possible.* Field staff and supervisors may prefer to live in larger towns rather than villages, but locations farther from farming communities increase commuting time
   and reduce work time. Living near to farmers increases trust and

---

BOX 5.2

Reaching Women Farmers

Government extension services have generally performed poorly in reaching women farmers and
in the number of women staff they employ. The reasons for this are complex and varied, but they
include factors such as (a) cultural constraints on women being mobile and away from the home;
(b) selection criteria for farmers or contact farmers that inadvertently discriminate against women;
and (c) women's multiple roles, which may make it difficult for them to attend meetings at the
appointed time and place.

   A recent review of approaches to extension for women highlighted the following (Colverson
and Mbo'o-Tchouawou 2014):

• The context in which men and women experience opportunities to adopt new technology can
  be quite different, so a careful analysis of the practical, socioeconomic, and cultural constraints
  to adoption is important.
• Training staff in gender sensitivity is important if reaching women is a priority.
• Using women community volunteers is an effective approach.
• There is good experience in using group-based approaches (women-only groups).
• ICT—including messaging via mobile phones and radio programs—has a good track record in
  reaching women.
• It is important to monitor the results (as discussed in more detail in chapters 7 and 9).

   Approaches may also combine messaging to include other issues that interest women
(for example, nutrition for infants and pregnant women).

knowledge about farming practices and problems. Basing staff at the village level may require special provisions, such as four-days-on, three-days-off schedules and allowances to furnish or improve village housing.

• *Establish realistic targets for farmer contact.* Consider farmer location and clustering when setting targets and determining the number of farmers that an agent may handle. Depending on travel time between farmer groups, an agent can typically meet with two groups per day.

• *Provide messaging support to extension officers.* This could include written material, videos that can be shown to farmers, or radio messages that reinforce the face-to-face visits.

• *Closely monitor the daily activities of field staff.* Extension staff work on their own most of the time. However, even with good planning and scheduling, field staff may not be working in the location where they are expected on a particular day—whether because of constraints beyond their control, such as weather or road conditions, or because of poor work habits. Given the expense of placing staff in the field, firms need the reassurance that training is being conducted as planned or they run the risk that objectives will not be realized. Unannounced visits by supervisors to observe training sessions are the best way to monitor extension staff performance and assess the effectiveness of extension messages. With declining costs for GPS-based systems, field staff location can be cost-effectively monitored using GPS units for motorbikes and vehicles, 3G phones, or the services offered by firms for remote vehicle monitoring. Software is now readily available to show, remotely, the location of all team members.

• *Purchase high-quality motorbikes and develop clear policies about their use.* Firms often provide their field staff with off-road motorbikes so they can manage back roads between farms. It is a good policy to provide training, to have a skills test that all staff must pass before receiving their motorbikes, and to have ongoing road safety awareness workshops. Even the best motorbikes will experience excessive repair costs after about three years of heavy use. Close monitoring of spare parts and fuel consumption will ensure proper service intervals and indicate when a bike has reached the end of its service life. Qualified shops are typically more capable of handling major repairs than village mechanics. A policy of giving (or selling) motorbikes to field staff at the end of their service life may encourage staff to take better care of them. Policies that prohibit riding without a helmet, outlaw drinking and driving, limit the number of riders, restrict use of motorbikes after work, and establish procedures for notification of accidents can improve safety.

• *Develop clear expense policies for staff, farmers, and lead farmers.* Per diems, meals, and transport costs are all areas of potential contention. Programs with clear policies that are communicated up-front to participants avoid extended negotiations and perceived favoritism.

Lead Farmers: Extending the Reach of Field Staff

Firms can extend the reach of field staff without significantly increasing costs by identifying lead farmers (also called contact farmers, lead contact farmers, or volunteer leaders) to transmit (or "cascade") training messages to 20 to 30 farmers (box 5.3). This is sometimes referred to as "farmer-to-farmer" training.

Lead farmers are typically community members with recognized leadership ability who volunteer to convey information from field staff

---

BOX 5.3

An Extension System Leveraging Lead Farmers

In the sample design (figure B5.3.1), five paid staff train and oversee the output of 800 farmers, transmitting a new message each week according to the crop production calendar. A field supervisor coordinates the work of four field staff who deliver messages and training to lead farmers and farmer groups in an assigned territory. As described in chapter 3, the farmer groups could be preexisting producer organizations or formed to receive agricultural training.

Depending on travel time between farmer groups, an extension agent can typically meet with two farmer groups daily. This enables an agent to visit eight farmer groups in four days, reserving the fifth workday for meetings, planning, report writing, and vehicle maintenance. The fifth day might also include training from a contracted agronomist who develops the messages and training materials used by field staff.

Firms often employ a "rolling design" that maximizes the number of trained farmers. If one crop cycle of intensive training is enough to reach a critical mass of trained farmers in a given area, the extension team will move on to a new location. The network of lead contact farmers and farmers' groups will then support the learning of late adopters in the first area. The extension program may periodically provide additional performance support through less-intensive refresher training to reinforce important messages.

box continued

BOX 5.3

An Extension System Leveraging Lead Farmers *(Continued)*

FIGURE B5.3.1 Sample Organizational Chart of Extension Program

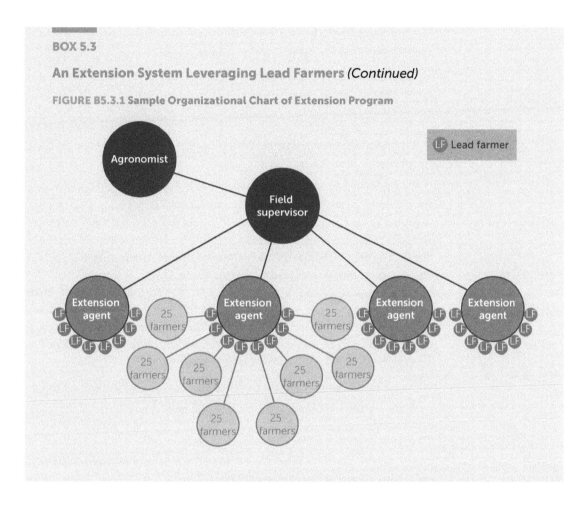

to individual farmers. Effective lead farmers are literate, dynamic community members who have their peers' respect and are willing to try new techniques. Well-organized farmer groups typically have someone who assumes the role of lead farmer.

Managing lead farmers. Lead farmers do not usually receive a salary, but their role may require significant time investment. Because they are potentially very cost-effective trainers, firms should look carefully at how to motivate them and maintain commitment with incentives such as the following:

· Fertilizer and other inputs for their demonstration plots

· Tools to facilitate training such as motorbike fuel, bicycles, hats, shirts, rain gear, backpacks, scales, notebooks, calculators, cell phones, and air time

- Opportunities to be the first in their community to learn or trial new techniques

- Opportunities to travel for meetings or visit other successful programs

- Community recognition during meetings or on radio programs

- Opportunities to win prizes based on the results of farmers in their groups.

Providing inputs is the most expensive but also the most effective incentive because (1) the lead farmer gets a tangible benefit from higher yields, and (2) there is a demonstration effect for neighbors, even if the lead farmer does no other training. Whatever incentive is chosen, it should motivate the lead farmer without negatively affecting other farmers. (See table 5.2 on the stated motivations of lead farmers in three African countries.)

Best practices. Lead farmers can be good representatives of the firm in the community, so it is essential to (1) give them appropriate incentives to play that role; (2) equip them with the knowledge, resources, and capacity to train farmers; and (3) keep track of them. Best practices for increasing their effectiveness include the following:

- *Involving community members* in the selection of lead farmers to foster local support for the program and increase the farmers' stake in its success

TABLE 5.2 **Motivations for Becoming Lead Farmers in Selected African Countries**
Percentage of lead farmers, by motivation cited

Motivation	Cameroon	Kenya	Malawi
Gain knowledge	64	62	58
Help others	69	42	56
Social status	26	28[a]	4
Social networking	34		4
Project financial or material benefits	30	27	8
Income from associated activities	—[b]	23	5

Source: Simpson et al. 2015.
Note: Surveys were conducted in 2014 and 2015. The motivations that respondents expressed for *continuing* to serve as lead farmers were similar except in three ways: (a) "gaining new knowledge" declined; (b) the importance of "helping others" increased; and (c) where the question was asked, "income from associated activities" became significantly more important (for example, selling seed or receiving a training fee).
a. The Kenya survey combined "social status" and "social networking" as "social benefits."
b. — = not available. The Cameroon survey did not include the "income from associated activities" motivation.

- *Carefully considering community dynamics* when identifying the right profile for a lead farmer—for example (although younger farmers tend to be energetic), preferably selecting older farmers because, in some cultures, they are more respected

- *Developing written contracts* between firm, lead farmer, and farmer groups to clarify roles, responsibilities, and expectations—and checking local labor laws to ascertain the firm's potential obligations to give salaries or benefits

- *Conducting off-site meetings and training sessions* with groups of lead farmers to help reinforce key messages, improve facilitation skills, and encourage sharing and learning

- *Disseminating weekly schedules* detailing each lead farmer's tasks, to help the firm, farmer, and farmer group track the lead farmer's progress and achievements.

Messages and Training Approaches

When developing messages for farmers, it is useful to begin with an agricultural calendar for the focus crop or crops. This should detail all necessary activities on a weekly or biweekly basis throughout the year. With climate change affecting weather patterns in many regions, traditional agricultural calendars may need to be adjusted for new conditions.

Extension messages should accompany each activity listed on the calendar. Depending on the roles of the field staff, these messages could include crop prices, agricultural productivity advice, or practices required for certification.

The calendar should also include information that the staff need to collect. Again, depending on the roles of the field staff, this information could include crop volumes, production information, and data (such as farm practices) needed for certification.

Training of smallholder farmers uses three main methodologies: demonstration and innovation, farmer field schools, and farmer training centers.

Demonstration and Innovation

Under this approach, the field staff instruct contact farmers to create demonstration plots (or "dem" plots) using best management practices and recommended types and levels of inputs. Firms may provide inputs both as a training tool and as an incentive for the contact farmers.

Best practices in organizing demonstration plots include the following:

- Farmer-led research to identify best practices is a proven approach (farmer field school), but extra time should be allowed because it requires more time than simple demonstration.

- Demonstrated practices should be economically and technically feasible for most of the surrounding farmers.

- The plot should be clearly laid out and marked—without attempting to demonstrate too many practices.

- Signs explaining the demonstration can provide information to passersby even when no one is present.

- Farmers, not extension staff, should work on the plots.

- Field days involving neighboring farmers are an effective way to increase reach.

Field staff then hold training sessions at the demonstration plots and on the farms of other group members. The sessions focus on instruction reinforced by hands-on practice. The plots can also be used for farmer-led research. Community field days can be held at the plots throughout the production cycle, highlighting best practices and giving farmers an opportunity to practice their learning. These events also help recruit new producers into the supply chain.

A related methodology—"train and visit"—offers group training sessions at central locations, followed by visits to individual farms to coach and mentor farmers. Although this approach is effective in transmitting messages, it is often considered too expensive given the time needed to visit individual smallholdings. However, the approaches can be combined if a farmer encounters a particular problem best resolved by a visit. By rotating the training location between the farmers in a group, individual assistance can be provided while still training the whole group.

Farmer Field Schools

Farmer field schools are a form of adult education, based on the concept that farmers learn optimally from field observation and experimentation. They were developed in Indonesia to help rice farmers tailor their integrated pest management practices to diverse and dynamic ecological conditions. Policy makers and donors were impressed with the results and the program was rapidly expanded (Van den Berg 2004).

FIGURE 5.3 How Farmer Field Schools Facilitate Experimentation and Discussion in Smallholder Training

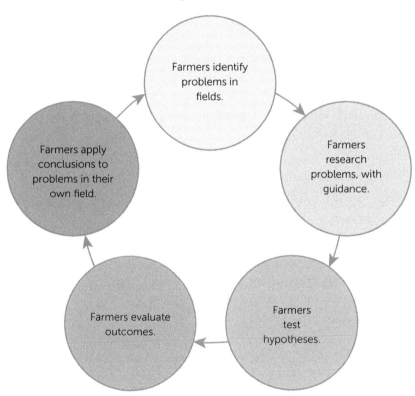

With this approach, farmers discover improved techniques themselves through facilitated research and discussion (figure 5.3). For example, farmers might look at pest control techniques across several farms and determine which practices led to higher yields and at what cost. Although the process is always guided by a trained extension agent, his or her role is not to instruct, but rather to facilitate experimentation and discussion. This participatory philosophy is an effective approach that leads to deeper learning and understanding, but its success is critically dependent on good facilitation skills.

The farmer field school approach may be too time-consuming for firms trying to maximize the reach of their training, but extension programs can incorporate elements of the methodology throughout the production cycle. For example, farmers can analyze the productivity of a dem plot by comparing it with neighboring fields. Dem plots can also be designed with several treatments, such as low, medium, and high levels of fertilizer application, which can facilitate an analysis and discussion about the optimal fertilizer amount.

A systematic review of 500 documents found that farmer field schools compare with other approaches to extension in the following ways (Waddington and White 2014):

- They better target less-poor male farmers than poorer farmers and women.

- Good facilitation is very important, or they become more top-down in approach.

- They can work well locally, but there's little experience of effective (national) scaling up.

- They are not a good way to reach those beyond the immediate participants.

- They are less cost-effective than other approaches for simple practices but are potentially cost-effective for disseminating complex practices (although extension visits are still more cost-effective).

Farmer Training Centers

Farmer training centers provide classrooms and associated plots where improved techniques are demonstrated and practiced. The demonstration plots can be used as nurseries to produce improved planting materials for sale or distribution. However, farmers learn techniques on *model* plots, so they may have difficulty transferring their learning to their own fields. Centers tend to be near the target communities, but some centers have dormitories to host farmers for multiday training events. A farmer training center can also serve as a base for the field staff in both demonstration and farmer field school systems. Nucleus estates may have farmer training centers serving their outgrowers.

Local schools can also be encouraged to incorporate agricultural themes into existing curricula or to use "garden-based learning" approaches. Mathematics can be taught using agricultural examples and farm management accounting principles, and biology classes can include discussion of plant nutrition. Such instruction lays a foundation for a new generation of more professional smallholders and, in the meantime, when children learn good agricultural practices, they may pass these on to their parents. Of course, any initiatives involving children must take care to avoid any direct or indirect encouragement of child labor.

Training in Business Approaches, Professionalism, and Markets

Most approaches to agricultural extension have tended to focus on the production and management of crops and animals. Sometimes training includes consideration of marketing issues, but generally this has not been a focus. In separate developments, some organizations have focused on the capacity development needs of producer organizations, addressing issues such as governance, record keeping, legal registration, access to banking, and how to self-organize for training and interaction with value chain stakeholders. Some of those programs have been successful, but the approaches and results have varied among providers and, when project-based, have often been too short-lived to build needed long-term capacities. Even when initially successful, leadership may change, and standards of governance may subsequently slip.

Farm productivity is important to companies, but agribusinesses are also keen to engage with farmers who are already integrated into national markets as suppliers of crops or livestock products and as buyers of inputs. Smallholders who understand the requirements of higher-value or external markets (for example, the importance of quality issues or other product specifications) and how to link with market players make easier business partners for agribusiness firms.

With the increasing recognition that farmer organization is essential for smallholder integration into global agribusiness supply chains, building the capacity of those organizations to engage in markets is a growing area of interest and new developments. For example, IFC's Agribusiness Leadership Program (box 5.4) and the Bayer Academy in the Philippines (box 5.5) are helping farmers become "agripreneurs."

BOX 5.4

The Agribusiness Leadership Program

International Finance Corporation's Agribusiness Leadership Program (ALP) prepares producer organizations (POs) to become more professional and more reliable supply chain partners. It uses an integrated system of assessment, training, and coaching to help POs (like cooperatives and agro-retailers) move from semisubsistence production to commercially vibrant operations linked to supply chains, finance, and other market opportunities.

box continued

BOX 5.4

The Agribusiness Leadership Program *(Continued)*

ALP goes beyond the usual smallholder training interventions. Its integration with assessment tools places a razor-sharp focus on the performance gaps preventing POs from integrating into markets. ALP instructional designers build a customized training and coaching program that responds to needs identified by the assessments and a training needs assessment. Following training and coaching, POs are reassessed using the same assessment tool. Thus, ALP can quantifiably measure their progress toward professionalism. Figure B5.4.1 summarizes the ALP implementation process.

At the end of the program (typically 6–24 months), the POs have a development plan, which they can turn into a business plan for lenders. After ALP, leaders of the POs also have the business management skills to fulfill contracts, making them more likely to attract new customers and strengthen existing customer relationships.

Since launching in July 2016, ALP has been deployed for five IFC clients on six projects in Africa. The program has trained 61 local trainers, who have subsequently trained and coached 620 farmer organizations serving 150,000 farming families.

FIGURE B5.4.1 Steps in IFC Agribusiness Leadership Program

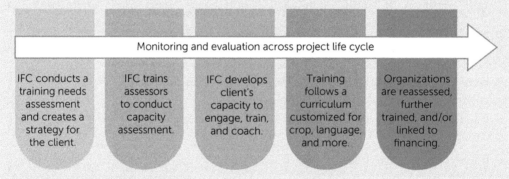

Monitoring and evaluation across project life cycle

| IFC conducts a training needs assessment and creates a strategy for the client. | IFC trains assessors to conduct capacity assessment. | IFC develops client's capacity to engage, train, and coach. | Training follows a curriculum customized for crop, language, and more. | Organizations are reassessed, further trained, and/or linked to financing. |

Note: IFC = International Finance Corporation.

In Practice: Helping Farmers Become "Agripreneurs" at Bayer Academy in the Philippines

In the Philippines, Bayer has been working with IFC to develop the Bayer Academy, an ambitious initiative launched in 2014. Over the five-year program, about 100,000 Filipino rice farmers are to learn business and financial skills as well as the advantages of using better seeds, more machinery, and new farming technologies.

Nearly one in three Filipino workers is employed in the country's agriculture sector. Yet, incomes and productivity are constrained by low investments in agricultural infrastructure, poor irrigation, inefficient transport and logistics, the high cost of improved seeds and other farm inputs, and farmers' lack of financial literacy and limited access to finance. As Hans-Joachim Wegfahrt (former managing director of Bayer CropScience Inc. in the Philippines) observed, "Local farmers need to change their mindset. From being subsistence farmers, they have to become agripreneurs who will see farming as a business where the entire value chain has to be efficient and sustainable."

Responding to this challenge, the Bayer Academy is unusual as a farmer training program in several ways:

- It is holistic—covering production as well as financial and business management skills.
- It uses learning techniques that are effective in engaging a more mature audience and the audience that might have low numeracy and literacy skills.
- It recognizes that farmers do not respond well to conventional teaching methods.
- It works through multiple outreach channels including farmer cooperatives, Bayer's own field teams, distributor networks, and other organizations including NGOs and government agencies like the Agricultural Training Institute.
- It plans to complement face-to-face interaction with radio, digital, and mobile technologies.

By 2017, the program had reached over 90,000 farmers and other agri-stakeholders with trainings and field activities that followed IFC's Agricultural Extension Training of Trainers module. Moving forward, Bayer Academy will continue its efforts to bring quality learning via training and improve the farmer livelihoods through its global Smallholder Initiative.

Training Materials to Support Field Staff

Experience is rapidly expanding in using a vast array of emerging ICT options to support farmer training and communication, but there is still a significant place for more-traditional hard copy and the use of mass media. Although the next section discusses communication outreach to farmers more generally, the options listed below are specific to the training context. A convenient checklist of guidelines for designing such materials uses the acronym ACTIONS (as shown in table 5.3).

TABLE 5.3 The ACTIONS Model for Designing Training Materials

A	C	T	I	O	N	S
Accessibility:	Cost:	Teaching style:	Interactivity:	Organizational support:	Novelty:	Sustainability:
The material must be accessible to the target audience. This means using the visual information for low-literacy audiences and ensuring that examples are culturally appropriate.	Consider the various costs of development, field testing, revision, layout, and dissemination. Some studies estimate that 40 hours of advance work are needed for one hour of instruction time.	Training materials that encourage active participation by students are more effective. Elements such as role playing, problem solving, and participatory field exercises make learning active. Radio programs that allow listener participation are more effective than passive broadcasts.	Training materials that promote interactivity between trainer and trainee reinforce learning. The farmer field school methodology is based on interactivity, using examples from farmers' fields and eliciting solutions from farmers, rather than providing prescriptive approaches.	Trainers require logistical (transportation and communication); administrative (salary, reimbursement of expenses, and record keeping); and managerial support so they can concentrate on preparing for training.	It is important to make training interesting. This can involve mixing media, such as videos with face-to-face training, and using new communication technologies such as SMS.	Training by private sector firms must pay for itself to be sustainable. In some cases, fees for training may defray costs. However, with smallholder farmers, this is rare. More likely, increased revenue from productivity and quality needs to cover training costs.

Source: Adapted from Bates 1995.
Note: The ACTIONS model—a decision-making framework for use of technology—is attributed to A. W. (Tony) Bates (Bates 1995). SMS = short message service.

Effective training tools to support face-to-face group learning include the following:

- *Reference guides for field staff:* These provide the theory behind the recommendations and a detailed list of diagnoses for nutritional deficiencies, pests, and diseases. An increasing amount of such material is available for use on tablet computers and smartphones.

- *Manuals for farmers:* Integrating simple, feasible messages into training materials for farmers increases the likelihood that those messages are understood and adopted. Farmer manuals do not need the same level of detail as the reference guides for field staff. They should be developed in the local language, use pictures and graphics, and reflect the local context. (In general, good drawings are preferable to photographs because they reproduce better.) Adult learning methodology and interactive practice exercises can promote learning more than rote memorization.

BOX 5.6

In Practice: Digital Green Helps Farmers Create Training Videos for Other Farmers

India-based Digital Green has developed a system for recording and disseminating agricultural training videos. It provides farmers with basic cameras and training to shoot short films. Subject experts review the videos to check that the content follows best practices, and the films are made available to other farmers via communal video showings and DVDs.

Where this approach is used, 70 percent of farmers are trying new practices, compared with just 10–15 percent under "traditional" extension models. Digital Green CEO Rikin Gandhi says that 1.4 million people in India are now watching these videos (80 percent of whom are women). Their content and audience has expanded, too, to include nutrition and health messages, with coverage in Sub-Saharan Africa as well as in other Asian countries. Youth are becoming engaged in rural issues, too, as Digital Green has developed a reality TV show and a Facebook game, to make the learning fun. Firms and organizations using the system combine the videos with training by field staff—a combination that has succeeded in influencing behavior change.

Source: Martineau 2017.

- *Flip charts and posters:* Hung in common meeting areas or used during trainings, these can be useful tools to supplement the trainer's presentation with pictures and diagrams.

- *Quick reference cards, pictorial guides, and crop-cycle calendars:* These are shorter, less dense versions of the farmer best practices guides. With more graphics, these tools can be especially helpful when farmers' literacy is low. Consider weatherproofing these materials to last longer and promote their use in the field.

- *Video:* This is a popular and effective medium for training farmers, who can watch individually or in groups with field staff. Some firms are using tablet computers provided to field staff to show training videos and collect data. Videos can be produced professionally or made by farmers themselves after some training. Box 5.6 discusses the experience of Digital Green in producing and disseminating videos with farmer training content.

- *Radio programming:* This can reinforce face-to-face training and ensure that consistent messages are transmitted. If the radio program precedes the training, farmers can discuss the messages and ask questions. Farmer interviews give early adopters the chance to convince other farmers about the benefits of new approaches.

- *ICT to support group training:* With the expanded reach of mobile-phone networks and declining costs of tablet computers and smart-phones, the development of applications to support farmer learning and decision making is a rapidly shifting area of growth, potentially opening a much wider menu of low-cost tools to support agricul-tural extension. Many such tools provide information to individuals, but creating opportunities to reinforce this learning is key to its impact. For examples, see the ICT section below.

Communication to Expand Reach

Communication Channels

Communication channels can be broadly grouped into four categories (figure 5.4), which firms will find suitable depending on factors such as the frequency of communication, its quality, and its reach among farmer suppliers. Effective communication strategies will likely use a combina-tion of mutually reinforcing channels.

Communication along supply chains, particularly complex ones, may flow in both directions—from firm to farmer and back to firm, such as through face-to-face interactions or various mobile applications. This two-way communication may be more useful than one-way communica-tion (for example, through written materials).

The amount and complexity of communication increases as supply chains become stronger and more developed. Basic supply chains may transmit delivery and payment information, while complex supply chains communicate crop prices, traceability information, training on

FIGURE 5.4 Communication Channels between Agribusiness Firms and Farmers

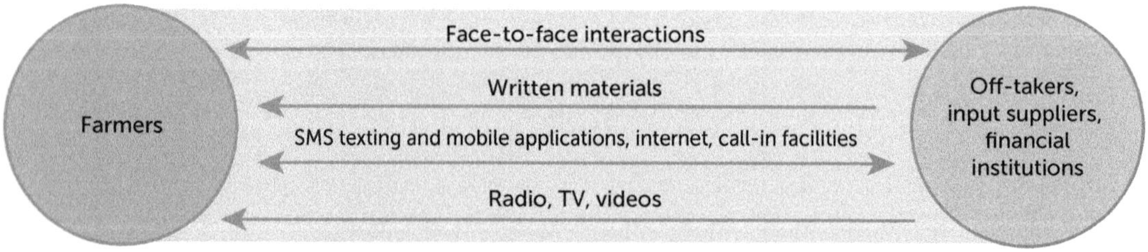

Farmers

Face-to-face interactions

Written materials

SMS texting and mobile applications, internet, call-in facilities

Radio, TV, videos

Off-takers, input suppliers, financial institutions

Note: SMS = short message service.

FIGURE 5.5 Types of Information Communicated in Agricultural Supply Chains, by Complexity and Impact Occurrence

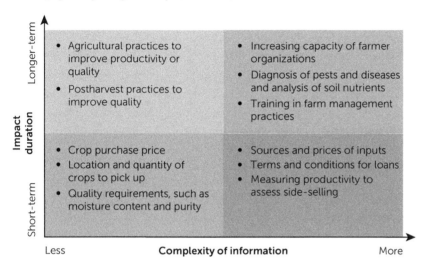

improved agricultural practices, certification data, product specifications, finance opportunities, and the weather. Figure 5.5 maps the types of information that firms may wish to convey according to their complexity and impact on the supply chain.

Mass Media: Print, Radio, and Television

Mass media are powerful tools for communicating with many farmers at low cost over a wide area, but opportunities to reinforce learning are also needed. Farm Radio International argues that using radio with interactive content increases its own reach and effectiveness (as described in box 5.7).

Print media, such as agricultural newspapers, can update farmers on market developments and provide timely reminders about good agricultural practices throughout the production calendar. In India and other populous countries, locally produced print media advertise agricultural inputs and opportunities for crop marketing. Pamphlets, instructional labels, and inserts are other types of print media that can communicate a variety of information to farmers.

Radio and television can be used in many ways including advertising, discussion programs about crops or products, farmer interviews, call-in programs, and radio or TV soap operas. They also have the advantage of

BOX 5.7

In Practice: Radio with Interactive Content Reaches Farmers in Africa and Southeast Asia

Radio has extensive reach in low- and middle-income countries, but the combination of radio with interactive content, facilitated by the spread of mobile phones, can magnify impact.

Farm Radio International has developed a series of interactive, radio-based approaches tailored to achieve outcomes such as awareness raising, knowledge change, market links, adoption of good practices, changes in attitude and behavior, citizen engagement, and women's empowerment.[a]

It partnered with the Gates Foundation to study the impact of radio programming on farmer practices in Africa. This five-country study found that 39 percent of farmers who listened actively (deliberately) to interactive radio programs changed their agricultural practices, compared with 21 percent of passive listeners (those who just happened to hear the program). Of those who did not listen at all (the control group), only 4 percent changed their practices. The cost of this program averaged less than $1 per "adopter." One station combined this programming with listener phone-ins to answer questions and bulk texting via short message service (SMS).

In Cambodia, IFC used radio to educate aromatic-rice farmers about the benefits of improved planting seed, which include higher yields and greater uniformity. This initiative supports client mills that are multiplying improved seed for sale or distribution in their supply chains. The radio programs, broadcast in eight provinces, included music, drama, interviews with successful farmers, and advice from rice agronomists. Farmers could also use their mobile phones to access information in their local language about aromatic-rice varieties—and to leave a question which would be answered on the radio broadcast.

A sample survey revealed that 101,000 Cambodian households had heard the broadcasts, and 22 percent of those gained a medium to large amount of information from the programs. The cost of development and airtime for 17 programs was $0.49 per listening household and $2.21 per household that gained knowledge. Moreover, this programming contributed to a multifaceted package of support to develop the rice value chain in Cambodia, which saw its recorded exports of rice increase from 100,000 metric tons in 2010 to 530,000 metric tons in 2015.

Sources: IFC 2014; Farm Radio International 2011, 2017.
a. Farm Radio International is a Canada-based international nonprofit organization dedicated to exclusively serving African farming families and rural communities through radio. For more information, see its http://www.farmradio.org/.

being accessible to illiterate farmers. Another effective strategy is to combine face-to-face training with radio—during which farmers listen to radio programs with field staff and then practice the skills together. Farm radio programs have a long history, generating a set of best practices (figure 5.6).

FIGURE 5.6 Best Practices for Communicating with Farmers by Radio

Base program development in field research. Use field research to identify the percentage and profile of radio owners, which stations farmers listen to, the extent of coverage areas, and when farmers tend to listen.	**Follow a set schedule**. Shows should air at times convenient to farmers, such as in the evening or early in the morning.	**Feature real farmers**. Whenever possible, include real farmers speaking in the predominant language of farmers in the coverage area.	**Keep messages simple**. Simple messages that are repeated multiple times in different ways are particularly effective. Using various formats such as drama, phone-in programs, and field interviews maintains audience interest and reinforces learning.	**Evaluate impact**. Assessing knowledge, attitudes, and practices is a good methodology to evaluate the impact of radio training programs.

ICTs Have the Potential to Reduce Costs and Extend Reach

ICTs have garnered much interest because they are less costly per farmer than face-to-face communications, can reach large numbers of farmers, and present opportunities for reinforcement and impact assessment, as the following data attest (GSMA 2017):[1]

- By the end of 2016, there were 7.9 billion cellular telephone subscriptions, held by 4.8 billion unique subscribers, representing 65 percent of the world's population. (In fact, more people have a mobile phone than have access to safe sanitation services.)

- With markets almost saturated in high-income countries, 90 percent of new subscriptions in 2016–20 will be in low- and middle-income countries.

- Fifty-five percent of the subscriber identity module (SIM) connections in 2016 were mobile broadband connections (3G and 4G technologies).

- 4G networks covered almost 60 percent of the world's population, including almost 50 percent of the population in low- and middle-income countries.

- Fifty percent of the world's population used the internet as of 2017, ranging from 28 percent in Africa to 45 percent in Asia and 88 percent in North America.

In much of the rural world, 2G (nondata) cellular telephones remain prevalent. They can be used to collect and disseminate small amounts of information via short message service (SMS) or other types of text messaging. Firms and NGOs have developed systems that use 2G platforms to disseminate prices and collect data on crop volumes and locations in a process known as "scout polling." Mobile payment systems also use 2G phones to purchase crops and pay for inputs (as discussed in chapter 2).

However, rapid developments in ICT are creating possibilities that previously seemed scientifically impossible or just prohibitively expensive. Communication and training in agriculture—and in smallholder systems linked to global value chains—are being transformed by systems that make a vast array of actions easier and quicker, providing for almost instantaneous analysis and reporting, with the potential for much more effective and powerful communication. These new systems are affecting, or have the potential to affect, smallholder agriculture in multiple ways:

- *Use of the internet or messaging for agricultural information* relating to standard practices, diseases, treatments and so on. In other words, knowledge can be available in rural areas not just through training and books but also via internet access or text messaging (such as routine mailings on particular topics or prompted by a farmer's query). The more-interactive systems can relay messages to call centers and expert input, if necessary, or combine face-to-face interaction with ICT backup. Hundreds of these systems are now available, either as subscription services that individual farmers can sign up for or included as a function of supply chain management and traceability systems (for example, the ability to send bulk SMS texts).

- *Availability of real-time, local, and customized information* including market data, weather forecasts, and area or crop surveillance (for example, eKutir, e-Choupal, Esoko, aWhere). In particular, big data can be used to target training (table 5.4). See also box 5.8, which illustrates how customized, localized, and timely information can be used to improve logistics.

- *Lower-cost, wider-reaching technology and scope for more interactive content* are making video, television, and radio more accessible, current, targeted, and effective as channels for transmitting information to and from farmers.

The use of ICT in agriculture is a rapidly developing field and there is now also online training available that explores the design considerations and technologies for agricultural production in frontier and emerging markets, with interactive inputs from experts in the field.

TABLE 5.4 ICT4Ag: Big Data Products for Smallholder Farmers

eKutir	e-Choupal	Esoko	aWhere
eKutir offers decentralized, risk-mitigating, transparent infrastructure for smallholder farmers. eKutir's product, the FarmChalo app, has three main components: • Khyeti for data-driven farming, providing farmers with personalized solutions throughout the crop cycle • Haat for connecting farmers to digital markets • FARM for generating a farmer's credit score based on farm data	e-Choupal, the model developed by ITC Ltd. of Kolkata, India, blends offline and online solutions through village internet kiosks. It enables access to information, in the local language, on the weather, market prices, innovative farm practices, and risk management. The model also facilitates the sale of farm inputs and purchase of farm produce directly from farmers.	Esoko offers a range of solutions for smallholder farmers and extension workers, among them Insyt and MIS: • Insyt primarily supports management of extension work and gathers respective monitoring and evaluation data. • MIS delivers timely information such as weather updates, market prices, and announcements to farmers through SMS and voice messages. It also offers call center support that allows farmers to connect with extension experts.	aWhere offers timely (updated four times a day), localized weather information that is crucial in the light of climate change to reduce farmers' weather vulnerability. This solution provides agronomic modeling based on weather data, soil information, and crop statistics to support timely decisions for needed adaptations.

Sources: "FarmChalo," eKutir Global (accessed February 6, 2018), http://www.ekutirglobal.com/farmchalo.html; "e-Choupal," Agri Business, ITC Ltd. (accessed February 6, 2018), http://www.itcportal.com/businesses/agri-business/e-choupal.aspx; "Products," Esoko (accessed February 6, 2018), https://www.esoko.com.
Note: SMS = short message service.

BOX 5.8

In Practice: ICT Addresses Challenging Logistics in Hazelnut Supply in Bhutan

Mountain Hazelnuts is a smallholder farmer-based company designed to take advantage of the growing demand for hazelnuts from European confectionery and Asian snack producers. The company operates in Bhutan, an environment that presents significant challenges for commercial agriculture. The country has limited suitable land for growing crops, while its geography and road conditions make logistics and market access costly.

To achieve operational efficiency, Mountain Hazelnuts has implemented numerous information and communication technology (ICT) solutions along its supply chains, mitigating risks and reducing costs. The most recent technical innovation the company has implemented addresses the unique logistical challenges presented in Bhutan. The company's operations cover the entire

box continued

In Practice: ICT Addresses Challenging Logistics in Hazelnut Supply in Bhutan *(Continued)*

country, with widely dispersed orchards in 18 out of 20 districts. The domestic road network is fragmented, its poor infrastructure necessitating two full days to drive the 500 kilometers from Bhutan's west to the east on the best-traveled roads, while significantly slower travel is required on the smaller, less-maintained farm roads that reach most of the hazelnut orchards. Natural and manufactured roadblocks are frequent, unpredictable, and ubiquitous—a situation also aggravated by the lack of timely traffic information.

Mountain Hazelnuts has developed an innovative solution to monitor and register road conditions as well as optimize the time required to travel between locations. More than 150 field staff are involved in updating information on road conditions and travel times. The data are further shared through OpenStreetMap and made accessible to all relevant employees to ensure that logistics operations are efficiently planned and safely completed.[a] This approach has proven successful in reducing transportation delays and costs. Increased transparency has enabled Mountain Hazelnuts to standardize truck hiring rates, cutting transport costs and reducing the challenge of negotiating ad hoc transport arrangements.

Sources: GAFSP and IFC 2016; Ishihara 2017.
a. For more information about the worldwide, open-data OpenStreetMap project, see https://www.openstreetmap.org.

A four-week program covers crop planning and financing, the crop cycle, postharvest and farm management, and the future for ICT for agriculture (including sensors, geographic information systems [GIS], big data, digital photo recognition, and data analytics).[2]

Considerations for Selecting an Engagement Strategy

Designing an effective extension system involves balancing multiple competing factors that influence budget and farmer reach. For example, extension costs are affected by various internal and external factors (figure 5.7). Depending on such factors, a firm or NGO using extension field staff might spend $50–$150 or more per farmer.

The factors to be considered include the following:

- *Farmer density:* How many farmers need to be trained at each location or village? What is the distance between villages? How many farmer meetings can an extension hold per day? If farmers are widely

FIGURE 5.7 Factors Affecting Extension System Cost per Farmer

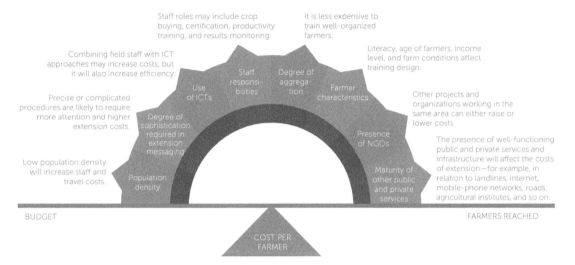

Note: ICT = information and communication technology; NGO = nongovernmental organization.

dispersed, only one meeting per day may be possible. In higher-density areas, up to four meetings per day may be possible.

- *ICT approaches:* Although combining field staff with ICTs will increase costs, it can also increase staff efficiency and effectiveness. For example, digital tablets are costly, but they allow staff to use training videos and collect data. Costs per farmer reached may be lower because ICTs reduce the need for face-to-face contact or reinforcement.

- *Degree of farmer organization:* It is less expensive to train well-organized farmers because some groups can transmit information among members without outside assistance. If farmers are not organized, field staff may need to help them form basic groups before beginning technical training.

- *Farmer characteristics:* Training must be tailored to farmers' socioeconomic characteristics, including literacy levels and income. In addition, farms' physical characteristics (including farm size) and conditions (such as slope, age of tree crops, and soil fertility) affect farmers' ability to use inputs and training. Firms should analyze and, if necessary, segment farm populations to ensure effective training.

- *Presence of NGOs:* The presence of local or international NGOs can be either an opportunity or a challenge. Costs may be reduced if the firm's objectives can be met by other organizations. However, the firm will likely have to match the NGO's salaries or risk having its staff poached. In either case, close coordination between the NGO and the firm is essential. A written memorandum of understanding would be useful to document the roles and responsibilities of each side.

- *Presence of other public and private services:* The amount and cost of a firm's reach will definitely be affected by the strength of internet and telephone services, as well as the density (and state) of the rural road network. Government research institutes may have useful information and outreach services, and may be willing to collaborate on applied research issues, potentially reducing costs of accessing specialist expertise.

- *Budget:* The costs, capacity, and intensity of various communication options vary widely. Increases in the amount of information and the intensity of the channel correlate with increased cost per farmer (figure 5.8). Information delivered by field staff via farm visits can transmit a large amount of detailed information, but the intervention

FIGURE 5.8 Indicative Comparison of Cost and Capacity for Various Communication Methods

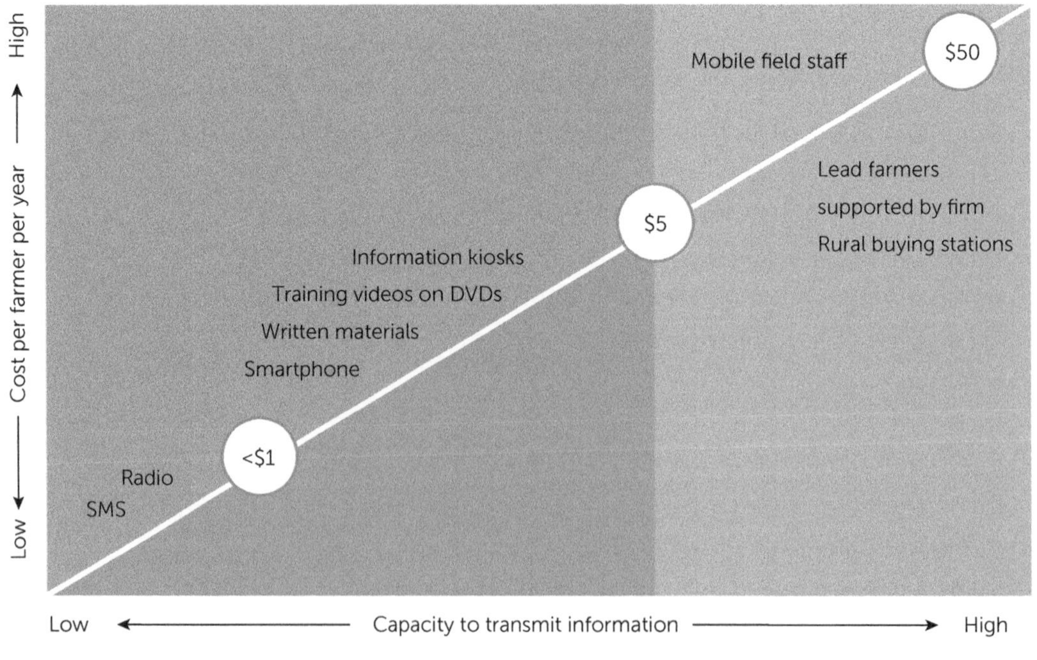

Source: Fischer 2014.
Note: SMS = short message service.

may cost more than $100 per farmer annually. Radio messages may cost less than $1 per farmer but transmit a limited amount of information, albeit with minimal interaction with message recipients. As a result, the impact of the message may be minimized, and the percentage of farmers adopting new behaviors will be lower. If the firm's objectives require mobile field staff to interact with farmers, it is important to design an extension system that meets these objectives while minimizing the cost per farmer. Wide variations in regional labor costs make it difficult to benchmark the cost per farmer of interventions that deploy mobile field staff. For example, hiring field staff in South Asia is significantly less expensive than in Africa, where competition with NGO programs elevates costs.

- *Impact of training and communication:* To effectively assess the benefits of various communication tools, clear training goals and a reasonable time frame for obtaining a positive return on investment should be established. This can help manage expectations among farmers, field staff, and the firm. For annual crops, measurable productivity gains may be seen within two seasons. In contrast, a program focused on tree crop renewal may not see increased productivity until five years after seedlings were planted.

Cost metrics such as cost per farmer trained and number of farmers per extension agent can be used. However, tracking the *impact* of training is more complex because short-term, tangible benefits such as crop quality, productivity, and certification are more easily measured than less-tangible, longer-term benefits such as increased goodwill among suppliers. Chapter 9, on results measurement, provides more detail on suitable metrics for measuring change in smallholder farming systems.

The following chapter on reducing yield gaps—including farm management and appropriate use of inputs—complements this review of farmer training.

Notes

1. Data exclude "machine to machine" mobile connections. "Internet World Stats: Usage and Population Statistics" [accessed June 10, 2017], http://www.internet worldstats.com/stats.htm)
2. "Agriculture, Innovation, and Technology," online course held June 6–July 1, 2017, by TechChange, Washington, DC (accessed July 9, 2017), https://www.techchange .org/online-courses/agriculture-innovation-technology/.

References

Babu, S. C., and Y. Zhou. 2016. "Knowledge Driven Development: Private Extension and Global Lessons. Synopsis." Book synopsis, International Food Policy Research Institute, Washington, DC.

Bates, A. W. 1995. *Technology, Open Learning and Distance Education.* London: Routledge.

Colverson, K., and M. Mbo'o-Tchouawou. 2014. *Increasing Access to Agricultural Extension and Advisory Services: How Effective Are New Approaches in Reaching Women Farmers in Rural Areas?* Nairobi, Kenya: International Livestock Research Institute.

Farm Radio International. 2011. "Agricultural Radio that Works." Brochure, Farm Radio International, Ottawa.

———. 2017. "Getting Results with Interactive Radio." Brochure, Farm Radio International, Ottawa.

Fischer, D. 2014. "Benchmarking the Costs and Benefits of Training Smallholder Farmers." Unpublished manuscript, International Finance Corporation of the World Bank Group (IFC), Washington, DC.

Fischer, T., D. Byerlee, and G. O. Edmeades. 2014. *Crop Yields and Global Food Security: Will Yield Increase Continue to Feed the World?* Canberra: Australian Centre for International Agricultural Research.

GAFSP and IFC (Global Agriculture and Food Security Program and the International Finance Corporation of the World Bank Group). 2016. "Bhutan: Blending Happiness and Hazelnuts with Finance." Case study, IFC, Washington, DC.

GSMA (Groupe Speciale Mobile Association). 2017. "The Mobile Economy 2017." Annual industry outlook report, GSMA, London.

IFC (International Finance Corporation). 2014. "Working with Smallholders: A Handbook for Firms Building Sustainable Supply Chains." IFC, Washington, DC.

Ishihara, Y. 2017. "When Technology Meets Agriculture in Bhutan." *End Poverty in South Asia* (blog), December 19.

Martineau, E. 2017. "Digital Green: How Videos Are Transforming Farming in India and across Africa." Interview with Rikin Gandhi, CEO of Digital Green, *Smart Villages* (website), March 22. http://e4sv.org/digital-green-videos-transforming -farming-rural-india/.

Simpson, B. M., S. Franzel, A, Degrande, G. Kundhlande, and S. Tsafack. 2015. "Farmer-to-Farmer Extension: Issues in Planning and Implementation." Technical Note, Modernizing Extension and Advisory Services, Urbana, IL.

Van den Berg, H. 2004. "IPM Farmer Field Schools: A Synthesis of 25 Impact Evaluations." Report for the Global Integrated Pest Management (IPM) Facility of the Food and Agriculture Organization of the United Nations, Rome.

Waddington, H., and H. White. 2014. "Farmer Field Schools: From Agricultural Extension to Adult Education." Systematic Review Summary 1, International Initiative for Impact Evaluation (3ie), London.

Additional Resources

Agricultural Extension

CARE USA. 2017. "Farmers Field Business School (FFBS) Brief." Food and Nutrition Security Brief, CARE USA, Atlanta. http://www.care.org/sites/default/files/docu ments/ffbs_innovation_brief.pdf.

COMPACI (Competitive African Cotton Initiative). "Farmer Business School. Sustainable Cotton Production Systems." Trainer's file, Zambia–Alliance Ginneries, German Agency for International Cooperation (GIZ)/COMPACI. http://www .compaci.org/en/training-material/farmer-business-school/56-fbs-trainers -file/file.

FAO (Food and Agriculture Organization of the United Nations). "Global Farmer Field School Platform." http://www.fao.org/farmer-field-schools/en/.

———. "Research and Extension." FAO resources on extension, http://www.fao.org /research-and-extension/en/.

G-FRAS (Global Forum for Rural Advisory Services). https://www.g-fras.org/en/.

IFC (International Finance Corporation of the World Bank Group). "IFC Agribusiness Leadership Program." http://www.ifc.org/wps/wcm/connect/industry_ext_con tent/ifc_external_corporate_site/agribusiness/priorities/enhancing+food+secu rity/agribusiness-leadership-program.

MEAS (Modernizing Extension and Advisory Services). http://meas.illinois.edu/. [Resources developed with the support of the U.S. Agency for International Development (USAID). The objective of MEAS is "to define and disseminate good practice strategies and approaches to establishing efficient, effective, and financially sustainable rural extension and advisory service systems in selected countries."]

SCOPEInsight. http:www//scopeinsight.com. SCOPEinsight has developed innovative, universally applicable assessment tools that measure the level of farmer professionalism in emerging markets.

ValueChains Knowledge Clearinghouse. "LINK Methodology." Online resources, including the LINK methodology (of the International Center for Tropical Agriculture [CIAT]) for linking farmers to value chains. http://www.tools4valuec hains.org/tool/link-methodology.

World Vision. "Management of Agriculture Demonstration Plots: What Are We Learning?" http://www.fsnnetwork.org/sites/default/files/Demo%20Plots%20 Presentation_GM%20Mar%2022.pdf.

Agricultural Training to Involve Young People

CNS (Center for Nutrition in Schools). "Garden-Based Learning." Resource page, CNS, University of California, Davis. https://cns.ucdavis.edu/resources/garden -based-learning. [Information on garden-based learning, using school gardens to promote learning about agriculture, nutrition, and other topics]

4-H Youth Development Program. https://4-h.org/. [Information on involving youth in agriculture]

World Bank and UNCTAD (United Nations Conference on Trade and Development). 2018. "Participation of Youth." Responsible Agricultural Investment (RAI) Knowledge into Action Note No. 21, World Bank, Washington, DC; UNCTAD, New York. https://openknowledge.worldbank.org/bitstream/handle/10986/29472 /124296-BRI-PUBLIC-KN21.pdf?sequence=1&isAllowed=y.

Information and Communication Technology

Digital extension and information services. Examples include

- *e-Agriculture.* http://www.e-agriculture.org/. [ICTs for agriculture: a global community of practice]

- *eKutir Global.* http://www.ekutirglobal.com/. ["digital technology solutions for farmers to grow more food"]
- *Esoko.* https://www.esoko.com/. [ICT services for agricultural markets in Africa]
- *Frontline.* http://www.frontlinesms.com/. [Helps enterprises develop messaging systems]
- *ITC Ltd., e-Choupal.* http://www.itcportal.com/businesses/agri-business/e-choupal .aspx. [Provides market information for farmers in India]

Digital Green. http://www.digitalgreen.org. [Works with ICT and grassroots organizations to develop solutions for improved small-farmer livelihoods]

FHI 360 (Family Health International 360). "Fostering Agriculture Competitiveness Employing Information Communication Technologies (FACET)." Technical project to support U.S. Agency for International Development (USAID) missions and implementing partners. https://www.fhi360.org/projects/fostering-agriculture -competitiveness-employing-information-communication-technologies.

TechChange. https://www.techchange.org/about/. [Provides online training in technology and agriculture]

United Nations Global Forum on ICT for Development (ICT4Dev). http://close-the -gap.org/discover-us/united-nations/un-gaid/.

Van Campenhout, B. 2012. "Mobile Applications to Deliver Extension to Remote Areas." Study of Grameen Foundation project in Uganda, Grameen Foundation, Washington, DC.

World Bank. 2017. *ICT in Agriculture: Connecting Smallholders to Knowledge, Networks and Institutions. Updated Edition.* Washington, DC: World Bank.

Other Information Resources

eGranary. https://www.widernet.org/eGranary/about. [Offline information store providing access to 35 million digital resources for those lacking internet access]

Plantwise Knowledge Bank. http://www.plantwise.org/KnowledgeBank/home.aspx. [Plantwise clinics, a program of the Centre for Agriculture and Biosciences International]

Woodard, J. 2012. *Integrating Low-Cost Video into Agricultural Development Projects: A Toolkit for Practitioners.* Washington, DC: U.S. Agency for International Development (USAID). http://ictforag.org/toolkits/video/resources.html#.WTe -JuuGPIU. [Online toolkit on the use of video for agricultural development, developed by FHI 360, a USAID-funded project]

World Bank and UNCTAD (United Nations Conference on Trade and Development). 2018. "Training and Integrating Local People into the Workforce." Responsible Agricultural Investment (RAI) Knowledge into Action Note No. 17, World Bank, Washington, DC. http://documents.worldbank.org/curated/en/619331521090484109 /pdf/124292-BRI-PUBLIC-KN17.pdf.

CHAPTER 6
YIELD GAPS

KEY MESSAGES

➡ Smallholder agriculture significantly underperforms relative to its potential.

➡ Reducing those yield gaps, through improved farm management and appropriate input use, is one of the most obvious ways to increase global agricultural output.

➡ Training, input packages, and finance, as well as insurance, can help improve productivity, but there is also a need to extend the reach of input companies.

➡ New technology helps reduce yield gaps with off-the-shelf systems to facilitate smallholder management, as well as with its increasing potential for site-specific analysis and recommendations that sharply improve the efficiency of input use.

➡ Climate-smart agriculture is an important and needed area of development.

➡ To be adopted, new input packages must be unambiguously better-performing.

➡ Categorizing farmers based on capacity to increase output and use credit—and customizing packages to gradually upgrade farmer capacity—is good practice.

➡ "Reversibility" is a key determinant of agricultural practice adoption that outweighs concerns such as level of investment or expected increase in income—so use graduated approaches.

The Business Case for Improving Farm Management and Input Use

Notwithstanding the role for breeding, the most obvious strategy for rapid yield gap closing is to improve the level of agronomic management practised by the millions of smallholder farmers involved in underperforming systems. (Fischer, Byerlee, and Edmeades 2014, *Crop Yields and Global Food Security*, 548)

What Is Farm Management?

Farm management is about organizing and operating a farm, with the available resources, to maximize profit while meeting other obligations or choices of the farm household. It therefore involves elements of

- *Know-how* about cultivation, rearing livestock, harvest, and storage

- *Understanding how farming practices interact* with one another and how they affect critical land and water resources

- *Management of risk and uncertainty*—to build resilience to normal patterns of variation in the weather and markets as well as to climate change-related shifts

- *Appropriate use of inputs and resources*

- *Access to current information*—for example, prices, product specifications, trader offers, and weather forecasts—to support decisions that affect incomes and sustainability

- *Keeping records* of practices, applications, prices, yields, and events

- *Analysis and calculation*, to assess trade-offs between alternative options.

Sometimes farm management is described in relation to two aspects: (1) agronomic and animal husbandry skills, and (2) financial literacy, business management, and market participation.

Why Is Farm Management Important?

Farm management affects the smallholders' bottom line, in the current year and in the future. It is especially important, if smallholders are to play a larger role in global food chains, for a host of reasons:

- Increasing pressure on natural resources, to meet the competing needs of the world's growing population, means that management of those resources is critical.

- Farmers play a pivotal resource management role in supplying global food chains.

- Some crops are based on smallholder production systems, and as demand increases, the smallholders need support to ensure supply.

- As smallholders become bigger players in global food supply, farm management solutions must be accessible to poorer and less-educated farmers.

- Smallholder farming systems present strong opportunities to close yield gaps, including scrutiny of how critical inputs are used in combination.

- Climate change has added new challenges: changes in weather patterns, more frequent but unpredictable extreme weather events, and increasing water salinity.

Smallholder Farmers: High Yield Gaps, Scope for Big Productivity Gains

In most low-income countries, yield gaps exceed 50 percent—a "yield gap" being the difference between farm yield and potential yield (the yield achievable using existing technology, expressed as a percentage of farm yield). High yield gaps reflect multiple constraints such as insufficient adoption of more-productive technologies, poor market integration, and gender inequalities in small-scale family farming (FAO 2017). Closing those yield gaps will require a multifaceted approach that addresses financial constraints; risk management; access to inputs, training, and markets; and infrastructure. Box 6.1 lists some typical characteristics of smallholder farms that affect farm management.

A recent study underlines the importance of farmers' concerns about risk, finding that the most significant factor in new practice or technology adoption rates was the degree of *reversibility* of the change. In fact,

BOX 6.1

Smallholders: Typical Characteristics Affecting Farm Management

Land and Soil
- A small landholding, often smaller than 2 hectares, that in many places gets smaller with each generation, limiting the number of crop cycles per year
- Traditional soil fertility management (including fallow periods) under pressure
- Shortage of labor (and little mechanization), which may limit conservation methods
- Weak incentives to manage common property resources (especially forestry)

Finances
- Scarcity of cash combined with seasonal labor constraints (reliance on family labor)
- Marked seasonality to cash flow: "the hungry period" before the new crop, strain on the household at the beginning of the school year, and difficulties in meeting unexpected outlays

Farming Knowledge
- Familiarity with traditional farming techniques, using largely on-farm inputs
- Knowledge of the farming calendar, based on "normal" weather patterns
- Risk management entailing primarily diversity of crops, intercropping, and off-farm income

Farm Records
- Low literacy and numeracy
- Lack of records and rarely knowing exact size of farm or field
- Difficulty of measuring benefits from improved practice

Access to Markets
- Distance from markets—and hence constraints on access to banks, inputs, advice, and buyers
- With poor records, difficulty in borrowing from banks (also lacking formal land title or collateral)
- Relative weakness of communications infrastructure in rural areas (landlines, 3G+ mobile, internet)
- Poor knowledge of quality requirements in global food supply chains

reversibility outweighed considerations such as the level of investment or the anticipated increase in income: "Case studies that enjoy rapid and widespread adoption are those that avoid engaging farmers into very long-term commitments. In those cases, farmers can go back to their previous practices if they so wish, at little or no cost. On the contrary, the case studies that struggle to achieve widespread adoption are 'one-way tickets,' whereby it becomes very difficult [or expensive] for farmers to go back to the status quo" (Hystra 2015, 20). This finding underlines the importance of stepwise approaches to improved productivity, whereby the change in farming practice is gradual.

Smallholder farmers tend to be low-level users of purchased inputs such as fertilizer, improved seed, and crop protection products, but they use high amounts of labor (predominantly family labor). This results in high *land* productivity but low *labor* productivity—making smallholders "efficient but poor" (as, with little land and capital, they try to maximize returns to these factors) (FAO 2014). This imbalance affects production in various ways (figure 6.1).

The low quality of smallholder supply can often be attributed to poor use of inputs—broadly defined to include planting seed, tree seedlings, fertilizer, chemical and nonchemical crop protection products, agricultural hand tools, irrigation products (like drip systems), and mechanized equipment for production or processing.

These generalizations mask a more nuanced reality and, inevitably, wide variation between and within countries. Many smallholder farmers

FIGURE 6.1 Symptoms of Inefficient Use of Agricultural Inputs

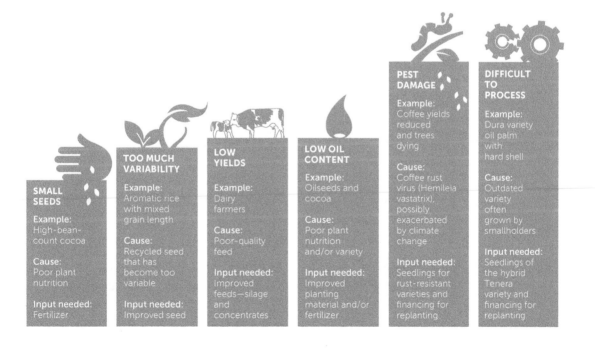

SMALL SEEDS

Example:
High-bean-count cocoa

Cause:
Poor plant nutrition

Input needed:
Fertilizer

TOO MUCH VARIABILITY

Example:
Aromatic rice with mixed grain length

Cause:
Recycled seed that has become too variable

Input needed:
Improved seed

LOW YIELDS

Example:
Dairy farmers

Cause:
Poor-quality feed

Input needed:
Improved feeds—silage and concentrates

LOW OIL CONTENT

Example:
Oilseeds and cocoa

Cause:
Poor plant nutrition and/or variety

Input needed:
Improved planting material and/or fertilizer

PEST DAMAGE

Example:
Coffee yields reduced and trees dying

Cause:
Coffee rust virus (Hemileia vastatrix), possibly exacerbated by climate change

Input needed:
Seedlings for rust-resistant varieties and financing for replanting

DIFFICULT TO PROCESS

Example:
Dura variety oil palm with hard shell

Cause:
Outdated variety often grown by smallholders

Input needed:
Seedlings of the hybrid Tenera variety and financing for replanting

make relatively intensive use of *on-farm* inputs such as animal manure. African smallholders often face *seasonal* labor shortages (for instance, when preparing land). The use of mechanization among smallholders is also quite different across regions: In Nicaragua, for instance, 27 percent of the population live on smallholder farms of 35 hectares or less, with the consequence that 44 percent of those (relatively land-rich) smallholders own or rent tractors, trucks, or other machinery. In Bangladesh, almost 60 percent of smallholders use threshing, husking, and ginning equipment. But this contrasts sharply with African smallholders, who generally make little use of mechanization.

Smallholders' use of irrigation technologies shows similar variation: the irrigated share of cropland in Sub-Saharan Africa is only 6 percent (less than one quarter of the irrigated share in other regions)—and most of that area is concentrated in just five countries (You et al. 2010). Meanwhile, fertilizer use (kilograms per hectare of arable land) in low- and middle-income countries in Sub-Saharan Africa is less than 12 percent of that in other countries with similar incomes (Morris et al. 2007).[1] These factors are interrelated: dependence on rainfed agriculture increases exposure to weather shocks, so farmers are less willing to use purchased inputs, fearing a loss should the rains fail (Rapsomanikis 2015).

Used together, reliable water supply, fertilizer, and improved seed make up a highly complementary standard input package; however, in many places, those farmers who use inorganic fertilizer or improved seed rarely use both and rarely use them along with irrigation. The reasons for this low or partial adoption of purchased inputs are complex, but they include the following:

- Difficulty buying inputs because of physical distance, cost, and poor access to finance

- High farm-gate prices for fertilizer in Africa, making its use less economical (Fischer, Byerlee, and Edmeades 2014)

- Unavailability of inputs in small quantities

- Absence of irrigation, thereby making the use of purchased inputs potentially risky

- Lack of knowledge of the benefits and proper use of purchased inputs

- Counterfeit products that give poor results, contributing to uncertainty and reticence.

Who Benefits from Improved Farm Management?

Improved farm management will generate benefits for all: farmers, off-takers, banks, input companies—and ultimately consumers, via the increased production volume in local and global markets. For farmers, it will help to increase their incomes, making farming a more viable and attractive option for current and future generations. Improved management can lift up the entire farm, not just that part linked to global markets.

Undoubtedly, the knowledge base on farm management is broad. Moreover, a growing array of tools and equipment is becoming economical at a much smaller scale, allowing, for example, much wider adoption of precision agriculture—reflecting advances in computing, satellite, and communications technology. The challenge is to make these advances available to small-scale producers. Ignoring that challenge would undermine attempts to incentivize smallholders through productivity gains—and could ultimately threaten global food security.

Strategies and Best Practices for Improved Farm Management

This section first provides some generalized guidelines on strategies that have proven successful in improving smallholder farm management and appropriate use of inputs— particularly, improvements in the following areas:

- Financial literacy and business management skills
- Agronomic calculations
- Resource conservation and land use planning
- Smallholder access to inputs
- New information and communication technology (ICT) tools.

The concluding section then briefly reviews different types of services and inputs as well as the specific issues pertinent to their increased use, including marketing, distribution, and training.

As for emerging developments and new needs in relation to farm management, chapter 10 explores the outlook on those topics. It covers climate-smart agriculture as well as the growing availability of the forecasting and granular information that will make precision agriculture accessible in much wider areas, even to small-scale producers.

Improving Financial Literacy and Business Management Skills

Some firms, nongovernmental organizations (NGOs), and other entities have developed training materials designed to improve farm management skills and financial literacy among rural households and smallholder farmers (as illustrated in box 6.2). Using these open-source materials or partnering with other organizations are cost-effective ways

---

BOX 6.2

In Practice: Low-Cost Financial Literacy Training in Malawi and Nigeria

Opportunity International: Educating Bank Customers by Video

Opportunity International—an NGO based in the United Kingdom that serves farmers with loans and other support—provides training on savings, credit management, budgeting, basic business skills, and insurance products to nearly 250,000 Malawian savings clients. This training is provided inexpensively, through a set of videos shown while clients are waiting at the bank to conduct their transactions.

The first video focuses on savings, budgeting, and debt management. Additional videos cover budgeting, basic business skills, insurance products, and more. Opportunity International plans to soon roll out this video program to additional countries, including Ghana, Mozambique, and Uganda.

Making Cents International: Using Role Playing to Teach Farm Management Skills

Making Cents International, a Washington, DC-based organization, has developed an interactive simulation to develop agricultural enterprise management skills. In this simulation, smallholder clients play the roles of input suppliers, producers, and processors as they navigate through an agricultural cycle. This allows them to practice the outcomes of planning, carefully timed input purchases and output sales, record keeping, savings, and working in groups. In Nigeria, this training tool is part of the organization's flagship Agricultural Enterprise Curriculum, which emphasizes a market-driven, commercial approach to farming activities through applied learning methods.

All producers who completed the training began to purchase planting inputs immediately after harvest instead of right before planting, realizing average cost savings of 43 percent. In addition, more than 80 percent of these producers waited several months after harvest to sell their products, when the sale price was 35 percent higher.

Sources: "How We Work: Training and Financial Advice," Opportunity International (accessed March 29, 2018), http://opportunity.org.uk/what-we-do/how-we-work/training-financial-advice; "Maximizing Agricultural Revenue and Key Enterprises in Targeted Sites," Making Cents (accessed March 29, 2018), http://www.makingcents.com/markets.

of providing financial literacy training. This is also the focus of International Finance Corporation's (IFC) Agribusiness Leadership Program, with its modules tailored for cooperative leaders, crop collectors, and agro-retailers (as further discussed in chapter 5).

Improving Agronomic Calculations

All farmers need to know the size of their production area, but in fact, many do not. This makes it impossible to calculate yields or produce useful farm records. Even when farmers have an idea of their farm size, it may include the house or other nonproductive areas such as steep hillsides. Precision is important in area measurement because errors make it difficult to track typical yield gains of 10–20 percent per year. Moreover, most certification programs require farm maps and production areas, so this is an important aspect of farm management for off-takers to include in training programs.

Smallholders can be taught to measure and map the productive area of their farms by pacing, by using a string with a measured length, or by using the Global Positioning System (GPS) function on more-advanced cell phones. Formulas for calculating rectangle and triangle areas may also be taught. Knowing the farm-area size helps with other basic agricultural calculations, such as yield. For field staff, the increasing use of GPS as well as ICT systems for the management of smallholder supply chains is making it much easier to obtain accurate area information.

Moisture content often gives rise to disagreement with buyers, so training on this can be included with other technical training. For example, training given at a demonstration plot during harvest time may include methods for yield calculation. Methods for estimating the moisture content of harvested crops may be discussed at training sessions on crop quality. Low-cost moisture meters, including one developed by the International Rice Research Institute in the Philippines, are becoming available.

Improving Resource Conservation and Land Use Planning

The use of farm management practices—such as crop rotation, soil moisture conservation, nitrogen-fixing intercrops, creating windbreaks, using animal manures, and incorporating integrated pest management (IPM) techniques in farm planning—can increase the profitability of smallholder farmers by increasing productivity and reducing costs. Off-takers have demonstrated that assisting smallholders with this type of planning can benefit their suppliers as well as their own businesses. Examples of these actions include the following:

- *Coffee farmers* who plant nitrogen-fixing shade trees and provide seedlings increase soil fertility and improve coffee quality.

- *Flower seed outgrowers* who plant *Jatropha curcas* as a border around their fields create a windbreak and can provide farmers with household energy or a second marketable crop.

- *Cashew tree farmers* who plant groundnuts as a cover crop while waiting for cashew seedlings to mature increase soil fertility and provide both firm and farmers with an interim income source.

- *Paprika farmers* who plant marigolds as a border crop reduce pests in the paprika and provide the firm and farmers with another marketable crop (marigold flowers used as a colorant).

- *Farmers of integrated crop-livestock operations* can exploit synergies such as using crop residues as livestock fodder and animal manure as fertilizer and an on-farm energy source (biogas).

- *Off-takers who pay attention to the other crops and livestock on smallholder farms* (not focusing exclusively on the crops of interest to the off-taker) help farmers to see wider benefits, which also helps build loyalty.

Some of these actions may be eligible for support through the United Nations (UN) Reducing Emissions from Deforestation and Forest Degradation (REDD+) program. With increasing numbers of agribusinesses committing to zero deforestation, there is considerable interest in how this can be supported through REDD+ (box 6.3).

BOX 6.3

REDD+: Results-Based Payments for Landscape Restoration by Smallholders

Reducing Emissions from Deforestation and Forest Degradation (REDD+) is a mechanism developed by the Parties to the United Nations Framework Convention on Climate Change (UNFCCC). It creates a financial value for the carbon stored in forests by offering incentives for low- and

box continued

BOX 6.3

REDD+: Results-Based Payments for Landscape Restoration by Smallholders (Continued)

middle-income countries to reduce emissions from forested lands and invest in low-carbon paths to sustainable development—that is, low- and middle-income countries receive payments based on the results achieved. REDD+ goes beyond deforestation and forest degradation. It includes conservation, sustainable forest management, and enhancement of forest carbon stocks.

Experience is growing in how REDD+ can work in practice, to safeguard global carbon stocks and reward rural communities for their stewardship role. With agribusiness increasingly committing to zero net deforestation, this is an area of particular interest.

A project in Côte d'Ivoire illustrates the potential that REDD+ may offer to smallholder value chains. The EU REDD Facility has engaged with the government, the private sector, the research community, and farmers to demonstrate how a zero-deforestation policy can be adapted to smallholder cocoa. It partnered with leading chocolate manufacturers to test the implementation of a zero-deforestation policy; it studied the feasibility of a national payment scheme targeting smallholders implementing zero-deforestation practices and participating in forest restoration initiatives such as agroforestry; and it has engaged with the national policy process. Although still at a preliminary stage, the initial results are promising, suggesting strong support from farmers, companies, and other stakeholders.

Sources: "About REDD+," UN-REDD Programme (accessed November 15, 2017), http://www.unredd.net/about/what-is-redd-plus.html; "Engaging with Smallholder Cocoa Farmers to Develop Deforestation-Free Supply Chains in Côte d'Ivore," EU REDD Facility (accessed March 29, 2018), http://www.euredd.efi.int/lo/publications/engaging-with-smallholder-cocoa-farmers.

Making Inputs More Accessible to Smallholders

Promoting improved farm management and appropriate use of inputs is not just about changing farmer behavior. In many frontier and emerging markets, input suppliers have a poor presence in rural areas, so there is also a need to address this. The use of agrodealers as a conduit for training benefits farmers and agrodealers alike (box 6.4). Another model is to develop a synergistic service bundle, which, in one example, brought inputs to within 1.5 miles of farmers (as discussed in box 6.6). Making inputs available in small package sizes is also highlighted in the discussion below of different types of farm input.

BOX 6.4

In Practice: Training Agroretailers to Increase Smallholders' Access to Inputs in Kenya

Training Model

The nonprofit Cultivating New Frontiers in Agriculture (CNFA) and its Kenyan affiliate, the Agricultural Marketing Development Trust (AGMARK), provided training to more than 3,000 agrodealers in 64 districts across Kenya. Dealers were trained in safe handling and the use of plant protection products, crop husbandry practices, and business management. The dealers were also linked to input-supply companies to increase the range of products they carried. More than 7.1 million Kenyans have access to the dealer network.

Results

After completing the program, agriretailers began to offer farmers a range of services, in addition to marketing an expanded range of inputs. They also created demonstration plots, held field days, and contacted village-based savings programs interested in purchasing inputs.

CNFA is now supporting International Finance Corporation's Agribusiness Leadership Program to develop financial literacy and business training for agrodealers, linked to independent assessments of their capacities and training needs and further supported by coaching (as further discussed in chapter 5).

Source: Okello et al. 2012.

Actions for Firms and Governments

For input suppliers seeking to develop retail networks to serve low-income dispersed farmers, the distribution costs can be high. Although there may be scope for economies of scale by selling to producer organizations (POs), some of those costs stem from government policies and poor public infrastructure.

Governments play an important role in promoting the development of input markets. Improvements in rural infrastructure help reduce costs for all types of private business. Also, governments sometimes intervene in agricultural input markets. Although such actions are intended to control prices, they can also stifle much-needed market development. Or governments may have onerous or lengthy procedures to license agricultural products, as illustrated in figure 6.2, which compares the time and cost required to register a new fertilizer product in countries of varying income levels. Recent analysis of fertilizer use data from 22,000 farm

FIGURE 6.2 Average Time and Cost to Register New Fertilizer Products, by Country Income Level

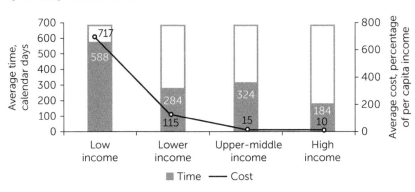

Source: World Bank 2017b.

households in six African countries found that an astonishing 45 percent of the variation in microscale inorganic fertilizer use was explained by country-level factors such as policy, institutional, or macroeconomic variables (Sheahan and Barrett 2017).

Firms can lobby for changes in these policies, probably most effectively in partnership with other sector stakeholders or via multilateral processes promoting policy change (for example, the Comprehensive Africa Agricultural Development Programme of the New Partnership for Africa's Development).[2]

Key Considerations in Promoting Access to Inputs

Promoting increased use of purchased inputs to improve smallholder yields will likely involve credit. Successful farmer credit programs involve credit (partly in-kind) that can be repaid at harvest when crops are sold—preferably with loan repayment deducted directly from crop revenues.

To encourage adoption and correct use of inputs, important considerations include the following:

· Input use must be unambiguously commercially viable for the farmer.

· Additional incentives or risk sharing may be needed if the change in agricultural practice is seen as irreversible.

· Information provision is important (on label or accompanying brochure).

· Incorporate demonstrations, training, and piloting—and engage POs and lead farmers.

- Short message service (SMS) reminders on application dates and procedures can be effective.

- Minimize input diversion to other crops by paying attention to those, too.

To ensure that input loans are repaid, good practices include the following (Hystra 2015):

- Use interlocking loans: deduct loan repayments when purchasing the farmer's crop.

- Provide the loan mostly in-kind but partly as cash to help farmers' cash-flow.

- Assess how "loose" the chain is—that is, how likely are farmers to side-sell?

- Follow the practice adopted by some companies of lending only 35 percent of the output value, so that the farmer can repay but still retain a significant surplus.

- Build loyalty via a value proposition—for example, by providing a wider range of services.

- Be present often and at the right time, making it convenient for the farmers to sell crops and repay loans.

- Review the repayment ethos in general: is it considered acceptable to default?

- Use new tools to monitor input use and yield—and identify side-selling.

- Time transactions to fit the farmer's cash-flow calendar (outlay and revenue).

- Plan for unexpected expense (for example, funeral or health costs).

- Reward good performance and apply penalties to deter potential defaulters.

- Follow up quickly on delinquency.

- Draw on the available experience with minimizing side-selling (box 6.5).

BOX 6.5

Best Practices to Minimize Smallholder Loan Defaults

There is always a risk of side-selling—where farmers sell the crop to other traders, thereby avoiding the loan repayment. However, there is a lot of experience in how to minimize side-selling. Several best practices can help, including the following:

- *Assess the context*—the ethos and the market chain—for risk of default. Bulky low-value crops are usually less susceptible to side-selling; high-value crops with multiple buyers, such as coffee and cocoa, are often the most susceptible. Plan accordingly.
- *Provide empty grain bags*, or other packaging, at harvest time, and collect crops frequently.
- *Customize loans* to farmers' needs and circumstances, as follows:
  o Gradually increase loan amounts year-on-year as the farmer repays.
  o Offer different technology packages based on repayment capacity.
  o Use metrics or scores to estimate credit capacity (for example, crop volumes).
- *Allow flexible repayments* or include insurance (health or funeral insurance).
- *Smooth out farmer cash flow*, which is often valued more than the "best price," by the following:
  o Offering minimum prices
  o Offering partial payment year-round
  o Helping farmers save.
- *Work with farmers' groups* to minimize default through use of the following:
  o Peer pressure
  o Group guarantee
  o Their ability to self-monitor.
- *Insist on partial payment* up-front.

Source: Hystra 2015.

Integrating Program Activities to Exploit Synergies

- *Link training and inputs*, making sure to emphasize even the less-obvious links, for example, when training on pruning, note that it will improve fertilizer response.

- *Build loyalty* by recognizing and providing synergistic support for the farmer's other agricultural needs (as the East Africa case study shows in box 6.6).

BOX 6.6

In Practice: One Acre Fund Combines Proximity and Integrated Packages to Increase Farmer Income in East Africa

Background

The One Acre Fund supports the efforts of more than 135,000 farmers in Burundi, Kenya, and Rwanda to increase their incorporation into agriculture value chains. With the motto of "farmers first," the nonprofit organization's operation is geared to treat smallholder farmers as customers to whom services are offered.

Integrated Service Model

This has led the One Acre Fund to develop a bundle of agricultural services that smallholder farmers need, implemented through a deep rural distribution chain. The service bundle includes farm inputs, financing, training, and market facilitation. The inputs (seed and fertilizer) are delivered within 1.5 miles of where customers live.

Those inputs are provided on credit, so farmers do not have to pay cash up-front before planting. Farmers repay the in-kind loan in cash over the course of the agriculture season. Meanwhile, they receive training on topics such as planting, composting, harvest techniques, and climate-smart agriculture. One Acre Fund staff also provide training and materials for safe postharvest storage as well as training on how to connect to traders. This service bundle forms a complete value chain for a small farmer.

Results

One Acre's harvest measurement program verifies that the farmers involved double their income per planted acre. In 2016, 98 percent of the loans extended to farmers were repaid. The organization plans to expand to serve 1.5 million farm families by 2020 with operations in five to eight countries and more than 7,000 staff. This expansion would make One Acre the largest network of smallholder farmers in Africa.

Source: "Farmers First," One Acre Fund (accessed March 29, 2018), https://oneacrefund.org/what-we-do/how -we-grow.

- *Incorporate nutrition and health messaging* where appropriate, including the promotion of biofortified crops (as discussed later in this chapter).

- *Engage the right expertise:* partner with NGOs or local governments for extension, and develop collaboration among off-takers, input companies, and banks.

- *Use new ICT tools* that integrate or simplify operations.

- *Nurture the next generation:* engage farm household youth where possible.

Using ICT Tools to Integrate and Simplify Farm Management

Management software to coordinate outgrower schemes in real time is key for scaling up. Many companies that aim to go beyond paper and spreadsheets have tried adapting systems for large farms or developing their own solutions. However, ICT systems specifically designed to support outgrower schemes are now available and widely used. Chapter 5 discussed ICT systems for extension content and supervision of field agents. In addition, there are systems to support supply chain management and traceability. For example, the Farmforce mobile platform illustrates the ways in which ICT is changing supply chain management in smallholder value chains (box 6.7).

BOX 6.7

In Practice: Farmforce—An ICT System for Outgrower Management

Background

A recent review of five off-the-shelf information and communication technology (ICT) systems for smallholder supply chain management found that although they differ in emphasis (for example, loan management or internal control), all covered the following functions: farm registration, input management, farmer training, field monitoring, traceability, and farmer payments.

Mobile Platform Model

One example is Farmforce, a product of the Syngenta Foundation for Sustainable Agriculture. Farmforce is a cloud-based, integrated mobile technology platform that simplifies outgrower management. It offers a suite of tools to manage outgrower schemes by organizing farmers, farmer groups, and field staff to manage production and harvest in compliance with a selected standard scheme and by providing full traceability starting from the farmer's field.

box continued

BOX 6.7

In Practice: Farmforce—An ICT System for Outgrower Management *(Continued)*

Advantages

Farmforce expansion apps allow users to communicate with farmers through SMS (short message service), track input loans, oversee movement of goods in storage facilities, monitor the quality of farmer trainings, and perform surveys and assessments. Potential side-selling can be flagged (low sales volumes) as can a certified farmer with improbably high sales volumes (indicating possible resale of purchases from other noncertified sources). It reduces the need for field staff input and can inform the development of more specific agronomic recommendations, thereby reducing input use and increasing yield response.

As a cloud-based platform, Farmforce can be used in any location, and users don't have to install a program on their own servers. Field officers working with farmers use the mobile phone with the Farmforce client and synchronize data with the cloud-based server. The management has access to real-time information through their web browser. This reduces start-up efforts and improves service. In addition, Farmforce offers onsite implementation support and training and ongoing support service.

Results

Farmforce started productive rollout in 2013 and, as of 2017, was being used in 15 countries in Asia, Africa, and Latin America; in six languages; and in vegetable, rice, cotton, cocoa, coffee, and potato value chains. IFC is working with coffee sector clients in Vietnam, where Farmforce has been introduced and is well-received.

Source: "Integrated Mobile Platform to Manage Smallholder Farming," Farmforce (accessed March 29, 2018), http://farmforce.com/.

Categories of Farm Input and Related Issues

Planting Material

Planting material—seeds, seedlings, cuttings, and grafts—is the most basic input for any farmer, affecting both crop yield and quality. In most of Africa and in isolated regions of Asia, farmers of staple crops such as maize, oilseeds, and rice use open-pollinated or inbred varieties and save their seed to replant year after year. Over time, this leads to increasing impurity in the seed, such that its attributes become more variable and the quality of the crop inconsistent.

In low- and middle-income countries elsewhere, where the "green revolution" has occurred, farmers tend to opt for more expensive hybrid seed because it is significantly more productive. In areas where farming is most advanced, genetically modified seed may also be available to smallholders. Seedlings and grafts to produce or improve tree crops can come from existing trees, seed, or cloned plant material.

Seed: Promoting Use of Open-Pollinated and Hybrid Seed

Bringing new seed to market involves significant costs, including research and development and registration (figure 6.3). Clonal, hybrid, and genetically modified organism planting material have higher costs and hence are more expensive than open-pollinated seed production. Yet in relatively thin and low-income markets, the development of more affordable but improved open-pollinated varieties is often unprofitable, leaving a gap in the market: the margins are low, and there is little repeat business because farmers retain seed at harvest for use and for sharing the following year.

Firms trying to encourage smallholders to adopt open-pollinated seed, as an initial step, must look beyond what is available on the market. In some countries and for some crops, this remains a significant gap, but it is often addressed via government, NGO, or private initiatives. For example, firms can contract farmers (smallholders or a PO or a larger farmer) to grow seed. They are typically paid 20–100 percent more than the crop price to compensate for the extra labor required to grow planting seed. After processing, packaging, and distribution, open-pollinated seeds usually retail for two to three times the crop price. For more on marketing and distribution strategies, see box 6.8.

In contrast, hybrid seed is a more attractive product for seed companies, but its production is more complicated and involves higher labor costs. This is reflected in the price: hybrid seed retails at up to 10 times the price of the same crop. Most hybrid varieties are selected to

FIGURE 6.3 Process to Bring New Seed Varieties to Market

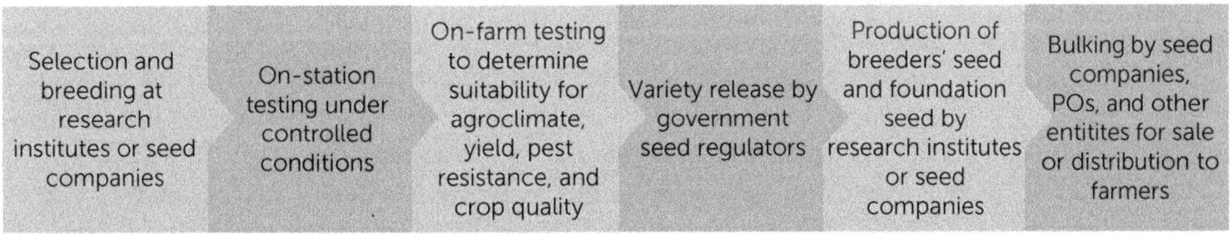

Selection and breeding at research institutes or seed companies	On-station testing under controlled conditions	On-farm testing to determine suitability for agroclimate, yield, pest resistance, and crop quality	Variety release by government seed regulators	Production of breeders' seed and foundation seed by research institutes or seed companies	Bulking by seed companies, POs, and other entitites for sale or distribution to farmers

Note: POs = producer organizations.

BOX 6.8

Marketing and Distribution Strategies for Planting Material

Off-Takers

Off-takers may reduce the cost of providing planting material if they grow planting seed or seedlings in house. Firms that produce some crops on plantations and purchase the balance from smallholders may already have facilities to grow high-quality seedlings. For some tree crops, such as cocoa, disease-resistant clones for grafting are the recommended option. Seed for open-pollinated vegetables, such as paprika, can be collected during processing and cleaned for redistribution.

Production of open-pollinated planting seed is straightforward as long as high-quality foundation seed is available. Winnowing, cleaning, and packing can be done manually using temporary labor. Motorized seed-cleaning equipment is also available in a range of capacities.

Seed Suppliers

Seed companies or off-takers may also contract producer organizations to produce seed or seedlings. Producer organizations with the right foundational material and training can earn additional revenue through these activities. The organizations may also market fertilizer and other inputs.

Sample packs accompanied by simple directions for sowing and production are a good way to allow farmers to experiment with a new crop or variety.

make effective use of fertilizer, and they underperform when grown with insufficient fertilizer, reducing their cost-effectiveness. In combination with improved practices, hybrid seed and fertilizer become a technical package. There are two risks, though:

- The following season, farmers might plant seed obtained from the previous season's crop to cut costs, leading to lower productivity.

- This higher-cost package is riskier for off-takers to provide on credit if side-selling is a problem.

Tree Seedlings

Firms may also market tree seedlings to smallholders. Because trees can produce fruit for 20–30 years, quality seedlings are important. Although this is a relatively low-cost input when amortized over the crop's life span, smallholders may find this a significant outlay, exacerbated by having to wait several years for the first crop.

Grafting can reduce the time between the investment in planting material and the first harvest, by making use of existing rootstock. Under the right conditions and with the proper facilities and training, off-takers and smallholders can produce quality scions (the part grafted onto the rootstock) and graft their own trees. Input suppliers must compete with these "in-house" techniques when marketing seedlings and scions, facing similar challenges to the marketing of open-pollinated seed varieties.

Planting Material Research Supported by Firms

Firms that produce crops on plantations have traditionally conducted strategic and applied research, and sometimes basic research (fundamental research), on the crops they produce. The agronomic research and variety development by firms in the oil palm sector is a good example.

More recently, firms have begun to support basic research on smallholder crops, too: notable examples are the collaborative efforts initiated by Mars and General Mills to map the genomes of cocoa and vanilla to accelerate the development of new varieties. Box 6.9 discusses IFC's experience of working with Cambodian rice millers and exporters to multiply improved rice seeds.

BOX 6.9

In Practice: Mills Produce Planting Seed to Improve Quality of Rice in Cambodia

Background

In 2008, Cambodian rice millers and exporters began working with IFC to support upgrading of the rice sector. After the success of the initial project, a further phase began in 2013, which covered many more elements, such as food safety, rice export promotion programs, and seed multiplication.

The "green revolution" that brought hybrid seeds to most of Asia never reached Cambodia's rice sector, and smallholders had recycled their rice seed for many years, resulting in variable yield, grain length, and color. This variation limited the quality of aromatic rice from Cambodia.

Distribution Model

Working with IFC, several mills began multiplying improved, aromatic rice seed for sale or distribution on credit to farmers in their supply chains.

box continued

BOX 6.9

In Practice: Mills Produce Planting Seed to Improve Quality of
Rice in Cambodia (Continued)

Results

The improved seed has uniform grain length and color, resulting in 4 percentage points higher head rice recovery[a] for the partner mills—a significant increase relative to more typical head rice recovery rates of 40–45 percent in Cambodia. For farmers, the improved inbred seed yields 20 percent more than recycled seed, but it can still be reused for up to four seasons.

The second project also had used a value chain approach to identify and address efficiency bottlenecks. This succeeded in kickstarting interest and investments by global lead importers and marketers in the Cambodian rice sector.

In addition, several development groups have since initiated projects in the rice sector, including the Asian Development Bank, the French Development Agency, and the World Trade Organization— expanded engagement important for addressing the remaining inefficiencies in the Cambodian rice value chain.

Source: World Bank 2017a.
a. "Head rice recovery" is a measure of rice quality referring to the percentage of head rice (whole, unbroken grains) obtained from a sample of paddy.

Breeding Stock, Young Animals, and Artificial Insemination

For poultry, dairy, and livestock farmers, the analogous inputs are artificial insemination services, breeding stock, or young animals selected for favorable attributes such as size, milk production, or ability to efficiently convert feed into meat. For example, chicks that reach market size in six weeks use feed far more efficiently than "village chickens" and are more profitable for smallholders.

Inputs for Healthy Soils

Most smallholders use traditional soil management techniques and a combination of organic and inorganic fertilizer. Box 6.10 describes different fertilizer types: inorganic, organic, and nitrogen-fixing cover.

Smallholder farmers in low- and middle-income regions face several soil management issues:

- Poor knowledge of management practices, when traditional techniques are insufficient

BOX 6.10

Types of Fertilizers and Specifics of Their Use

Inorganic Fertilizer

- Soil testing is critical to understand soil deficiencies.
- It should be the correct blend of nitrogen, phosphorus, and potassium (NPK) and other elements for the soil and crop in question.
- It needs to be applied in the right location at the correct time.

Organic Fertilizer

- Compost can be made from manure, crop waste, or vegetation.
- It can be difficult to move from production areas to fields if farmers lack transport.
- Organic mulch reduces weeds and retains soil moisture.
- It is necessary in organic production to avoid low yields.

Nitrogen-Fixing Cover

- There are numerous leguminous cover crops that can be used in every situation.
- Some of these crops, like groundnuts, produce a food crop as well as improve the soil.
- Cover crops also reduce weed growth.
- Leguminous tree crops can provide shade for coffee and cocoa.

- Limited availability of soil testing, resulting in fertilizer recommendations that may be incorrect (and potentially loss-making for farmers)

- In rainfed agriculture, uncertainty that may make the application of chemical (purchased) fertilizer particularly risky

- Poor local availability and affordability of purchased soil conditioners (such as lime and fertilizer), coupled with the absence of credit and sometimes transport.

Soil Health

Healthy soil is essential because it provides nutrients, water, and structure for the plants it supports. Soil helps control how water flows and hence the amount of erosion and nutrient loss. Soil can filter manure, agricultural chemicals, and other compounds that may pollute air and water. It is also a storehouse for carbon (organic matter)—an increasingly important role as concern grows about atmospheric carbon dioxide.

Farmers can influence soil health through their choices about tillage, crop rotations, and the application of lime or nutrients as well as physical structures that aid water retention or focus nutrients. Thus, it is possible to change the structure, biological activity, and chemical content of soil and hence influence erosion, pest populations, nutrient availability, and ultimately crop production.

The following practices improve soil performance (Lewandowski 2001; Morris et al. 2007):

- *Adding organic matter.* Farmers can apply manure, cover crops, residues, or roots (off-farm inorganic inputs such as chemical fertilizer or lime can also be used).

- *Avoiding excessive tillage and soil compaction.* This practice helps to preserve soil structure and minimize the decomposition and loss of organic matter, thus protecting the soil surface and reducing erosion and the loss of habitat of helpful organisms. Reducing compaction helps maintain sufficient air, water, and space for roots and soil organisms.

- *Managing pests and nutrients efficiently.* Pesticides and chemical fertilizers, as well as nutrients from organic sources, can harm nontarget organisms and cause pollution if misapplied or overapplied. Efficient pest and nutrient management means applying only the necessary chemicals, at the right time and place; testing and monitoring soil and pests; and using nonchemical approaches (for example, crop rotations, cover crops, and manure management).

- *Keeping the ground covered.* Bare soil is susceptible to wind and water erosion and to drying and crusting. Ground cover protects soil, provides habitats for helpful organisms, and can improve water availability. Crop residues can be left on the surface between crops, or living cover crops can create new organic matter and help feed soil organisms. Ground cover must be managed to prevent diseases and excessive buildup of surface phosphorus.

- *Increasing diversity.* Each crop contributes a unique root structure and type of residue. A diversity of soil organisms helps control pest populations, and a diversity of cultural practices reduces weed and disease pressures. Diversity across the landscape can be increased by using buffer strips, small fields, or contour strip-cropping. Diversity can be increased by adding crops to the crop rotation or by varying tillage practices. These practices increase plant diversity and the insects, microorganisms, and wildlife that are present.

- *Monitoring soil performance.* Casual observations of change are important, but to fine-tune management practices and promptly determine whether changes in soil or crops are significant, systematic monitoring is important.

Some soil-health requirements may vary by region. For example, many tropical soils have low fertility and, in the humid tropics, high acidity. Marked seasonality and extremes in rainfall also increase vulnerability to soil erosion and nutrient leaching.

Smallholders typically use traditional soil management techniques (such as rotations, cover crops, mulches, intercropping, windbreaks, terracing, and structures to trap water). However, as pressure to intensify (produce higher yields per hectare) grows—even as, in some regions, farm size is declining—and as flood irrigation (with its nutrients) declines, these practices are insufficient to maintain or improve soil health, particularly in the face of less certain and more extreme weather events. For example, in Ethiopia, land degradation is associated with an estimated 2–3 percent fall in productivity per year. Moreover, for smallholders in many countries, even basic soil tests are rarely available and neither are a range of chemical fertilizer blends.

Soil Management

Improving soil management on smallholder farms requires a judicious mix of the following;

- Training on and use of good soil management techniques

- Use of available on-farm or local organic inputs, as well as other management practices, in combination with careful use of purchased inputs

- Determination of the latter based on tests of soil fertility and timely application of the appropriate fertilizer blend at levels that will maximize net income (not yield).

The last point may sound straightforward, but it poses multiple dilemmas for smallholder agriculture: the availability of testing, the availability of the required blend of fertilizer, and calculations on the appropriate application rate. The calculation requires a knowledge of the prices, for purchased inputs and output, actually faced by smallholders, effectively "at the farm gate." This might sound like a detail, but the wrong numbers may mean that farmers do not see the benefits of purchased inputs—and could even face losses because of their use.

Smallholder reluctance to use purchased inputs may also reflect an entirely rational assessment of the risk associated with rainfed agriculture—hence the importance of emerging smallholder crop insurance programs.

Fortunately, soil analysis is becoming more accessible with relatively low-cost handheld devices (as discussed in chapter 10). Moreover, the International Fertilizer Development Center (IFDC) has developed a number of techniques and technologies for more effective fertilizer use, by concentrating its effects and reducing leaching, including the following:[3]

- *Banding:* placing the fertilizer in proximity to the crop

- *Controlled-release pellets*

- *Deep-placement fertilizer* for rice production to prevent losses during irrigation

Several poor practices reduce the effectiveness of programs that promote use of chemical fertilizers:

- Using too little fertilizer

  - Hybrid seeds (especially) do not reach their potential.

  - Farmers do this to economize at planting time, when they lack funds.

- Applying fertilizer at the wrong time

  - Farmers may lack adequate funds or knowledge.

  - Rainfall (which may be unpredictable) and crop stage are both important.

- Applying fertilizer incorrectly

  - The recommendation may be incorrect (not based on maximizing net revenue).

  - Farmers may lack the knowledge, equipment, or labor to apply fertilizer correctly.

  - Depth is important, as is avoiding potential for fertilizer to be washed away.

  - If weeds are present, they are fertilized instead of the crop.

- Using an inappropriate type of fertilizer

  ○ Farmers may use the wrong blend for the crop and soil characteristics.

  ○ Soil and leaf-testing services, if available, can help identify the right blend.

- Diverting the fertilizer

  ○ Farmers may sell the fertilizer for cash or use it on other crops.

The soil-testing case study (box 6.11) shows how some of these points can be addressed.

BOX 6.11

In Practice: Soil Testing to Improve Fertilizer Application in Rwanda, Kenya, and Algeria

Rwanda

The nonprofit organization TechnoServe worked with the Rwanda Coffee Authority to conduct a national soil and leaf survey to determine the levels of key soil nutrients in all coffee production areas. This study found that highly acidic soils in many parts of Rwanda require application of lime to increase soil pH. The survey also found low levels of zinc, boron, and sulfur—contributing to poor yields and coffee quality. As a consequence, two NPK fertilizer blends were recommended for Rwandan coffee farmers. These have been demonstrated to 30,000 farmers via demo plots.

Kenya

IFC is now working with the Kenya Tea Development Agency and CropNuts Laboratory Services on soil testing and leaf analysis to optimize fertilizer formulas and provide tailored advice to tea farmers, to contribute to lower costs and higher yields.

Algeria

IFC investment client Fertial is the largest fertilizer manufacturer in Algeria. The Fertial-IFC partnership has improved productivity for approximately 650 small and medium-size farmers as well as access to high-quality services, such as soil analysis and technical support on fertilizer use.

The partnership achieved these results by training 1,000 farmers, 45 fertilizer intermediaries, and 30 technical advisers; developing a comprehensive technical fertilization manual; and building the capacity of Fertial's network of seven soil analysis laboratories. Fertial found that fertilizer sales to small- and medium-scale farmers increased after the training.

Fertilizer Marketing and Distribution Strategies

Strategies for Off-Takers

If storage facilities are available in rural areas, it may be cost-effective to supply fertilizer and other inputs using the same trucks that take crops out. Such systems have functioned in southern Africa where many villages have underused warehouses. This is helpful to farmers who can purchase fertilizer when they receive payment for crops, rather than at planting time, when they may not have the funds.

Strategies for Input Supply Companies

Demonstration is the most effective way to market new products to smallholders. For production inputs, such as seed and fertilizer, demonstration plots managed by lead contact farmers are a good option (see chapter 5). Product information should be provided on the label and in accompanying brochures.

Smaller package sizes for fertilizer and crop protection products may help make these products more affordable and safer for smallholder farmers. Smallholders typically lack both the cash to buy large quantities and the appropriate storage for partially used containers. Because channeling fertilizer to smallholders may entail various risks, input suppliers should implement several mitigating strategies (table 6.1).

TABLE 6.1 Risk Mitigating Strategies for Channeling Fertilizer to Smallholders

Risk		Mitigating Strategy
Farmers divert fertilizer to other crops or sell it to raise cash. Because the fertilizer was not used as anticipated, yields do not rise.	→	Loans that combine cash and physical inputs alleviate farmers' cash needs at planning time. The combination loan increases the likelihood that fertilizer will be applied as intended.
Productivity does not increase as expected, so farmers' net income declines after paying the loan's principal and interest.	→	Test input packages among smallholders to ensure their efficacy.
Weather or disease reduces yields, again affecting farmers' ability to pay.	→	Facilitate farmers' effort to obtain crop insurance.
Crop prices rise and off-takers are unable to pay competitive prices.	→	Create written agreements between all parties, specifying harvest price relative to prevailing prices, quality, and penalties for side-selling.
Farmers side-sell to other firms that offer higher prices and are not collecting loan repayments.	→	Perform field surveys during the production cycle to estimate harvests so that side-selling can be detected. Schedule rapid pickup of harvested crops, settlement of loans, and payment. Provide empty grain bags to speed marketing and reduce side-selling. Monitor closely and build loyalty.

Crop Protection

Crop protection strategies may use IPM (as illustrated in box 6.12) or purchased crop protection products, such as pesticides and herbicides.

Crop Protection Products

Purchased crop protection products are available in a wide variety of chemical and nonchemical solutions. Applied correctly, most can be used within sustainable production systems. However, many countries have banned approximately 20 chemicals, which farmers in environmental certification programs are not allowed to use because of their high toxicity and environmental persistence.

BOX 6.12

In Practice: Using IPM against the Coffee Berry Borer

Background

Integrated pest management (IPM) comprises strategies to minimize pest damage through the careful integration of available pest control technologies. It gives priority to nonchemical control components such as host-plant resistance and biological and cultural controls, only using chemical controls when alternatives are clearly unlikely to afford sufficient protection (NRI 1992).

IPM Advantages

In tropical agricultural systems, where pesticides are increasingly expensive and pose risks to farmers and consumers, reduced use of pesticides through IPM has many economic and social as well as environmental advantages. Reduced use of chemicals implies reduced cash and other capital inputs into production systems, and for this reason IPM approaches tend to be more sustainable in small-scale agricultural systems. At the same time, IPM strategies minimize environmental damage and health risks. For example, vegetables can be protected from climate extremes and pests by plastic row covers, which is a nonchemical IPM method. In some cases, off-takers can produce these technologies in house, reducing their cost.

IPM Solutions for Coffee Berries

Coffee crops may benefit from two types of IPM technologies. One is a naturally occurring soil fungus called *Beauveria bassiana* that is used to combat coffee berry borers. Another nonchemical technology, the Brocap® trap, uses red color and a sweet smell to attract the coffee berry borer (the latter developed by the French Agricultural Research Centre for International Development [CIRAD]).

Source: NRI 1992.

The capacity of smallholders to effectively use crop protection products varies, and some firms engage specialized companies to spray smallholder crops to reduce the risk of high pesticide residues. A farmer with limited exposure to proper application techniques may misapply and waste crop protection products. If protective gear and basic application equipment is lacking, such as backpack sprayers, application may cause health risks to the farmer and the farmer's family.

Farmers with access to proper equipment and the ability to correctly diagnose pests and diseases can properly apply these products, but they may need advice to help them distinguish between genuine brands, good-quality generic products, poor-quality generic products, and counterfeits.

Marketing and Distribution Strategies for Crop Protection Products

Fertilizer and crop protection products are often sold in generic form or diluted, and completely ineffective counterfeits are also available. If intellectual property enforcement is weak, the only way for farmers to tell whether products are effective may be to try them.

One strategy that has been developed for the same problem in the health sector is the use of codes hidden by scratch-off material that enables the consumer to verify the product's authenticity by sending the firm a text message. An added benefit is that the firm collects contact information from its customers.

Irrigation Equipment

A variety of relatively affordable irrigation technologies use surface water and subsurface groundwater. If surface water is inaccessible and groundwater is deep below the surface, irrigation becomes a more expensive proposition.

Although irrigation may be a cost-effective investment over the medium-term, because the initial outlay is relatively large with benefits generally spread over more than one year, smallholders may find it hard to finance this investment. For the same reasons (cost and longer payback period) off-takers generally do not provide this equipment on credit, but might do so if the supply chain is tight (relatively few buyers and little scope for side-selling) and the crop is valuable.

The range of technologies available—at different scales and costs—lends itself to a stepwise approach, where farmer capacity to use and repay the costs of technology is tested successively as she or he gradually upgrades to more expensive but more effective systems.

Affordable Irrigation Technologies

For those smallholders with access to surface water or subsurface groundwater, the following types of irrigation technologies may prove affordable:

• *Small farm reservoirs and check dams:* These small-scale civil works trap rainwater runoff for irrigation or livestock. Construction is manual or using basic equipment. (See box 6.13 on a cotton processor's support of rainwater-capture systems, complemented by other technologies, for farmers in Burkina Faso.)

BOX 6.13

SOFITEX Water Management and Irrigation Program for Smallholder Cotton Farmers in Burkina Faso

Background

Société Burkinabè des Fibres Textiles (SOFITEX) is the leading cotton processing company in Burkina Faso, with about 160,000 smallholder farms in its supply chain. In Burkina Faso, Africa's second largest cotton producing country, cotton has historically been grown as a rainfed crop.

SOFITEX sources from regions in the south of Burkina Faso, where irregular rainfall patterns, combined with inadequate soil and water management, threaten SOFITEX's cotton supply and diminish yields (owing to poor absorption of fertilizers, soil erosion, and failed germination). In trials conducted in SOFITEX's research and development facility, the combination of supplementary irrigation and soil and water management in the cotton crop resulted in higher yields.

Complementary Irrigation and Service Model

SOFITEX partnered with IFC to make its supply chain more sustainable. The project supports the adoption of improved soil and water management practices, supplementary irrigation technologies, and rainfall harvesting by farmers via extension service agents in SOFITEX's supply chain. The project included two main components:

• *Farmer training* that is focused on construction and use of small-scale infrastructure for rainwater capture and the use, operation, and maintenance of irrigation equipment
• *Engagement with local financial institutions,* through SOFITEX, to prefinance infrastructure and irrigation equipment with loans to the farmers.

box continued

SOFITEX Water Management and Irrigation Program for Smallholder Cotton Farmers in Burkina Faso *(Continued)*

The company uses its own network of extension agents to train farmers to build stone contour lines that help retain water in the soil after heavy rains, avoiding the runoff of fertilizer, topsoil, and organic matter. The program is also preparing farmers to build small ponds to capture rainwater, which can be used for irrigation at critical growth phases of the cotton plants, and to operate and maintain equipment for water pumping and distribution.

SOFITEX's overall strategy is to stabilize and ultimately increase cotton yields, strengthen food security through improving rotational crop yields, and boost farmers' incomes.

Source: Riveras 2017.

- *Well-auguring and jetting systems:* These systems use hand augurs or small, motorized pumps to insert low-cost tube wells into shallow water tables. They are often used in combination with treadle pumps.

- *Treadle pumps:* These low-cost, foot-operated pumps draw water from up to 7 meters and irrigate up to 0.5 hectare of land. They are ideal for vegetable and small-scale rice production. The price of treadle pumps ranges from $20 in Asia to $100 in Africa. *Small motorized pumps* are also popular, but cost several hundred dollars for equivalent capacity.

- *Drip irrigation:* Low-cost drip systems increase productivity and conserve water by delivering the optimal amount of water to crop roots. They are typically used with tree crops and vegetables. (See box 6.14 for a case of successful use with sugarcane crops in India.) The least expensive systems cost less than $500 per hectare. A very basic form of drip irrigation uses clay water containers buried next to plants.

- *Solar power to support irrigation:* Recent developments in renewable energy have led to significant expansion in the products available and falling costs. Solar panels today offer farmers a cheap and renewable source of power for pumping water, whether from ground or surface water bodies. Although larger pumps make it possible for service providers to deliver irrigation to others, smaller units create

---

BOX 6.14

In Practice: Netafim Achieves Scale with Drip Irrigation in India

Background

Drip irrigation offers huge potential for smallholder farmers to increase productivity and reduce water use. However, global uptake has been slow because of high up-front costs and lack of knowledge. Irrigation equipment manufacturer Netafim has made significant progress in overcoming these challenges in India, where the company has sold more than 1.5 million drip irrigation systems. These farmers use drip irrigation to cultivate sugarcane, fruits, vegetables, and field crops on an average land holding of 1.1 hectares.

Benefits to Sugarcane Farmers

Sugarcane is a water-intensive crop, which is typically grown using surface irrigation. Farmers using surface irrigation lose more than 50 percent of the water from evaporation and infiltration. This makes it an ideal crop for drip irrigation and a major focus for Netafim India. The average yield for sugarcane in India is 77.6 tons per hectare.[a] With drip "fertigation," the yield can increase to more than 120 tons per hectare. Other benefits include higher sucrose content, reduced pumping costs, and reduced labor costs.

Results

More than 95 percent of Indian sugarcane farmers who installed Netafim drip irrigation systems reduced their water use and increased productivity. For more than 65 percent of the farmers, the water savings and productivity gains exceeded 25 percent. Independent research showed that a sugarcane farmer with 10 hectares could repay the cost of a drip irrigation system in one year, based on cost savings and increased productivity. In an IFC-designed program in Madhya Pradesh and Maharashtra, more than 500 hectares of drip irrigation were installed, and sugarcane farmers increased water use efficiency by 30 percent.

Challenges

Despite highly favorable economics for Indian sugarcane farmers, the initial cost of drip irrigation equipment has been a barrier to adoption. In Andhra Pradesh and elsewhere, the Indian government has overcome this hurdle with a combination of a 50–70 percent subsidy and access to low-interest bank loans. Ongoing technical support by Netafim has also been important to ensure that farmers have access to training and service.

a. FAOSTAT, http://www.fao.org/faostat/en/#data/QC.

the potential for smallholders in rainfed agriculture to provide supplementary irrigation, thus boosting productivity and enhancing resilience (IWMI 2017).

Marketing and Distribution Strategies for Irrigation Equipment

Given the relatively larger investment that irrigation and other technologies represent for smallholders, adoption may be a challenge. Some extension programs begin with a rent-to-own policy on technology. This reduces the risk for initial adopters while getting products into the field for demonstration purposes. Another strategy is to demonstrate products at market days, when farmers are gathered and have cash. Yet another strategy is a road show, during which a truck drives through villages conducting demonstrations, screening promotional videos, and selling the product.

Vendors of irrigation pumps and other mechanical equipment should ensure the availability of spare parts and after-sales service. Agro-input agents may offer this service, but many small shops do not have qualified technicians on staff. Another option is to train the most dynamic customers to make simple repairs, because these farmers understand the technology and are accessible to other farmers.

Production and Postharvest Handling Technologies

Technologies that support farmers during planting, cultivating, and postharvest processing can improve efficiency and productivity, as well as increase and maintain quality after harvest. They can also improve farmers' welfare by reducing manual labor, including for women, who often play a prominent role in some postharvest activities.

Inputs for production and postharvest handling comprise a wide variety of technologies that are suitable for smallholders. They tend to be crop-specific, so the following list provides examples only:

- *Conservation agriculture packages:* Conservation agriculture is based on three principles: minimal soil disruption, permanent soil cover (with cover crops or crop residues), and crop diversification (through rotations, cover crops, or intercropping). These packages include techniques and tools for producing field crops such as soy, groundnuts, maize, and cotton in low-rainfall conditions. They have been developed for manual, animal-traction, and motorized farming. At each technology level, the packages are designed to use inputs efficiently while conserving soil moisture, nutrients, and structure. One interesting technology is the "weed wipe," which allows smallholders to apply contact herbicide directly to weeds rapidly and safely.

- *Biofortified crops:* Interest is growing in biofortification: increasing the nutritional value of a crop through breeding, transgenic techniques, or agronomic practice. HarvestPlus and its partners have focused on locally produced food crops to improve accessibility to smallholder farmers, who can integrate biofortified crops into mixed food and cash crop farming systems.[4] Globally, biofortified crops are now grown by 20 million farmers, contributing to increased food security, reduced micronutrient deficiency, and better health outcomes.

- *Seeding tools:* These tools reduce labor by automating the planting process and help farmers grow the optimum number of plants per hectare. Examples include the International Rice Research Institute's manual drum seeder for rice and the affordable seed drill for zero tillage agriculture, both of which are popular in India.

- *Pollination:* Insect pollinators are a crucial input for certain crops. For example, sunflower yields are improved if farmers keep bees nearby, so bee hives can be an important input.

- *Manual and motorized equipment for harvesting, threshing, and winnowing:* There are a wide variety of technologies for different crops, at varying levels of sophistication, that reduce labor costs, protect crop quality, and reduce the time from harvest to market. Small rural businesses often use these technologies to provide services to smallholders.

- *Tractors and transport:* A new area of development is the increasing availability of mobile or GPS-enabled services that match dispersed demand for relatively expensive machinery with providers. Hello Tractor is one example,[5] and similar services are available for transport. Other areas of development include linking surplus cold storage with demand from small-scale dairy farmers or retailers.

- *Ultraviolet (UV)-resistant plastic film for crop drying:* Firms provide plastic film to their suppliers to enable them to build low-cost bamboo drying racks for coffee and cocoa. The use of covered racks speeds drying and protects quality.

- *Large grain bags:* Hermetic or open grain bags can hold up to one ton. This may reduce handling costs and pest infestation (and can reduce side-selling, too).

A Key Consideration: Will the Input Package Deliver Expected Benefits?

An off-taker interested in advancing inputs to suppliers will want to confirm that the investment is cost-effective. Most farmers will benefit from improved input use, but this depends on their existing use of inputs and the suitability of land and climate. Comparative analysis will determine whether producers of a particular crop are significantly less productive than producers in other similar locations. Farmland that is less productive than comparable locations would likely benefit from improved inputs.

Input producers may also consider a similar analysis to identify marketing opportunities. This step-by-step guide offers recommendations for conducting the analysis:

- *Identify yield gaps.* Use the online FAOSTAT database of crop statistics compiled by the Food and Agriculture Organization of the UN (FAO) to compare yields in the target country with global and regional yields and with yields in competitor countries with a similar climate. The dataset also includes the volume of commercial seed produced for each crop, while the "Resources" section contains information about fertilizer and pesticide use by country.[6] In estimating the yield gaps, note also the following: a review of time series data (over a decade or more) helps identify trends and intrayear variability.

- Cross-check FAO data with country-specific yield and production data, often available from government sources; note that FAO data is usually more reliable and comparable across regions.

- Ultimately, recommendations to farmers on fertilizer use should be based on agronomic measurements because aggregate statistics from governments or the FAO may not be accurate enough.

1. *Determine the extent to which inputs can reduce productivity gaps or quality gaps.* Low productivity almost always results from a combination of limited input use and poor agricultural practices. Usually a combination of inputs and training will be necessary. However, in some cases, training to improve production and postharvest practices may be as effective as the introduction of new inputs. In other cases, neither training nor inputs will improve production because, for example, farmers lack sufficient labor during planting and harvest. Sometimes, the climate and terrain is not suited for the crop, in

which case any investment in improved input supply or administration will bring marginal results.

2. *Determine the type and quantity of inputs farmers use.* Farmer surveys, fieldwork, and interviews with agriretailers can contribute data to identify the input packages already being used by farmers. Firms may conduct a survey of randomly selected farmers to research their use of inputs and crop-protection products (for an example, see box 6.15). Surveys may be supplemented by the fieldwork and observations of trained agronomists concerning crop varieties and agricultural practices. Fieldwork allows agronomists to take physical measurements of farms to check the accuracy of recall data about input application rates.

3. *Consider losses to side-selling and consumption.* An apparent productivity gap may be the result of side-selling to other off-takers or on-farm consumption of the food crop. Comparing reported yields with the quantities sold to an off-taker provides an indication of the amount lost to side-selling or consumption. If a large proportion of the crop

---

BOX 6.15

Farmer Surveys Generate Localized Data on Input Use

A farmer survey, as described further in chapter 9 ("Measuring Results") is a good first step toward understanding the causes of low productivity. Sample questions for a survey on fertilizer use might include the following:

Do you use fertilizer?	□ Yes	□ No	
What form is the fertilizer?	□ Chemical	□ Manure	□ Compost
Where do you obtain fertilizer?	□ Shop	□ Other farmer	□ Other
How often do you purchase?	□ Annually	□ Other frequency ————	
Specify quantity and type: ———————————		(Choices will depend on what is available.)	
Which crops are fertilized? ———————————		(Choices will depend on what is being grown.)	
How is fertilizer applied? ———————————		(Choices will depend on what is being grown.)	

is diverted, it is important to understand the underlying reasons before deciding what action is appropriate.

4. *Determine production and postharvest best practices for the crop in question.* The results of the analysis can be compared with global best practices for the crop being studied. The FAO, CGIAR (formerly the Consultative Group for International Agricultural Research) centers, and other national and international research institutions are a good source of this information. It is also useful to determine the production practices in countries with similar climates but higher crop yields and quality. Unfortunately, the new varieties and knowledge that are available at these centers are rarely accessible to smallholders, especially those who rely on government extension services. Firms and NGOs can be an ideal conduit for widespread dissemination.

5. *Design a package of technical advice and inputs.* An agronomist should design the package to test it with a carefully monitored group of farmers before it is widely disseminated. Best practice involves implementing the proposed package of inputs and training with a pilot group of farmers under normal conditions. Using a "quasi-experimental design" technique (described in chapter 9), firms can measure the impact and cost-effectiveness of the intervention.

The following chapters build on the content here:

- *Chapter 7, "Women's Participation,"* explores these topics in relation to women's role in supply chains, including ways in which training and farm management may need to be adjusted.

- *Chapter 8, "Partnerships for Efficient Value Chains,"* elaborates the types of partnerships needed to work effectively with smallholders.

- *Chapter 9, "Measuring Results,"* looks at methods for measuring results.

- *Chapter 10, "Future Outlook,"* concludes with a look at pressing issues for the future, how these will affect smallholder agriculture, and the emerging possibilities to address them.

Notes

1. World Bank 2014 fertilizer consumption data (accessed June 18, 2017), http://data .worldbank.org/indicator/AG.CON.FERT.ZS.
2. For more information about the Comprehensive Africa Agriculture Development Programme (CAADP) of the New Partnership for Africa's Development, see the

CAADP http://www.nepad.org/cop/comprehensive-africa-agriculture-development
-programme-caadp.
3. For more about the IFDC's research and technologies, see https://ifdc.org/.
4. http://www.harvestplus.org/biofortification-nutrition-revolution-now.
5. For more information about Hello Tractor, see http://www.hellotractor.com/.
6. For the FAOSTAT database, see Data tab->Inputs http://www.fao.org/faostat
/en/#data.

References

FAO (Food and Agriculture Organization of the United Nations). 2014. *The State of Food and Agriculture 2014: Innovation in Family Farming*. Rome: FAO.

———. 2017. *The Future of Food and Agriculture: Trends and Challenges*. Rome: FAO.

Fischer, T., D. Byerlee, and G. O. Edmeades. 2014. *Crop Yields and Global Food Security: Will Yield Increase Continue to Feed the World?* Canberra: Australian Centre for International Agricultural Research.

Hystra. 2015. "Smallholder Farmers and Business: 15 Pioneering Collaborations for Improved Productivity and Sustainability." Research report, Hystra, Paris.

IWMI (International Water Management Institute). 2017. "Solar Powered Irrigation: Adding Value through a Business Model Approach." R4D Capabilities brief, IWMI, Colombo, Sri Lanka.

Lewandowski, Ann. 2001. "Introduction to Soil Management." University of Minnesota Extension, St. Paul, MN.

Morris, M., V. A. Kelly, R. J. Kopicki, and D. Byerlee. 2007. *Fertilizer Use in African Agriculture: Lessons Learned and Good Practice Guidelines*. Directions in Development Series. Washington, DC: World Bank.

NRI (Natural Resources Institute). 1992. *Integrated Pest Management in Developing Countries: Experience and Prospects*. Chatham, UK: NRI.

Okello, B., S. Paruzzolo, R. Mehra, A. Shetty, and E. Weiss. 2012. "Agrodealerships in Western Kenya: How Promising for Agricultural Development and Women Farmers?" Assessment report for the International Center for Research on Women, Washington, DC.

Rapsomanikis, G. 2015. "The Economic Lives of Smallholder Farmers: An Analysis Based on Household Data from Nine Countries." Report, Food and Agriculture Organization of the United Nations, Rome.

Riveras, Inaê. 2017. "Sowing Seeds of a Bright Future for Burkinabe Cotton Farmers." Article for Creating Markets Advisory Window, IFC (International Finance Corporation of the World Bank Group), Washington, DC.

Sheahan, M., and C. Barrett. 2017. "Ten Striking Facts about Agricultural Input Use in Sub-Saharan Africa." *Food Policy* 67 (C): 12–25.

World Bank. 2017a. "Case Study: Modernizing the Rice Sector in Cambodia." infoDev case study, World Bank, Washington, DC.

———. 2017b. *Enabling the Business of Agriculture 2017*. Washington, DC: World Bank.

You, L., C. Ringler, G. Nelson, U. Wood-Sichra, R. Robertson, S. Wood, Z. Guo, T. Zhu, and Y. Sun. 2010. "What Is the Irrigation Potential for Africa? A Combined Biophysical and Socioeconomic Approach." Discussion Paper No. 00993, Environment and Production Technology Division, International Food Policy Research Institute (IFPRI), Washington, DC.

Additional Resources

Agricultural Research and Development

ACIAR (Australian Centre for International Agricultural Research). http://aciar .gov.au/.

AGRA (Alliance for a Green Revolution in Africa). https://agra.org/.

CABI (Centre for Agriculture and BioScience International). https://www.cabi.org/. [United Kingdom-based with centers in Kenya, Malaysia, Pakistan, and Switzerland]

CGIAR (Consultative Group for International Agricultural Research). http://www .cgiar.org. [international agricultural research centers]

CIRAD (French Agricultural Research Centre for International Development). https://www.cirad.fr/en.

CNFA (Cultivating New Frontiers in Agriculture). https://www.cnfa.org/.

Conservation Farming Unit. https://conservationagriculture.org/. [conservation farming and climate-smart agriculture]

eLEAF. http://www.eLeaf.com. [uses satellite images to analyze farms for nutrition, irrigation, and disease problems]

EnterpriseWorks/VITA. http://enterpriseworks.org/. [technology for small farmers]

FAO (Food and Agriculture Organization of the United Nations). http://www.fao.org. [online resources covering diverse topics on agriculture]

Hello Tractor. http://www.hellotractor.com/.

ICIPE (International Centre of Insect Physiology and Ecology). http://www.icipe.org. [based in Kenya, its work includes integrated pest management]

IDE (International Development Enterprises). http://www.ideglobal.org. [works on small-scale technology and models for its commercialization]

IFC (International Finance Corporation of the World Bank Group). 2015. "Agricultural Lending: A How-To Guide." Toolkit, IFC, Washington, DC.

IFDC (International Fertilizer Development Center). http://www.ifdc.org.

Making Cents International. http://www.makingcents.com/markets.

NRI (Natural Resources Institute). [research for development]

ODI (Overseas Development Institute). 2002. "Soil Fertility and Nutrient Management." Resource Management Key Sheet No. 7, ODI, London.

One Acre Fund. http://www.oneacrefund.org. [nongovernmental organization working with smallholder farmers]

Opportunity International. http://opportunity.org.uk/what-we-do/how-we-work /training-financial-advice.

Scholten, M. C. Th., I. J. M. de Boer, B. Gremmen, and C. Lokhorst. 2013. "Livestock Farming with Care: Towards Sustainable Production of Animal-Source Food." *NJAS - Wageningen Journal of Life Sciences* 66: 3–5.

Syngenta Foundation for Sustainable Development. http://www.syngentafoundation .org.

TechnoServe. http://www.technoserve.org.

Wageningen University and Research Centre, The Netherlands. http://www.wur.nl.

Climate Change and REDD+

CSA (Climate-Smart Agriculture). n.d. "What Is Climate-Smart Agriculture?" https://csa.guide/csa/what-is-climate-smart-agriculture.

FCPF (Forest Carbon Partnership Facility). https://www.forestcarbonpartnership.org/what-redd.

IPCC (International Panel on Climate Change. http://www.ipcc.ch/.

UN-REDD (United Nations Reducing Emissions from Deforestation and Forest Degradation Programme). http://www.un-redd.org.

World Bank and UNCTAD (United Nations Conference on Trade and Development). 2018. "Environmental and Social Impact Assessments." Responsible Agricultural Investment (RAI) Knowledge into Action Note No. 14, World Bank, Washington, DC; UNCTAD, New York. https://openknowledge.worldbank.org/bitstream/handle/10986/29477/124289-BRI-PUBLIC-KN14.pdf?sequence=1&isAllowed=y.

———. 2018. "Water Access and Management." Responsible Agricultural Investment (RAI) Knowledge into Action Note No. 13, World Bank, Washington, DC; UNCTAD, New York. https://openknowledge.worldbank.org/bitstream/handle/10986/29478/124288-BRI-PUBLIC-KN13.pdf?sequence=1&isAllowed=y.

CHAPTER 7
WOMEN'S PARTICIPATION

KEY MESSAGES

➡ Apart from compelling development arguments for more equal participation of women in the global economy, there is also an important
business rationale.

➡ A body of evidence shows that companies benefit in diverse ways
from investing in women as employees, entrepreneurs, customers,
and community partners.

➡ Closing gender-based agricultural yield gaps of 20–30 percent would
increase agricultural output by 2.5–4 percent in frontier and emerging
markets.

➡ Agribusinesses benefit from closing gender gaps through improved
quality of produce, better use of inputs, increased farm productivity,
more numerous and loyal suppliers, and reduced management costs.

➡ There are also market opportunities in products tailored to women's
needs—and in women-produced products.

➡ Focusing on women may yield opportunities to improve community
health and education because of women's additional roles in these areas.

➡ Gender diagnostic tools and approaches—supported by, for example,
more gender-inclusive use of information and communication technology (ICT)—can be used to develop gender-smart agribusiness solutions.

The Business Case for Increasing Women's Participation in Smallholder Supply Chains

The yield gap between men and women averages around 20–30 percent, and most research finds that the gap is due to differences in resource use. Bringing yields on the land farmed by women up to the levels achieved by men would increase agricultural output in developing countries between 2.5 and 4 percent. Increasing production by this amount could reduce the number of undernourished people in the world in the order of 12–17 percent. (FAO 2011, vi)

Scope for Increased Profit, Growth, and Innovation

Compelling development and equity arguments can be made for more equal participation of women in the global economy. There is also an important business rationale: women are, after all, half of the potential human capital pool and half of the potential market. "Realizing women's full economic potential is good for business and for development" (World Bank 2016). Most often cited is the evidence that gender equality strengthens national economies and that investing in women in senior leadership also strengthens the companies in which they work. These are strong arguments indeed, but they nonetheless understate the numerous and diverse ways in which women's economic participation is good for business.

International Finance Corporation (IFC) and its partners have been developing a portfolio of evidence on the ways in which—and by how much—women contribute to business growth and how that contribution can be promoted. Some of the more notable findings include the following (IFC 2017b, 4):

- Companies with gender-diverse boards generate a higher return on equity (MSCI 2015).

- Companies with gender-diverse boards outperform those with no women in terms of share price performance during times of crisis or volatility (CSRI 2012).

- High-performing companies are almost 50 percent more likely than low-performing companies to report that men and women have equal influence on strategy development (EY 2015).

Investors in companies with strong gender diversity strategies receive excess returns running at a compound annual growth rate (CAGR) of 3.5 percent (CSRI 2016).

Companies benefit in diverse ways from investing in women as employees, entrepreneurs, customers, and community partners. Strong evidence supports this argument in three key domains (IFC 2017b):

- *Human capital:* Expanding women's workforce participation and leadership promotes business growth via its effect on the following:

    ○ *Production quality and output.* For example, ECOM Agroindustrial Corporation saw farm yields increase by 131 percent when it trained both men and women, compared with 95 percent when only men were trained (IFC 2016b, 24).

    ○ *Staff retention, reduced absenteeism, and lower turnover.* For example, investments in childcare and women's clinics reduced staff turnover by one-third in a Vietnamese factory with which IFC worked (IFC 2013a, 86–90).

    ○ *Marketing.* A gender-diverse supplier base is a strong selling point in markets with high ethical and sustainable sourcing standards such as the European Union.

    ○ *Innovation capacity.* A study of 4,000 research and development teams found that gender diversity "generates dynamics conducive to radical innovation" (Díaz-García, González-Moreno, and Sáez-Martínez 2013).

- *Market growth and innovation:* Because women tend to be the principal decision makers on consumer spending globally (Silverstein and Sayre 2009),

    ○ *Designing and marketing* in response to gender-differentiated customer needs and preferences can produce new ideas or take old ideas in new directions.

    ○ *Targeting women* specifically, particularly by opening up a market previously closed to them, can be a key driver of growth. For example, Garanti Bank in Turkey found that women entrepreneurs used more of their services and generated higher profits for the bank (IFC 2016a).

- *Operating environment:* Many gender-related challenges that affect the private sector originate outside the workplace. For instance, access to education affects workforce participation, land title (often assigned to men only) affects access to finance, and so on. Companies can influence these sectorwide issues by working in multistakeholder groups.

Women's Unrealized Potential in Smallholder Agriculture

Women make up an average of 43 percent of the agricultural workforce in frontier and emerging markets (and at least 50 percent in many African and Asian countries) and produce more than half of the world's food. However, they are 20–30 percent less productive than men (FAO 2011) because they have limited access to productive resources, including land, financing, inputs, and technology (table 7.1).

TABLE 7.1 Constraints on Women in Smallholder Agriculture

Resource type	Constraint
Land	Formal land title, when it exists, is usually assigned to men in both traditional and modern land tenure systems, even when women contribute significantly to agricultural production. For example, less than 2 percent of African women have ownership rights to their land. Lack of official land ownership reduces women's ability to access finance and other resources.
Supply chain links	Women are underrepresented in the membership and governance of established producer organizations from which agribusinesses source. They are also less likely than men to participate in sustainability certification schemes. Fewer women are contract farmers or outgrowers. They miss out on income from crop sales and the services such as training, financing, and provision of inputs that off-takers provide.
Training	Only 5 percent of participants in extension services and capacity-building programs are women. Male field staff tend to interact with male farmers—meaning that training and inputs may be provided to a person in the household who is not necessarily responsible for the associated task. Poor transfer of agricultural knowledge within households in turn means that extension messages do not reach the appropriate person.
Finance	Women have less access to finance as a result of lower education levels, cultural restrictions, and collateral requirements that exclude them. Yet much anecdotal evidence suggests that women are often better than men at repaying loans and managing finance.
Technology	Women tend to use technology less than men, in part because of perceptions that women's labor is less onerous or important than that of men, so there has been less development and dissemination to women of appropriate technologies.
Attitudes to risk	Women's limited access to resources and their focus on other household responsibilities mean that women tend to be more risk-averse than men.
Household decision-making authority	Limited land ownership is one reason that women often contribute a disproportionately large share of work undertaken by the smallholder households but have poor access to or influence over the crop revenues. In other situations, women may not identify as farmers even though they have access to farmland, decide with their husbands what farm inputs to use, hold the household income, and influence how household finances are used.

table continued

TABLE 7.1 Constraints on Women in Smallholder Agriculture *(Continued)*

Resource type	Constraint
Time	Demands on women's time at home reduce their ability to participate in training or sourcing programs. Women visit demonstration plots and attend extension services less frequently than men, but the gender gap narrows when extension services are offered at home.
Mobility	Women's different social networks may reduce their ability to develop vertical and horizontal value chain links.

When agribusiness firms help to close gender gaps by addressing these constraints, they create opportunities to develop stronger supply chains, benefiting the agriculture sector overall (figure 7.1). Some specific benefits merit more attention—and action—from agribusiness companies (IFC 2016b):

- *Improved quality.* Women are conscientious with detail at points in the supply chain that can improve quality, such as postharvest handling and the identification of pests and disease. Women also often bring particular strengths to the cultivation of high-value, organic, and indigenous crops (IFC 2016b).

- *Better use of inputs.* Wherever women influence household financial decisions (for example, on input purchase and use), providing training for women increases the likelihood that inputs are purchased and used correctly.

- *Increased productivity.* In certain commodities and sectors, female family members are responsible for most of the field labor. Including women in training will contribute to improved yields, and promoting more equal sharing of farming revenues will increase women's interest in improving farm productivity.

- *More numerous and more loyal suppliers.* Responsibility for different crops is often gender-differentiated at the household level. Understanding those dynamics can lead to more effective targeting by firms. Moreover, in some areas, rural outmigration is significant, resulting in large numbers of women-headed farm households—again meriting more business attention than they often receive.

- *Reduced management costs.* Female representation in the management of producer organizations (POs) can improve their management

FIGURE 7.1 **Smallholder Gender Gap Reduction: Solutions and Benefits for Agribusiness Value Chains**

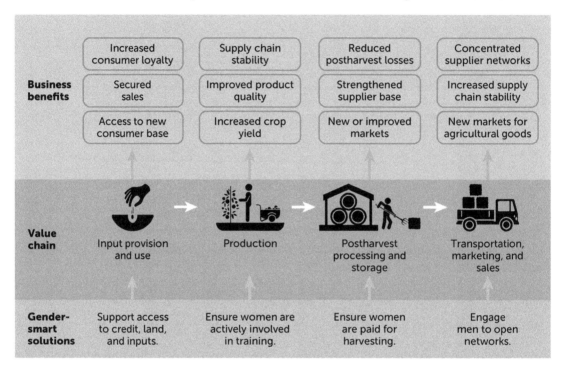

Source: IFC 2016b, ©International Finance Corporation (IFC). Reprinted, with permission, from IFC; further permission required for reuse.

and efficacy. Female committee members tend to be more willing to share information, help resolve disputes, and represent the interests of the wider membership, whereas male representatives are often unwilling to share too much information.

Men and women may perceive their roles in a particular crop sector in starkly different ways (figure 7.2). Clearly, an understanding of both perspectives can contribute to much better design and targeting of interventions.

The findings in figure 7.2 come from a survey that used gender mapping as a diagnostic tool in a collaboration between IFC and an agribusiness client. The remainder of this chapter elaborates on good practices for understanding and addressing the important roles of women in many value chains.

FIGURE 7.2 Differing Gender Perspectives on Male-Female Division of Labor in Cocoa Production

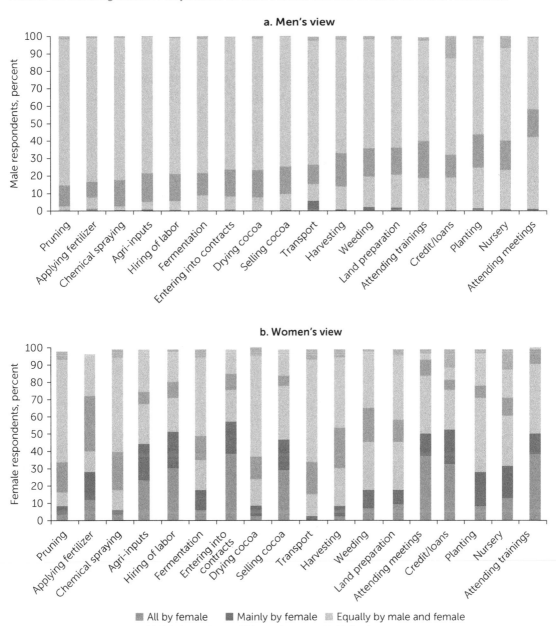

Strategies and Best Practices for Increasing Women's Participation

Understanding how women contribute to value chains and taking that into account when designing supply chain interventions creates value for the firm and for women. To that end, a gender lens can be used at each stage of program design and implementation (figure 7.3).

Understanding Roles and Motivations of Women Farmers

- Gender mapping is a type of survey tool designed to provide insight into women's roles throughout the production process and along the supply chain. It probes four key dimensions of the different roles of men and women within the household and the farming business:

- *Access:* Does the intervention create opportunities for women to be involved?

- *Participation:* Are both men and women involved? What explains any differences?

FIGURE 7.3 Gender-Related Considerations for Supply Chain Interventions, by Step of Program Design and Implementation

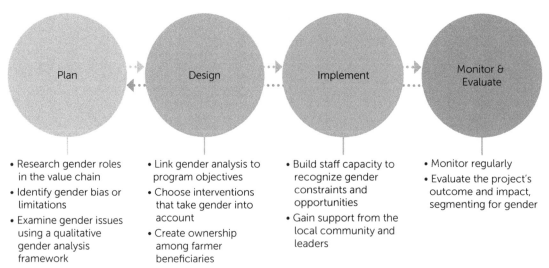

Plan
- Research gender roles in the value chain
- Identify gender bias or limitations
- Examine gender issues using a qualitative gender analysis framework

Design
- Link gender analysis to program objectives
- Choose interventions that take gender into account
- Create ownership among farmer beneficiaries

Implement
- Build staff capacity to recognize gender constraints and opportunities
- Gain support from the local community and leaders

Monitor & Evaluate
- Monitor regularly
- Evaluate the project's outcome and impact, segmenting for gender

FIGURE 7.4 Questions Addressed by Gender Mapping in Agriculture Supply Chains

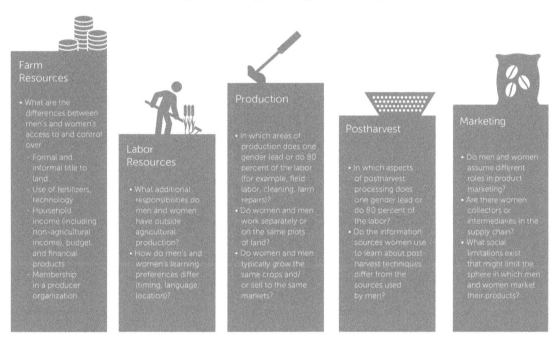

Farm Resources

• What are the differences between men's and women's access to and control over
  - Formal and informal title to land
  - Use of fertilizers, technology
  - Household income (including non-agricultural income), budget, and financial products
  - Membership in a producer organization

Labor Resources

• What additional responsibilities do men and women have outside agricultural production?
• How do men's and women's learning preferences differ (timing, language, location)?

Production

• In which areas of production does one gender lead or do 80 percent of the labor (for example, field labor, cleaning, farm repairs)?
• Do women and men work separately or on the same plots of land?
• Do women and men typically grow the same crops and/or sell to the same markets?

Postharvest

• In which aspects of postharvest processing does one gender lead or do 80 percent of the labor?
• Do the information sources women use to learn about postharvest techniques differ from the sources used by men?

Marketing

• Do men and women assume different roles in product marketing?
• Are there women collectors or intermediaries in the supply chain?
• What social limitations exist that might limit the sphere in which men and women market their products?

Source: IFC 2013b.

• *Control:* How are decisions made?

• *Benefits:* Do both men and women benefit? How? In equal measure?

To answer these questions, gender mapping draws on information from multiple sources such as questionnaire surveys, key informant interviews, focus group discussions, and analysis of PO membership. The gender-mapping analysis can provide useful insights into women's roles in several areas of the supply chain (figure 7.4).

Among the techniques used for gender mapping, one type of informal survey—a participatory rural appraisal (also called a rapid rural appraisal)—can be particularly useful for understanding the demands on women's time in a 24-hour period and women's roles in agricultural production and marketing. A participatory rural appraisal uses group discussion, usually in an informal outdoor setting, and simple markers such as pebbles and sticks to construct visual maps of complex household dynamics. Consulting women and men separately may ensure that participants feel comfortable sharing their priorities, needs, and motivations.

It is important that the gender mapping analysis seek to understand how any proposed supply chain intervention will affect the following:

- Women's workloads, access to resources, financial independence, and relationship with other household members

- Decision making within the household (for example, relating to resource allocation, budgets for food and education, and how women's and children's time is used)

- Membership, participation, and leadership in POs, which in turn affects access to resources and training.

This analysis will highlight issues that may either inhibit or encourage women's involvement. Understanding these issues—and, for example, finding ways to compensate for a negative aspect of an activity that is otherwise positive for women—will be instrumental in any enhanced value chain role for women. At the same time, gender mapping is contextual, and any recommendations for interventions should take note of existing cultural structures.

Determining How to Best Include Women in Supply Chains

Promoting women's roles and interests in the value chain means taking account of their capabilities and limitations and designing the program to make that value chain a win-win arrangement for companies and for women. As discussed, gender mapping (IFC 2017a) will highlight areas where women's contribution is strong as well as areas where they could potentially play a larger role, in ways that are good for women and good for business. With careful analysis and consultation, that information can be used to design interventions—and an approach—that promote women's interests and value chain development. This section elaborates on approaches to (a) effective outreach to women and (b) addressing specific areas where women's interests may be underrepresented.

As with other tools for rural surveys, some of these approaches can be time-consuming—for both the implementing team and the groups being surveyed—so they should be used selectively. Ideally, baseline and other surveys should be designed to include gender. Consideration could also be given, for instance, to initial interviews about women's roles in value chains, which could then be used to focus more detailed follow-up investigation. If resources are limited, project teams may focus on ways in which the proposed intervention directly links to women, though this approach risks missing potentially important issues and opportunities.

Although tools such as the Women's Empowerment in Agriculture Index (IFPRI 2012) can provide useful information (as described more fully at the end of this chapter), gender mapping gives greater attention to

- The division of labor at the farm, household, and community levels

- Women's access to institutions such as banks, nongovernmental organizations (NGOs), government, and off-takers

- Women's leadership in POs, which are important conduits for economic empowerment, particularly for high-value agricultural commodities.

Ensuring Effective Outreach to Women

Make sure that *training and extension* use inclusive methods. Content should be tailored to fit farmers' literacy, numeracy, language preferences, and cultural norms (as illustrated in box 7.1). In doing so, note that women and men may not share the same learning profiles. Women may have lower literacy rates or be monolingual in a traditional language. Segmenting the needs of male and female farmers will help to identify how training content can be tailored to reach both.

Include gender-awareness modules in training of trainers and training content for farmers. In some contexts, the perceptions of farmers and field staff may be that a woman's role is limited to that of an assistant. Increasing awareness of and appreciation for women's important roles and contributions can improve recognition of women's contributions.

BOX 7.1

In Practice: Video Viewing Clubs for Women Cocoa Farmers in Ghana

In Ghana, the Sustainable Tree Crops Program—founded in 2000 by the International Institute of Tropical Agriculture, the United States Agency for International Development, and the World Cocoa Foundation—has developed video viewing clubs for illiterate women who are cocoa smallholders. The program ensures that training is accessible for women by involving them in selecting the training venue, length, and frequency. Trainees can easily capture content conveyed through short films, discussions supported by picture guides, and practical demonstrations at trainee's farms.

Source: David and Asamoah 2011.

Their increased presence at training events and meetings may reinforce awareness and help improve gender equality.

Ensure that staff promote women's participation. Staff and extension agents are critical for ensuring that women feel safe, welcome, and valued in supply chain programs. Strategies to sensitize staff to this role include the following:

- *Training on women's roles, constraints, and concerns.* Such training should extend to field staff, producer group leaders, extension agents from other organizations, and service providers.

- *Ensuring gender-balanced training teams.* Hire female trainers and volunteers, but don't absolve male staff of addressing women's concerns. Women in leadership positions are often more effective at reaching and supporting female farmers, especially in contexts where social norms limit women's interactions with men (as shown in the Pakistan case study, box 7.2). However, a mix of female and male extension agents can reduce barriers for women's participation in the program. Firms may need to adjust selection criteria to recruit

---

BOX 7.2

In Practice: Integrating Women Suppliers into Livestock Value Chains to Improve Output and Quality in Pakistan and South Africa

Background

In many countries, particularly among the poor, women play an important role in livestock husbandry and marketing. Yet when marketing activities scale up and link to growing urban markets, the control over decisions and income often shifts to men (FAO 2011). Targeted actions are needed to include women in these new opportunities and thereby seize the benefits their participation confers.

Dairy Goat Initiative in Pakistan

In Pakistan, vulnerable women were deliberately targeted in a dairy goat initiative by Plan International—through the provision of goats and enterprise development training. This increased the women's voice and decision-making power through their representation in local cooperatives and the District Livestock Farmers' Association. With women playing a more active role, not only did milk output increase but quality did as well—reflected in a 60 percent increase in the sales price.

box continued

BOX 7.2

In Practice: Integrating Women Suppliers into Livestock Value Chains to Improve Output and Quality in Pakistan and South Africa *(Continued)*

Poultry Supplier Opportunities in South Africa

South Africa's third largest poultry supplier (Supreme Poultry) employs women at all levels of the business. The contract farmer manager is a woman, and women are well-represented in her field team. Supreme Poultry estimates that 25 percent (114) of the jobs provided by the contract growers are filled by women, although only one of the *named* contractors is a woman. "Women workers are seen as disciplined, determined, and able to organise their workloads and handle the chickens well" (IFC 2016c).

The company can build on its technical relationship with its outgrowers to encourage more employment of women in nontraditional jobs, using the examples set by existing growers (IFC 2016b). It could consider helping establish and train *women-run agrodealerships* and *microfranchises* to promote more effective outreach to women farmers and improve women's knowledge of farm input use. Tailoring products to meet women's needs can also be effective in promoting women's use of agro-inputs: smaller units of input purchase may better suit their pockets and small plot sizes.

Sources: IFC 2016b, 2016c.

---

female trainers by, for example, selecting women whose community leadership roles substitute for educational and professional qualifications. A strong, gender-balanced team can promote women's participation by the following:

○ Ensuring that event invitations are extended directly to women farmers, including female household members of male contract farmers (although, in some cultures, firms may need to obtain men's approval before extending invitations directly to women to avoid backlash or violence)

○ Encouraging women's participation and respecting women's opinions during discussions

○ Creating opportunities for women to lead group discussions and present group opinions

○ Using women's perspectives to help design and implement interventions in ways that are clearly more effective and more inclusive.

Promote gender inclusiveness within the firm's organizational culture and at all levels. In some situations, gender awareness may be dismissed as being "politically correct," and the benefits of increased gender awareness may be lost (or even resented) if there is an organizational culture of disrespect for women. Changing such cultures requires leadership and systems that reinforce that shift. Although women field staff may be more effective at reaching women farmers, male staff may be more influenced by the views of their bosses and male peers.

Ensure convenience to promote participation. Restrictions on women's time and social activities, including possible cultural norms prohibiting their interaction with men, can make it difficult for women to attend program events. Firms may need to actively engage women through POs or women-only groups. There are a few key points to consider:

- The location, timing, and duration of program events greatly affect women's participation rates. An accessible location to which women can travel safely and conveniently will increase their comfort levels. Ask women to suggest suitable places and times to hold events.

- Women's preferences may require flexible arrangements to accommodate weekend or evening meetings, for example, as well as childcare needs to relieve distractions.

- "Crop calendar" tools can help determine the ideal dates for arranging event and training schedules, but the schedules need to be cross-checked with women's availability. For example, March may not need much work on cash crop production, but women may be busy harvesting important food crops.

Respect social norms and context. Working with POs and other membership groups can give firms an opportunity to lead by example by valuing and respecting women's participation in agriculture. However, promoting women's active engagement in traditionally male environments is not always the right strategy: women and men may operate in different social spheres, and disregarding that may create conflict. The outcomes, though, are context-specific. Consult with women and others with relevant country experience. Working with women-only groups can be an alternative to promoting women's participation and leadership in established (male) POs. Firms can leverage existing women's self-help, savings, or water user groups to build capacity and to source from women farmers. Each approach—working with mixed-gender or with women-only groups—has advantages and disadvantages (figure 7.5).

FIGURE 7.5 Mixed-Gender versus Gender-Segregated Working Groups

ENGAGE WOMEN IN MIXED-GENDER GROUPS		ENGAGE WOMEN IN GENDER-SEGREGATED GROUPS	
(+) Improves women's access to producer groups and value chains (+) Provides access to marketing, inputs, credit, and information	(−) May not improve women's decision-making power (−) Social norms and expectations can limit women's participation (−) Group priorities may not meet women's needs	(+) More socially accepted (+) Women are better able to voice opinions and needs (+) Women can develop leadership skills	(−) Women-only groups lack vertical supply chain linkages that men typically control (−) Men can feel excluded and attempt to sabotage the group

Identify "quick wins" by empowering women through activities that were already planned. For example, if a firm is already planning to provide training, ensuring that a significant proportion of trainers are women can encourage women farmers without additional cost. By contrast, building capacity within women's producer groups would require a greater level of investment and careful consideration of the expected impacts.

For more about outreach to female smallholders, see also "Reaching Women Farmers" in chapter 5, box 5.2.

Addressing Areas Where Women's Interests Are Underrepresented

Evaluate opportunities to increase women's *access to finance*. Entry and guarantee requirements for credit schemes may be too burdensome for women or may require documents or assets they do not have and cannot obtain. A group guarantee may provide a collateral substitute. New technologies create new opportunities, and mobile payments may be more accessible to women or more easily managed than bank transfers or cash. Engage with insurers to see whether index-based insurance could be available, as women may be particularly vulnerable because of small farm size, less-productive land, and family responsibilities (see chapter 2).

Make sure that *eligibility requirements for technology*, equipment, and protective clothing do not unintentionally exclude women. ICT can be a low-cost tool that expands the impact of an agricultural extension program. Some technologies, such as radio, are particularly effective at reaching otherwise isolated communities—and can be a good way to reach women who, for whatever reason, are less likely to leave the house. To make the use of ICT tools more gender-inclusive, firms can follow several recommendations:

- *Include a gender component when assessing the benefits of an ICT-based intervention.* Men and women may use different types of technology and use them differently. It is important to understand (1) men's and women's different reasons for using technology, (2) whether they own or borrow that technology, (3) whether the technology is a subscription-based or pay-as-you-go service, and (4) whether the users prefer written or oral communication. Women may prefer communication transmitted via radio or other "hands-free" devices so they can listen as they work on other tasks.

- *Address the ongoing maintenance and costs of the ICT, not just the initial acquisition.* Like other assets, ICTs require ongoing, costly maintenance. For example, a mobile phone needs to be charged with airtime and electricity. If women face mobility barriers, charging a mobile phone can be more challenging for them than it is for men. Or they may have less income to purchase the airtime and phone-charging services. Identifying these differences is the first step to finding the best way to include women.

- *Advocate for gender-balanced staffing at agriculture-related ICT service providers.* Female extension agents may find it difficult to travel to remote districts, and female farmers may feel intimidated asking men questions when they contact an ICT service provider. One solution is to hire female agents as call center consultants and operators. Women staff can also act as intermediaries, liaising between community members and agricultural information providers. Their participation in content development will mean that they gain skills, earn income, and address women's information needs.

- *Combine ICT interventions with face-to-face learning.* Although mobile services are expanding and providing opportunities for reaching large populations, not all women have access to mobile phones or text-based information services. Using multiple approaches ensures that services reach a wider base of rural women through appropriate channels. For example, the Kenya Agricultural Commodity Exchange uses information kiosks in local markets, a radio program, a short message service (SMS), and an interactive voice-responsive service to provide market information (Mukhebi 2004).

- *Use new opportunities with Global Positioning System (GPS) and mobile phones to match service demand and supply.* Women may need agricultural storage, transport, or equipment in smaller measure than their male counterparts, or they may not find it easy to travel far from the home, making it harder to purchase or hire these services. A new area of development is the increasing availability of mobile or GPS-enabled services that match dispersed demand with providers. Hello Tractor is one example (as mentioned in chapter 6), and more will emerge, particularly with increased penetration of mobile-phone services and lower-cost smartphones or GPS. For example, a solution is proposed in Pakistan that would link last-mile rural microdistributors and cold-storage demand from farmers to underutilized capacity in corporate cold chain systems.[1]

Ensure inclusiveness in POs. Firms may need to proactively recruit women into outgrower or contract-farming schemes if women assume it will be difficult to join. Firms should assure women that land ownership is not a prerequisite and that women are encouraged to join. Information about company contract programs and benefits should be communicated to women.

Context permitting, sensitize POs to the beneficial roles and contributions of women in agricultural supply chains. Traditional values or historical economic structures may create unequal barriers to women's participation in producer groups. Caution may be needed so as not to generate resentment of women (as noted earlier), but firms may be able to encourage POs to address underrepresentation of women in their membership or production by

- Suggesting men give a share of their land or crops to their wives so women can join the group or program in their own right

- Ensuring that outgrower registration and contracts are completed in the name of the individual who is the main producer or decision maker (as sometimes a woman registers under her husband's name because it is more socially acceptable, consequently giving her less direct control over the resources and decision making at the group level)

- Proposing joint contracts that require both the husband and wife to sign the contract

- Requiring that the money earned be distributed to both the husband and wife

- Discouraging membership guidelines that effectively exclude women, such as those that, for example, (1) require members to possess legal or traditional land rights, (2) set minimum production volumes, and (3) register only heads of household as members.

Box 7.3 explains how women's roles were promoted in Indonesia coffee.

BOX 7.3

In Practice: Understanding Women's Farm Labor Contributions to Increase Training Effectiveness in Indonesia and Vietnam

Background

Female farmers constitute nearly 80 percent of coffee farm labor in North Sumatra, Indonesia, and 50 percent of farm labor in Lam Dong, Vietnam. Despite these high female participation rates, women are often excluded from extension services and other development activities. A 2010 IFC partnership with the ECOM Agroindustrial Corporation included a project promoting sustainable coffee cultivation practices among smallholder farmers that prioritized women's engagement in training.

The implementation team identified the following barriers to women's engagement:

- *Limited free time.* In addition to farm work, female farmers are in charge of most of the household's domestic work and rarely have time to attend training/workshops.
- *Few assets.* Family assets, especially land, are primarily owned by men.
- *Poor outreach.* Farmers' associations, which organize extension training, mostly work with household heads, more than 90 percent of whom are male.
- *Insufficient gender awareness.* Lead firm staff and local extension staff lack the knowledge on gender issues necessary to apply a gender-sensitive approach to extension training activities.

Gender-Specific Training Model

The implementation team's approach aimed to increase women's farming skills and improve overall coffee productivity and quality. To do so, the team identified women's roles in on-farm supply chain work and deployed women trainers, volunteers, and the leaders of women's unions, farmers' associations, village heads, and extension staff to underscore the project's prioritization of gender.

Trainers adjusted training schedules to accommodate women's needs and used gender-specific training materials. More visual aids, such as videos and pictures, accompanied traditional training materials to reach illiterate women in the audience. Recognizing women's traditional role in managing household income, the team also introduced a simple financial management tool to enable female farmers to document and analyze household and farm expenditures.

Results

By the project's close in 2012, 1,596 Indonesian women received training, increasing women's participation in training from 4 percent to 26 percent. In Vietnam, 2,317 women received training, more than doubling female participation in training workshops—from less than 12 percent in 2010 to 25 percent in 2012. The project improved the adoption rate of improved agricultural practices that are primarily done by female farmers, such as pruning and fertilization.

box continued

BOX 7.3

In Practice: Understanding Women's Farm Labor Contributions to Increase Training Effectiveness in Indonesia and Vietnam *(Continued)*

Two key benefits emerged from integrating women into the farmer training program. First, women's access to technical training, extension services, and productive input has increased the adoption of good agricultural practices. Coffee productivity was found to be higher among trained groups that included both men and women than among trained groups consisting only of men as well as a control group that received no training from the project. (In Indonesia specifically, the productivity increase were 131 percent among the mixed groups and 95 percent for men-only groups.)

Second, women applied the knowledge and skills they received through training to increase their household productivity. This additional knowledge helped farming families use their resources more efficiently, improving their livelihoods beyond the project's expectations.

Participants also expressed satisfaction with shifts in traditional household responsibilities as a result of the program. Men started taking on a greater role in childcare to free women's time to participate in the program. Women who normally controlled much of the household budget started to include men in the decision-making process.

Address underrepresentation of women in leadership or management positions. Producer groups and contract farming programs can accomplish the following:

- Introduce quotas for women's representation on boards and committees of contract farming programs and producer groups

- Encourage and support women to stand for election to committees

- Explain the importance and benefits of women's representation to men to help overcome likely cultural barriers and resistance to change.

Ensure that women benefit fairly from participation *in sustainability certification programs.* In general, sustainability standards do not specifically target women, but they do affect areas that are important to women, such as women's workload. For instance, an organic or fair trade scheme may increase women's involvement in preharvest and postharvest labor. A carefully balanced approach is needed to ensure that women can access training, markets, and market information; do not take on a disproportionate share of additional labor needs; and benefit from premiums distributed to groups. Such an approach should do the following:

- Assess additional labor burdens generated for women (and men) as a result of the adoption of certification standards

- Address additional burdens at an early stage through informal labor-sharing agreements at the community or household level or through labor-saving recommendations

- Ensure that, when certification generates a premium paid to the group (such as fair trade premiums), the funds are spent on projects benefiting women as well as men (more likely when women are represented on the committees responsible for allocating such funds)

- Support the development of women-driven brands, as in the case of coffee labeling that support women's enterprises in Latin America (box 7.4).

BOX 7.4

In Practice: Café Femenino: Woman-Driven Branding in Latin America

Branding Model

Café Femenino is a label that markets organically grown coffee and represents an emerging strategy to promote women's brands. Originating out of eight Latin American countries—Bolivia, Brazil, Colombia, the Dominican Republic, Guatemala, Mexico, Nicaragua, and Peru—the brand aims to create a niche market within the specialty coffee market that attributes a higher value to coffee produced entirely by women.

Results

In addition to creating opportunities to increase women's vertical and horizontal links across the value chain, the label has strengthened women's self-esteem and leadership skills. Café Femenino members in Peru produce in a "women-only" space in a mixed-gender producer organization, but as their technical skills improve, more women are taking on leadership positions within the larger organization. Although the label may remain a niche-market player, it has expanded women's roles and participation in the supply chain.

Source: Riisgaard, Fibla, and Ponte 2010.

Address *systemic issues* **that affect women's participation and value chain performance.** Sometimes firms encounter issues that originate outside the value chain and over which the firm has little purview. Such issues could be quite diverse in nature, including, for example, gender-based violence, a local law that acts to limit women's land ownership, poor nutrition habits, or the prevalence of human immunodeficiency virus and acquired immune deficiency syndrome (HIV-AIDS). These issues are clearly very context-specific, and there may be little the firm can do, but it is also possible that a firm could lend its support to cross-industry or multistakeholder initiatives promoting change. If an issue has direct and very negative consequences for women (or other groups employed or contracted by the firm), it may be appropriate for the firm to develop a policy on the issue and make sure that it is followed in house. This is how businesses and NGOs have responded to HIV-AIDS in countries or sectors where it is prevalent.

Monitoring and Evaluation

As chapter 9 discusses in greater detail, the use of project monitoring and evaluation techniques during a program can help keep activities and outcomes on track. Developing an early understanding of women's priorities and constraints can inform the development of appropriate outcome and impact indicators for gender, and collecting gender-disaggregated monitoring data will help highlight areas and issues for further development or adjustment. This allows a firm to ensure that a project attains its overall goals as well as to understand the separate contributions of both men and women. The rapidly changing context for data collection and analysis (as covered in chapter 9), including the use of ICT tools, makes it a lot easier to both collect and analyze gender-disaggregated data.

Gender indicators must meet the same standards as any other indicator (also discussed in chapter 9) and should capture changes in gender-related norms. The use of baseline data allows subsequent changes to be monitored as a percentage change in behavior. So, for example, monitoring the number of hours that women spend farming can be used to calculate the percentage reduction or increase in the time spent farming. Other gender-specific indicators for production and welfare outcomes include the following:

- Percentage of group leadership positions held by women

- Percentage of meeting time during which women speak

- Percentage of women among all recipients of fertilizer credit
- Percentage of household budget spent on inputs
- Percentage of women among total participants who have access to farm equipment
- Percentages of women and men owning a mobile phone.

Firms may also wish to track indicators relating to the sensitive or systemic issues discussed earlier so that they know the extent to which such issues are present and potentially affecting business.

Surveys that capture observations at the level of household members are more useful than those that aggregate responses for the whole household. Gender-segregated focus groups are a less costly means to probe possibly different concerns and opinions that men and women have about an agribusiness initiative. If farmer logbooks or other forms of farmer record keeping are used to track progress, the firm should identify whether it is more appropriate for men or women to be assigned the task. In some cases, women may control the household budget and can therefore track spending more precisely.

Women's Empowerment in Agriculture Index

The Women's Empowerment in Agriculture Index (WEAI) was developed to track the change in women's empowerment as a direct or indirect result of interventions under Feed the Future, the U.S. government's global hunger and food security initiative (IFPRI 2012). The index is a collaborative effort of the U.S. Agency for International Development (USAID), the International Food Policy Research Institute (IFPRI), and the Oxford Poverty and Human Development Initiative (OPHI).

Women play a critical and potentially transformative role in agricultural growth in frontier and emerging markets, but they face persistent obstacles and economic constraints limiting further inclusion in agriculture. The WEAI measures the empowerment, agency, and inclusion of women in the agriculture sector to identify ways to overcome those obstacles and constraints. The index aims to increase understanding of the connections between women's empowerment, food security, and agricultural growth.

The WEAI measures the roles and extent of women's engagement in the agriculture sector in five domains: decisions about agricultural production, access to and decision-making power over productive resources, control over use of income, leadership in the community, and time use.

It also measures women's empowerment relative to men within their households. The WEAI is a composite measurement tool that indicates women's control over critical parts of their lives in the household, community, and economy. It allows us to identify women who are disempowered and understand how to increase autonomy and decision making in key domains.

The WEAI is also useful for tracking progress toward gender equality. Ultimately, the index will be used for performance monitoring and impact evaluations of Feed the Future programs. Toward that end, in 2011, pilot surveys were conducted in regions of three countries: Bangladesh, Guatemala, and Uganda. The WEAI can be used by policy makers, development organizations, and academics seeking to inform efforts to increase women's empowerment.

Note

1. "An 'UBER' for Small-Holder Farmers: Linking Farmers to Urban Markets while Leveraging Under-Utilized Capacity in Corporate Cold-Chains," OpenIDEO "Challenge" post, June 21, 2016 (accessed April 2, 2018), https://challenges .openideo.com/challenge/agricultural-innovation/improve/an-uber-for-small -holder-farmers-linking-farmers-to-urban-markets-while-leveraging-under -utilized-capacity-in-corporate-cold-chains/comments.

References

CSRI (Credit Suisse Research Institute). 2012. "Gender Diversity and Corporate Performance." Research report, CSRI, Zurich.

———. 2016. "The CS Gender 3000: The Reward for Change." Research report, CSRI, Zurich.

David, S., and C. Asamoah. 2011. "Video as a tool for Agricultural Extension in Africa: A Case Study from Ghana." *International Journal of Education and Development using Information and Communication Technology* 7(1).

Díaz-García, C., A. González-Moreno, and F. Sáez-Martínez. 2013. "Gender Diversity within R&D Teams: Its Impact on Radicalness of Innovation." *Innovation: Management, Policy & Practice* 15 (2): 149.

EY (Ernst & Young). 2015. "Women. Fast Forward | The Time for Gender Parity is Now." Survey report, EY, London.

FAO (Food and Agriculture Organization of the United Nations). 2011. *The State of Food and Agriculture 2010–11. Women in Agriculture: Closing the Gender Gap for Development.* Rome: FAO.

IFC (International Finance Corporation of the World Bank Group). 2013a. "Investing in Women's Employment: Good for Business, Good for Development." Report of the IFC Gender Program and its *WINvest* (Investing in Women) initiative, IFC, Washington, DC.

———. 2013b. *Working with Smallholders: A Handbook for Firms Building Sustainable Supply Chains.* Washington, DC: IFC.

———. 2016a. "Garanti Bank Turkey: Combining SME Banking Excellence with a Proposition for Women Entrepreneurs in Turkey." Learning study on impact of banking on women programs in Europe, Central Asia, Middle East, and North Africa, IFC, Washington, DC.

———. 2016b. "Investing in Women along Agribusiness Value Chains." Report by the IFC Gender Secretariat, IFC, Washington, DC.

———. 2016c. "Supreme Poultry: Poultry Processing, South Africa." Case study, IFC, Washington, DC.

———. 2017a. "Handbook for Integrating Gender Smart Solutions in MAS-AS Smallholder Supply Chain Projects." Draft document, IFC, Washington, DC.

———. 2017b. "Investing in Women: New Evidence for the Business Case." Report by the IFC Gender Secretariat, IFC, Washington, DC.

IFPRI (International Food Policy Research Institute). 2012. "Women's Empowerment in Agriculture Index." IFPRI, Washington, DC.

MSCI (Morgan Stanley Capital International). 2015. "Women on Boards: Global Trends in Gender Diversity on Corporate Boards." Research report, MSCI, New York.

Mukhebi, Adrian. 2004. "Kenyan Agricultural Commodity Exchange Limited (KACE)." Paper presented at the CTA Seminal on the Role of Information Tools in Food Security, Maputo, Mozambique, November 8–12. https://courses.cs.washington.edu/courses/cse590f/07sp/docs/Mukhebi.pdf.

Riisgard, Lone, Anna Maria Escobar Fibla, and Stefano Ponte. 2010. "Gender and Value Chain Development." Danish Institute for International Studies, Evaluation Study. Copenhagen. https://www.oecd.org/derec/denmark/45670567.pdf.

Silverstein, M., and K. Sayre. 2009. "The Female Economy." *Harvard Business Review* 87 (9): 46–53.

World Bank. 2016. "World Bank Group Gender Strategy 2016–2023: Gender Equality, Poverty Reduction and Inclusive Growth." Report No. 102114, World Bank, Washington, DC.

Additional Resources

Arlotti-Parish, Elizabeth. 2014. "Gender in Agribusiness: An Analysis of Gender Dynamics in Cash and Food Crop Marketing Clubs in Southern Malawi." Final report, Catholic Relief Services, Baltimore.

Baden, Sally. 2014. "Women's Economic Empowerment and Collective Action in Agriculture: New Evidence and Measurement Challenges." Policy Brief No. 68, Future Agricultures Consortium, Institute of Development Studies (IDS), University of Sussex, Brighton, U.K.

CGIAR (Consultative Group on International Agricultural Research). CGIAR Collaborative Platform for Gender Research. http://gender.cgiar.org/.

Chan, M.-K. 2010. "Improving Opportunities for Women in Smallholder-Based Supply Chains: Business Case and Practical Guidance for International Food Companies." Guidebook prepared for the Bill & Melinda Gates Foundation, Seattle, WA.

DFAT (Department of Foreign Affairs and Trade, Australian Government). 2015. "Gender Equality and Women's Economic Empowerment in Agriculture." Operational Guidance Note, DFAT, Canberra.

Dross, C. 2017. "Women and Agricultural Productivity: Reframing the Issues." *Development Policy Review* 36 (1): 1–16.

Farming First. https://farmingfirst.org/women_infographic/. [Resources on women in agriculture]

GMSA (Groupe Mobile Speciale Association). 2014. "Women in Agriculture: A Toolkit for Mobile Services Practitioners." Guidebook prepared by the mWomen and mAgri programs of GSMA, London.

ICRW (International Center for Research on Women). https://www.icrw.org/.

IFC (International Finance Corporation of the World Bank Group). 2017. "The Business Case for Women's Employment in Agribusiness." Report, IFC, Washington, DC.

IFPRI (International Food Policy Research Institute). "Topic: Gender." https://www.ifpri.org/topic/gender. [Webpage on gender with links to useful resources]

Jiggins, J., R. K. Samanta, and J. E. Olawoye. 1998. "Improving Women Farmers' Access to Extension Services." In *Improving Agricultural Extension: A Reference Manual*, edited by B. E. Swanson, R. P. Bentz, and A. J. Sofranko, 104–19. Rome: Food and Agricultural Organization of the United Nations.

KIT Publishers, Agri-ProFocus, and IIRR. 2012. *Challenging Chains to Change: Gender Equity in Agricultural Value Chains*. Amsterdam: KIT Publishers.

Oxfam GB. "Gender Transformative and Responsible Agribusiness Investments in South East Asia (GRAISEA)." Program overview: https://policy-practice.oxfam.org.uk/our-work/food-livelihoods/graisea.

UN Women (United Nations Entity for Gender Equality and the Empowerment of Women). http://www.unwomen.org/en.

UN Women, UNDP (United Nations Development Programme), UNEP (United Nations Environment Programme), and World Bank. 2015. "The Cost of the Gender Gap in Agricultural Productivity in Malawi, Tanzania, and Uganda." Report of UN Women, UNDP, and UNEP, New York; World Bank, Washington, DC.

World Bank. 2011. *World Development Report 2012: Gender Equality and Development*. Washington, DC: World Bank.

———. 2017. "Women in Agriculture: The Agents of Change for the Global Food System." Feature story, March 7. http://www.worldbank.org/en/news/feature/2017/03/07/women-in-agriculture-the-agents-of-change-for-the-food-system. [World Bank resources on women and food systems]

World Bank and UNCTAD (United Nations Conference on Trade and Development). 2018. "Empowering Women." Responsible Agricultural Investment (RAI) Knowledge into Action Note No. 20, World Bank, Washington, DC; UNCTAD, New York. http://documents.worldbank.org/curated/en/283681521091071945/pdf/124295-BRI-PUBLIC-KN20.pdf.

CHAPTER 8
PARTNERSHIPS FOR SUSTAINABLE VALUE CHAINS

KEY MESSAGES

⇒ Partnerships among diverse stakeholders including private, public, not-for-profit, and community actors proliferate in smallholder-based supply chains.

⇒ Multistakeholder partnerships help businesses navigate multiple issues that affect smallholder agriculture, bridge cultural divides, manage risks, and address broader sectorwide issues (regarding, for example, labor or the environment).

⇒ Partnerships often enable stakeholders to address sectorwide issues that would not be addressed by business without additional support.

⇒ Maximizing Finance for Development (MFD) is a new approach to crowd in and leverage private sector investment while optimizing the use of scarce public resources to achieve the 2030 sustainable development goals.

⇒ Partnerships are often essential for companies seeking to deliver on the public commitments they have made on environmental and social issues.

⇒ They also provide a vehicle for the public- and private-good interventions needed to unlock win-win farmer-community-business solutions.

⇒ Partnerships can be transaction-cost-intensive, but agribusiness can avail itself of the growing experience on best practices and the key pillars for strong collaboration.

Types of Agribusiness Partnerships

Agribusiness partnerships generally fall into several categories:

- *Commercial partnerships based on contracts or agreements with other single entities.* If such partnerships involve smallholder produce, the business partners may be producer organizations (POs), traders, or other intermediaries. This type of relatively standard business partnership—covered earlier in chapter 3 (on POs) and chapter 6 (on yield gaps)—is not the focus of this chapter.

- *Multistakeholder partnerships for value chain or sector coordination.* These partnerships are often mechanisms for precompetitive collaboration—that is, multistakeholder collaboration to address important issues that are central to all commercial players and more cost-effectively tackled together (for example, deforestation, upholding labor standards, or smallholder capacity development).

- *Public-private partnerships (PPPs) that involve coinvestment from public finances because of the expected public-good benefits.* Examples include MFD agriculture area development programs, food security programs, climate change initiatives, and other issues covered by the United Nations (UN) Sustainable Development Goals (SDGs).

This chapter explores the multistakeholder partnerships that are ubiquitous in global smallholder-based value chains—be they for value chain coordination or the larger-scale PPPs that have far-reaching commercial and development goals.

Drivers of Multistakeholder Partnerships in Smallholder-Based Value Chains

If you want to go quickly, go alone. If you want to go far, go together.

This African proverb is an apt one for the benefits of partnerships. For many agribusinesses, until recently, the preferred modus operandi would have been to focus on areas of core competence: sourcing from their own plantations or global markets or selling inputs through their own distributor networks. For important linked activities, they could either contract with another provider or take on new roles themselves. Some companies specialized in smallholder crops for sustainability reasons or because smallholders were an important source of that product, but, in general, these were the exception.

However, as the drive to source more produce increases, fewer parts of the world have the scope to establish plantations or acquire large tracts of land. Working with other suppliers, including smallholder farmers, is therefore—of necessity—becoming more important in global value chains. Even if land were available for the required concessions, there are attendant reputational risks, such as perceived loss of sovereignty and threats to national food security. Hence, sourcing from smallholders is an alternative strategy. For some firms, this is uncharted territory, while others have already embarked on this journey. Both groups realize that smallholder sourcing requires different ways of working, perhaps having to consider factors that historically they would have considered well outside their remit.

Interest in partnerships is a response by firms to the need to navigate this expanding branch of the supply chain. There is an element of inherent tension: firms and smallholders do not share identical goals, concerns, and perspectives, and sometimes they may seem worlds apart. There are private- and public-good benefits to developing those supply chains, with the latter normally outside the purview of a global firm. The pace may seem slow for the firm and perhaps transaction-cost-intensive, but the effort is worthwhile if it helps secure future supply. In addition, such partnerships are essential for companies if they are to deliver on their public commitments regarding environmental and social issues. Hence the relevance of the African proverb: going together, to go far.

There has been a clamor around partnerships in food supply chains—as seen, for example, in these statements by Cargill, Unilever, Nestlé, and the International Business Leadership Forum, respectively:

- "We know we cannot achieve our goals alone, therefore we work in partnerships with a wide range of public, non-governmental and private stakeholders. We harness the scale, expertise, and reach of our business to these partnerships to achieve change in key areas. . . ."[1]

- "We believe that market transformation and the conversion to a fully sustainable palm supply chain can only be achieved through partnership and collaboration with all stakeholders, including customers, governments, suppliers, civil society groups, and [nongovernmental organizations]."[2]

- "We benefit from engaging with diverse stakeholders and, by working together, we maximise what can be achieved."[3]

- "Sourcing of agricultural products from smallholder farmers is a classic example in which companies may need to work with government extension services to provide technical support, [nongovernmental organizations] to help develop cooperatives, and finance institutions to help fund farmer capital costs" (Stibbe 2012).

There is nothing new in business partnerships—whether business-to-business or business cooperation with the not-for-profit sector, government, and communities. At their best, partnerships promote efficiency gains, allowing each partner to focus on what it does best. Similarly, when firms engage with smallholders, they must tackle issues that can be more effectively addressed in collaboration with other organizations in the following ways:

- Interactions between a (single) company and multiple smallholders create a need for a coordinating and organizing role, to link those parties.

- Differences of culture, connectedness, business outlook, education, and wealth between globally oriented firms and smallholders in underdeveloped rural areas can give rise to misunderstanding and distrust, creating a need for facilitation by trusted intermediaries able to bridge these different worlds and perspectives.

- Improving smallholder access to training, inputs, and finance in rural areas with weak services and markets is more easily achieved through coordinated actions among businesses, trainers, researchers, local government, and donors.

- The need to navigate multiple interests in rural economies—not just those of the smallholder suppliers—means there is a need to build understanding around shared objectives, linking with other rural stakeholders including local leaders.

- Certain challenging issues are most effectively tackled across multiple fronts with different partners, such as concerted action on environmental and labor issues.

- Issues of market failure and free riders (for example, side-selling) can be tackled by actions that coordinate, include, and enforce—underlining the role of partnerships.

- Risk of various types can be reduced or mediated through partnerships (for example, partial underwriting of smallholder income risks via blended finance arrangements or managing political risks by involving local leaders).

- The paramount need for innovation to promote productivity gains— of both a technological and an institutional nature—underscores the role of partnerships as a key factor in institutional innovation.

In addition, working with smallholders gives rise to valid questions about funding. Some activities may be appropriately and justifiably funded by the private sector. Other activities may support market development and integration but generate longer-term and wider social or economic benefits to which government and civil society can also contribute.

Value Chain or Sector Coordination Partnerships

The agricultural value chain is a continuum of diverse actors that play different roles in getting products from the fields to the shelves. Building partnerships along this continuum can strengthen the value chain and help rural households increase their food security and income. The partners with which firms engage can be diverse and include communities, POs, and nongovernmental organizations (NGOs); local government entities (extension services, research institutes, and training centers); commercial actors in the same sector (including off-takers, input suppliers, specialist training services, and banks); third parties engaged to help resolve disputes or certify production; and donor or development agencies.

Partnerships can play many important roles in value chain development:

- Contributing different areas of expertise, focus, and contacts or networks

- Involving researchers in needed applied or adaptive agricultural research

- Supporting technology transfer (see example of poultry production in box 8.1)

- Promoting scale by multiplying the resources available (for example, skilled trainers)

- Cutting costs through partner specialization in areas of comparative advantage

- Helping resolve disputes, particularly via an "honest broker" (third-party) role

- Permitting risk sharing

- Helping manage political risk

- Speeding up learning by being connected to parallel but relevant new developments

- Improving foresight via the varying reach, connections, and knowledge of partners

- Building coalitions of interest to address difficult sectorwide or multisector issues

- Allowing coordination and synergies among programs with linked but different interests (for example, using smallholder engagement as an opportunity to strengthen public health and nutrition messaging)

- Creating opportunities for innovation through synergies and learning among different players.

Value chain partnerships may be either formal (having a clear agreement or a memorandum of understanding) or informal (entailing collaboration or regular meetings, with a shared understanding of and benefit from a certain amount of coordination or complementarity). Usually bringing benefits to all parties, these partnerships may or may not include a financial agreement between the partners.

These partnerships tend to develop from one or more of the following situations:

- Companies seeking partners to address precompetitive issues

- NGOs, researchers, projects, or government agencies trying to link farmers to markets

- Government and donor program planning and project identification processes.

Public-Private Partnerships for Development

Partnerships are a way to address economic performance and reduce poverty. Among the UN SDGs for 2030, SDG 17 seeks to "strengthen the means of implementation and revitalize the global partnership for sustainable development."[4] The targets and indicators for SDG 17 highlight the role that partnerships can play in finance, trade, technology, capacity development, and policy and institutional coherence.

PPPs for agricultural development will work only if they have both commercial and development value. These partnerships take many forms, and different organizations use the term to mean different things.

BOX 8.1

In Practice: EthioChicken: Leveraging Public Support for Small-Scale Poultry Producers in Ethiopia

Background

EthioChicken is an innovative poultry company in Ethiopia that produces improved-breed day-old chicks (DOCs); affordable, blended feed; and technical advice aimed at the smallholder farmer market. The company has a unique distribution model to reach rural households, using a network of field agents. The improved breeds are dual-purpose chickens (combination genetics of both broilers and layers) that can lay up to 240 eggs per year—which is 5 times more than local chickens—and gain up to 2 kilograms in bodyweight in 90 days (male).

Distribution Model

Among the agents, 54 percent are small and medium enterprises that started their businesses through loans from microfinance institutions, while 46 percent are private agents who started their businesses using their own capital or loans from relatives. The average order size of the agents is 1,500 DOCs per cycle, which varies from 45 to 56 days among different regions.

The agents use different market channels to reach out to smallholders, including government livestock extension workers (or direct sales in local markets) or using commissioned individuals. EthioChicken provides each agent with door-to-door service delivery of DOCs, along with commercial feed, vaccines, and regular advisory services using its area sales managers. The company also provides information on where to source medicines, equipment, and other necessary inputs.

Partnership Model

Recognizing the importance of government support, EthioChicken entered into memorandums of understanding with the respective governments to get its support for poultry extension and access to improved breeds. As a result, the government leased out three of its hatcheries and breeding facilities to EthioChicken. The hatcheries and breeder facilities were refurbished by EthioChicken to meet international production standards, thereby making it possible for EthioChicken to produce 9 million DOCs per year by 2017—more than a sevenfold increase over previous production. The regional government also allowed the use of government livestock extension workers for the sale and promotion of new breeds to smallholder farmers and permitted importation of parent stock, quality vaccines, and equipment.

Results

EthioChicken's distribution model created jobs for more than 950 full-time employees and a network of more than 3,500 rural agents in 518 districts nationwide. The model has allowed EthioChicken to distribute 20 million DOCs and 20,000 metric tons of poultry feed since inception seven years ago, excluding 2018. This equates to approximately 2.5 million households within seven years of starting operations receiving improved poultry genetics—and a further predicted 1.5 million households in 2018. Independent studies indicated improved nutritional status for women and children under age seven, made possible through a distribution system that resulted in more chickens in villages and hence greater availability of eggs and meat.

There is no widely accepted definition of a PPP, but it generally involves a long-term agreement between government and the private sector in which services are provided to the public (often infrastructure services but increasingly in the social sector, too). This partnership is governed by a number of agreements, which could include a concession arrangement or a management contract (Moseley 2015).

PPPs are relatively new in the agriculture sector. The Food and Agriculture Organization of the United Nations defines a PPP for agribusiness development as a "formalized partnership between public institutions and private partners designed to address sustainable agricultural development objectives, where the public benefits anticipated from the partnership are clearly defined, investment contributions and risks are shared, and active roles exist for all partners at various stages throughout the PPP project lifecycle" (Rankin et al. 2016, viii). Its recent review highlights the following points:

- Partners have disparate interests but must reach a shared vision and objectives for the PPP to be successful.

- Clearly defined roles with rewards and incentives are important.

- Risks must be fairly shared, and the inclusion of risk management mechanisms is needed to protect the most vulnerable partners.

- Although small farmers may be included, there is little evidence to suggest that the poorest can benefit from such arrangements.

- There is ample scope to involve financial institutions in most agribusiness PPPs.

- Collective action is essential to promote inclusion and reduce transaction costs.

- Judicious land governance and transparent decision making and budgetary processes are needed.

- More monitoring and evaluation of PPPs is needed to distill lessons from this rapidly developing modality.

PPPs to Promote Transformative Change at Scale

In recent years, there has been strong and growing interest in large-scale PPPs to transform country or area economies, with public finance to support infrastructure development as well as other activities. These partnerships result from multistakeholder dialogue, consultation, and planning, particularly in the public sector at the early stages (at the country level and internationally). But private sector engagement and direction is key to their ultimate success.

MFD is a new approach based on working with governments to crowd in the private sector while optimizing the use of scarce public resources. The rationale is that the investments needed to achieve the 2030 SDGs are far greater than those available from governments and donors alone. Crowding in more private investment requires increasing the space for private sector activity, improving the policy and regulatory environment, and considering options for using public financing to improve private incentives and to reduce transaction costs and risks, including blended finance solutions.[5]

While these actions can help induce more private investment, there is still a critical need for public resources to finance essential public goods and services such as human capital, agricultural research, and complementary public infrastructure. In the agribusiness sector, the MFD initiatives can be focused on where the private sector is already investing in agricultural value chains. MFD requires multistakeholder partnerships among firms, financial institutions (including multilateral financial institutions), governments, and donor organizations. Such partnerships ensure comprehensive approaches that foster innovation, strengthen markets, and promote competition (box 8.2).[6]

BOX 8.2

Maximizing Finance for Development in Afghanistan

An example of the Maximizing Finance for Development (MFD) approach is Afghanistan, where the World Bank Group is supporting a transformation of the underdeveloped raisins sector. The World Bank is providing financing to enhance farmers' agricultural practices and introduce new drying technologies through the National Horticultural and Livestock Project; IFC will provide a working capital facility and advisory services; and the Multilateral Investment Guarantee Agency (MIGA) will provide guarantees against the risk of war and civil disturbance. The combination of these interventions will catalyze private sector investments in Rikweda Fruit Process Company who will develop a greenfield, modern, local raisin processing facility. These efforts are expected to improve yields and incomes for about 3,000 small-scale farmers who will gain access to a reliable processor and reap higher prices for their raisins.

Among the PPPs spearheaded by the World Economic Forum's (WEF) New Vision for Agriculture initiative Grow Asia and Grow Africa are prominent examples (ASEAN and WEF 2015; Grow Africa 2017). Grow Africa—founded by the WEF and the African Union's development program, New Partnership for Africa's Development—facilitates collaboration by governments, international and domestic agriculture companies, and smallholder farmers to lower the risk and cost of investing in agriculture and to improve the speed of return to all stakeholders.

The Grow Africa partnership consists of the founding members and 230 companies that have signed letters of intent to invest, along with their government countersignatories, the donor organizations that fund the Grow Africa Secretariat, and a small number of expert collaborators (companies that work with Grow Africa on specific issues). The broader Grow Africa network includes farmers, civil society, and development and research organizations.

The Beira Agricultural Growth Corridor (BAGC) Initiative in Mozambique is another example of a PPP promoting transformative change in agriculture and agribusiness. In partnerships such as this one, public and private players each contribute their own complementary solutions: public funds are leveraged to support the infrastructure development and public-good aspects of the development, helping create the conditions in which private players are willing to invest. The BAGC shows how agribusinesses can work with smallholders to create value added and market-based growth (box 8.3).

Various mechanisms help fund these partnerships. For example, the World Bank Group created a $2.5 billion International Development Association (IDA) Private Sector Window to catalyze private sector investment, with a focus on fragile and conflict-affected states.[7]

BOX 8.3

Matching Grants for Partnerships Targeting Value Chain Development

Matching grants are frequently used to support multistakeholder partnerships for value chain development. Companies find these a useful mechanism to support work on precompetitive and public benefit issues, including smallholder organization and training.

Broadly speaking, matching grants fall into two categories: partnership mechanisms such as challenge funds, and market system development programs.

box continued

BOX 8.3

Matching Grants for Partnerships Targeting Value Chain Development *(Continued)*

Partnership Mechanisms

Often used to initiate partnerships with the private sector, challenge funds and other types of partnership mechanisms have clearly defined strategies for sharing the costs and risks of private investments in a frontier or emerging market, based on proposals from businesses. Private companies are invited to submit proposals, subject to specified criteria.

Examples include the Food Retail Industry Challenge Fund (United Kingdom); the Innovation Fund of the Ethiopian Netherlands Trade Facility for Agribusiness (ENTAG); the Africa Enterprise Challenge Fund (an initiative of the Alliance for a Green Revolution in Africa [AGRA]); and the U.S. Agency for International Development's (USAID) Agribusiness Market Development matching grants.

Market System Development Programs

These grants aim for sustainable improvements in the systems in which the poor live, through catalytic interventions. They tend to result from development planning (by donors or NGOs or governments) and can include a wide range of activities, based on a thorough analysis of market failures and weaknesses. For example, they may combine technical assistance, brokering, business environment reforms, and a matching grant. In this case, commercial partners are often identified proactively by the development actors.

Both types of matching grants will require a legally binding agreement up-front, usually specifying the matching grant or cost sharing. Market system development programs will often involve complementary activities outside the collaboration, such as advocacy for improving the business environment through other partners. With partnership mechanisms, donor involvement tends to be more arm's-length, whereas market systems development programs tend to have more hands-on involvement by donors, with a strong focus on performance data.

Source: DCED 2015.

Another funding mechanism is the Global Agriculture and Food Security Program (GAFSP), which supports both public and private initiatives. GAFSP is a global effort that pools donor resources to fund programs focused on increasing agricultural productivity to reduce poverty and increase food and nutrition security. GAFSP targets countries with the highest rates of poverty and hunger.

The GAFSP public sector window, managed by the World Bank, helps governments with national agriculture and food security plans.[8] Its private sector window managed by IFC (and supported by the governments of Australia, Canada, Japan, the Netherlands, the United Kingdom, and the United States) provides long- and short-term loans, credit guarantees, and equity to private sector companies to improve productivity growth, deepen farmers' links to markets, and increase capacity and technical skills.[9]

GAFSP's private sector window uses blended finance solutions and IFC's expertise and knowledge to support projects in the agriculture sector, which might not otherwise attract commercial funding because of perceived high risks in the sector. GAFSP funding is coinvested alongside IFC funding, but the private sector window takes it one step further: addressing market failures by providing affordable funding with less demanding terms. This model allows GAFSP to invest in early-stage or riskier projects that hold high potential for development impact and financial sustainability as well as to partner with companies that include farmers as part of their overall value chain. The private sector window also helps to build capacity through its extensive advisory services, providing on-the-ground training and advice for businesses and farmers in improving farmer productivity, strengthening standards, reducing risks, and mitigating climate change effects.

To date, GAFSP's private sector window has approved 51 investment projects in 25 countries for total funding of $260.4 million, of which more than $158 million has been disbursed. In addition, a total of 47 advisory service projects in 27 countries have been approved for a total of $13.2 million. The private sector window has reached more than 874,000 farmers, most of whom are commercial smallholders, semi-commercial smallholders, or subsistence farmers living in extreme poverty. More than 152,000 of these smallholders are women. The GAFSP private sector window has also provided direct employment to 4,178 people, more than half of whom are women.

GAFSP is committed to helping meet the UN SDGs to end poverty and achieve food security in every corner of the globe by 2030. It focuses exclusively on the regions and sectors where significant progress will be required to meet several of the SDGs, including ending poverty (SDG 1) and meeting the hunger and food security (SDG 2), gender equality (SDG 5), and climate change (SDG 13) goals (UN 2015).

Effective Strategies and Best Practices for Building Strong Partnerships

Conducting a Stakeholder Analysis

In the initial planning stages of a program, it may be useful to conduct a stakeholder analysis—particularly if the firm does not know the area or actors well. A stakeholder analysis is the process of systematically gathering and analyzing qualitative information to determine whose interests should be considered when developing or implementing a policy or program. It is usually conducted by a consulting or research organization with appropriate experience, although many excellent guides are available that clearly explain the steps involved. For a firm, this analysis can help identify potential partners and may highlight potential conflicting interests in the proposed catchment area (Grimble 1998).

Understanding Key Elements of Successful Partnerships

There is no single formula for successful partnerships for agricultural innovation and productivity, but pillars of good practice include the following (BIAC 2014):

- Make sure there are mutual benefits.

- Develop clear agreements.

- Identify obstacles.

- Build in an appropriate level of transparency.

Although partnerships have much to offer, it is prudent to anticipate and seek to address certain potential issues from the outset—namely concerning shared objectives; transaction costs; clarity about roles, funding, and reporting; dispute resolution; and how risk is shared and managed.

Shared Objectives

It is clear that having shared objectives and a shared vision is a prerequisite for successful partnerships, but all guides and case studies emphasize the importance of this. The reality is that partnerships can beneficially connect different organizations from different spheres with different perspectives, so time may be needed to work through where they agree (and disagree) as well as how they will work together.

Companies may need to identify staff who understand development perspectives or provide training, while government and NGO partners will also find they need to adapt to and embrace the different views and approaches of their partners. In some circumstances, it may even be useful to use a professional facilitator initially. However, there is no point in including any more partners than are needed; there should be mutual benefits and clear roles for all partners. It is certainly worth taking time over this at the outset, to reduce later problems.

Transaction Costs

Partnering creates its own transaction costs: to meet, to travel, to coordinate, to communicate effectively, and to reach agreement—all of which can be exacerbated by differences of organizational culture, language, and emphasis. Some organizations are used to holding long meetings, where everyone has their say, while others are accustomed to shorter coordinating meetings, with detail reserved for follow-up discussions among those directly involved. Thus, it is worth considering ways to minimize these transaction costs, including the following:

- *Simplifying the collaboration and meeting agendas,* sticking to what really needs to be worked at together (and using the principle of subsidiarity: the idea that the central body should focus only on those tasks that cannot be performed at a more local level)

- *Holding informal events* that support team building and foster more effective working relationships, particularly because individuals from different organizations are unlikely to know one another well

- *Selectively using new technologies that facilitate communication,* where possible, but recognizing that face-to-face contact is important in building relationships

- *Rotating meeting places* among partners unless one obvious place is clearly the best place to meet

- *Acquiring or using staff who understand development—and NGOs,* such as in Heineken's interesting approach: it seconds one of its local sourcing staff to the NGO that is providing agronomic assistance.

Clarity about Roles, Funding, and Reporting

It is important to divide tasks and agree on clear roles and responsibilities, based on each partner's unique skills, experience, and resources available. Incentives to reward those roles are needed to generate commitment. Partnerships work best where all partners have a strong incentive for the initiative to succeed but where there is also interdependency among the partners.

Clarification on costs and funding is also important. Some partners may show interest because they have unrealistic funding expectations of other partners or external sources. There should be agreement on priority activities and their costs. Those issues need to be surfaced and worked through early in the collaboration. If the partners plan to seek funding from third parties such as donors, a strategy should be agreed upon. In its absence, partners may be competing for the same funds, giving outsiders the impression of poor coordination.

Sometimes partnerships emerge in response to a donor funding opportunity for which collaboration among, for example, communities, firms, NGOs, and government is a requirement. However, if the partnership is not really based on shared objectives and complementarity, it is likely to be frail and short-lived.

If external funding is involved, there will be a reporting requirement. With development funding, this role will often fall to the NGO or technical partner, which is likely to have more experience in this type of reporting. Nonetheless, there should be clarity on which partner will lead and coordinate the reporting; what type of information is needed from which partners; and when, and with whom, it may be shared (noting that commercial information may be sensitive). Some development organizations and programs support partnerships with matching grants (box 8.4), including funds to cover the costs of activities of a public-good nature (those generating longer-term or wider social and economic benefits, whose costs firms find it hard to recoup).

Dispute Resolution

It is useful to anticipate the potential for misunderstanding and give attention to areas where this might arise. Although roles and funding are common causes of disagreement, there are a few areas where it is helpful to have a clear agreement and strategy:

- *Confidentiality and intellectual property.* Some partners may attach more importance to intellectual property matters. The development of a memorandum of understanding (MoU) is good practice for clarifying these points and reducing the scope for disagreement. The MoU can also specify how disputes will be resolved (including potentially different mechanisms, depending on the issue of concern), as further noted below.

BOX 8.4

In Practice: The Beira Agricultural Growth Corridor: A PPP Promoting Agribusiness Growth and Smallholder Development in Mozambique

Partnership and Financing Model

The Beira Agricultural Growth Corridor (BAGC) Initiative, launched in 2010, aims to promote increased investment in commercial agriculture and agribusiness in Mozambique. It is a partnership between the government of Mozambique, private investors, producer organizations, and international agencies including International Finance Corporation and the World Bank. London-based AgDevCo, a BAGC partner, leverages funds from public and private sources to provide long-term, flexible risk capital structured to help early-stage businesses reach profitability and scale. It combines financial support with advisory input for the agribusinesses in which it invests.

Empresa de Comercialização Agricola (ECA) was established in 2011 with start-up capital support from AgDevCo (with funding from the BAGC initiative). As an agriprocessing company focusing on maize, ECA's approach illustrates many of the best practices highlighted earlier in this handbook: leveraging farmers' groups to work with large numbers of smallholders; offering different packages of support from which farmers can choose (the basic package being the most popular, although even this has enabled farmers to double their incomes); and offering both rewards and penalties to promote loyalty. In addition, it purchases maize from neighboring communities, where yields and output have also improved.

Results

By 2016, it is estimated that more than 6,000 smallholders had seen their incomes increase, and ECA's purchases of maize from noncontracted farmers exceeded those from contract farmers. By this time, ECA's staff had also grown to 98 full-time staff. ECA's state-of-the-art milling facility has enabled it to secure markets with large buyers (SAB Miller and Cargill) while also developing products that can be sold to local retailers.

For the BAGC initiative, this is just one example of how public and private resources can be mobilized to achieve a $1.7 billion investment target and annual farming revenues of $1 billion per year—ultimately promoting economic growth in Mozambique by realizing the potential of its local resources to supply growing domestic markets for agriproducts.

Sources: "ECA," AgDevCo (accessed April 3, 2018), https://www.agdevco.com/our-investments/by-investment/ECA; Hystra 2015.

- *Connections between groups.* Firms should consider employing some team members with strong "bridging skills"—people who can connect easily across these potentially different groups and perspectives. This ability will be important, anyway, in connecting firms to smallholders. It is important to listen to partners' concerns; they are only likely to deepen if ignored.

- *Dispute resolution procedures.* Partnerships should provide for how disputes will be resolved. One option is to have an "honest broker" partner. NGOs often play this role in partnerships between smallholders and the private sector, particularly if the former are weak in their negotiating position with companies.

How Risk Is Shared and Managed

Risk should be shared fairly among partners, and appropriate risk management mechanisms should be included where necessary. These could include insurance, guarantees, subsidized loans, secure purchasing or minimum price contracts, business management training for POs, and appropriate provisions in the case of force majeure (Rankin et al. 2016).

The final chapter of this handbook highlights some new and emerging partnership developments in sector transformation—underscoring the potential of win-win partnerships for increased productivity and development.

Notes

1. "Enhancing Livelihoods through Partnerships across the Value Chain," Unilever (accessed June 22, 2017), https://www.unilever.co.uk/sustainable-living/global -partnerships/enhancing-livelihoods-through-partnerships-across-the-value -chain.
2. "Partnership and Collaboration," Cargill Palm 2020 Roadmap (accessed June 22, 2017), https://www.cargill.com/sustainability/palm-oil/palm-partnership-collaboration.
3. "Partnerships and Collective Action," Nestlé in Society, Creating Shared Value (accessed June 22, 2017), http://www.nestle.com/csv/what-is-csv/stakeholder -engagement/partnerships-alliances.
4. "Sustainable Development Goal 17," Sustainable Development Knowledge Platform, United Nations (accessed June 27, 2017), https://sustainabledevelopment.un.org /sdg17.
5. Blended finance is the strategic use of development finance for the mobilization of additional commercial finance toward the SDGs in low- and middle-income countries (http://www.oecd.org/dac/financing-sustainable-development/development -finance-topics/blended-finance.htm).

6. https://www.ifc.org/wps/wcm/connect/7a43aec7-0164-4ec7-bfe8-82b99d293a26/IFC-AR17-Section-1-About-IFC.pdf?MOD=AJPERES.

7. "IDA18 Private Sector Window," International Development Association (accessed November 15, 2017), https://ida.worldbank.org/financing/ida18-private-sector-window.

8. For more information, see "Public Sector Window," Global Agriculture & Food Security Program (GAFSP) (accessed April 3, 2018), http://www.gafspfund.org/content/public-sector-window.

9. For more information, see "Private Sector Window," GAFSP (accessed April 3, 2018), http://www.gafspfund.org/content/private-sector-window.

References

ASEAN and WEF (Association of Southeast Asian Nations and World Economic Forum). 2015. "Grow Asia Partnership." Overview brochure, WEF, Geneva.

BIAC (Business and Industry Advisory Committee to the Organisation for Economic Co-operation and Development [OECD]). 2014. "Public-Private Partnerships for Agricultural Innovation and Productivity: Views from the Private Sector." BIAC Issues Paper, OECD, Paris.

DCED (Donor Committee for Enterprise Development). 2015. "Matching Grant Schemes & Systemic Approaches for Private Sector Development: Differences and Complementarities." Private Sector Development Synthesis Note, DCED, Cleveland, OH.

Grimble, R., 1998. *Stakeholder Methodologies in Natural Resource Management.* Chatham, UK: Natural Resources Institute.

Grow Africa. 2017. "Grow Africa: Partnering for Agricultural Transformation." Brochure, Grow Africa Secretariat, Johannesburg.

Hystra. 2015. "Smallholder Farmers and Business: 15 Pioneering Collaborations for Improved Productivity and Sustainability." Research report, Hystra, Paris.

Moseley, M. M. 2015. "What Are Public Private Partnerships?" Vimeo presentation (last updated October 3, 2015), World Bank, Washington, DC. http://ppp.worldbank.org/public-private-partnership/overview/what-are-public-private-partnerships.

Rankin, M., E. Gálvez Nogales, P. Santacoloma, N. Mhlanga, and C. Rizzo. 2016. *Public-Private Partnerships for Agribusiness Development: A Review of International Experiences.* Rome: Food and Agriculture Organization of the United Nations (FAO).

Stibbe, Darian. 2012. "To Achieve Inclusive Business, Companies Must Ramp Up Their Understanding and Capacity for Partnering with Other Societal Sectors." *The Leadership and CSR Blog from IBLF* (International Business Leaders Forum), June 21.

UN (United Nations). 2015. "Transforming Our World: The 2030 Agenda for Sustainable Development." A/RES/70/1, UN, New York.

WFP (World Food Programme). 2016. "WFP Boosts Food Security by Connecting Smallholder Farmers to Global Markets." News release, January 20. https://www.wfp.org/news/news-release/wfp-boosts-food-security-connecting-smallholder-farmers-global-markets.

Additional Resources

Brouwer, H., and J. Woodhill. 2015. *The MSP Guide: How to Design and Facilitate Multi-Stakeholder Partnerships.* Wageningen, Netherlands: Wageningen UR Centre for Development Innovation.

FSG (Foundation Strategies Group). 2015. "Ahead of the Curve: Insights for the International NGO of the Future." Report, FSG, Boston.

Nelson, J., and B. Jenkins. 2016. "Tackling Global Challenges: Lessons in System Leadership from the World Economic Forum's New Vision for Agriculture Initiative." Report of the Corporate Social Responsibility (CSR) Initiative at the Harvard Kennedy School, Cambridge, MA.

PBA (Partnership Brokers Association). http://www.partnershipbrokers.org/. [An international professional body for those managing and developing collaboration]

PPP Knowledge Lab. https://pppknowledgelab.org/. [World Bank-hosted resource of several multilateral organizations with links to resources on public-private partnerships]

PPP Lab. http://www.ppplab.org/. [Links to resources on public-private partnerships]

Pynburn, R., and J. Woodhill, eds. 2014. *The Dynamics of Rural Innovation.* Amsterdam: KIT Publishers.

Thorpe, J., and M. Maestre. 2015. "Brokering Development: Enabling Factors for Public-Private-Producer Partnerships in Agricultural Value Chains." Report, Institute of Development Studies (IDS), Brighton, U.K.; International Fund for Agricultural Development (IFAD), Rome. https://www.weforum.org/projects/new-vision-for-agriculture.

WEF (World Economic Forum). 2010. "Realizing a New Vision for Agriculture: A Road Map for Stakeholders." Report of the New Vision for Agriculture initiative, WEF, Geneva.

———. 2016. "Building Partnerships for Sustainable Agriculture and Food Security: A Guide to Country-Led Action." Report by WEF's New Vision for Agriculture Initiative in collaboration with Deloitte Consulting. WEF, Geneva, January. http://www3.weforum.org/docs/IP/2016/NVA/NVAGuidetoCountryLevelAction.pdf.

CHAPTER 9
MEASURING RESULTS

KEY MESSAGES

➡ Just as firms routinely monitor and measure business performance results, so they must also evaluate their smallholder agriculture supply chain performance.

➡ Companies find it hard to measure development or social impact.

➡ Farm-level impacts are important: farmer well-being is key to supply chain security, and companies can use this to self-promote and account to others, too.

➡ The applications that are transforming agribusiness engagement with smallholders can also provide important monitoring information.

➡ New tools are available that simplify and speed the collection and analysis of field data, including computer-assisted personal interview systems using smartphones and tablet computers.

➡ Income can be measured using rapid assessment tools including poverty scorecards and a new computer-assisted survey tool called "SWIFT"; such tools are also available to measure food insecurity and diet diversity.

The Business Case for Measuring Results

As with any new initiative and investment—whether commercial, governmental, nongovernmental, or even personal—it makes sense to monitor the implementation to see whether it is working as intended and delivering the anticipated results. Companies often refer to key performance indicators (KPIs): metrics of business performance or progress against a set of targets or industry benchmarks. A firm running an advertising campaign to boost sales will review the outcome to see whether the campaign was successful—and wish to understand the relative performance of certain aspects, such as whether the message or medium or target group was right.

That logic applies equally to a new development in the value chain. For example, a bank with a new credit line for farmers will want to know whether there has been uptake, whether farmers are paying back their loans, whether the initiative has been profitable, and whether there are future prospects for expanding the program. Going a step further—depending on its mandate, business strategy, and perhaps the origin of the fund—the bank will wish to know whether and how farmers have benefited. Or a veterinary medicine company that has decided to train local agrodealers (so they can provide better sales backup and train farmers at their stores) will want to know whether the training has made its products more likely to be used correctly, whether sales are increasing because of that intervention, and so on.

The collection and analysis of data is important, useful, and pervasive in business and development practice. It is common practice to initially test a new approach via a pilot and use the data collected from the pilot to modify the approach. The growth of mobile computing capacity and internet access has fueled expectations about data quality and availability—and if impact can be demonstrated with convincing data, it will attract more attention from senior management. With wider rollout, timely monitoring data can signal a need to adapt approaches, or it may support "kaizen" continuous improvement approaches.[1]

Moreover, agribusiness firms increasingly want to substantiate claims of positive impact on local farming populations. They also need to understand outcomes to reduce exposure to brand-damaging risks, such as from poor working conditions or environmental harm. Independent evaluation findings can underscore a firm's commitment to sustainability among the broader public.

In short, "what gets measured, gets managed." Rigorous results measurement allows a firm to

- *Track progress, steer activities, and plan*: for example, crop volume projections may signal the need for more storage capacity.

- *Account for the use of resources*: perhaps to the board, donors, farmers, and certification agencies.

- *Learn*: for example, what really works, and what are the costs and benefits?

- *Self-promote* and convince others.

This chapter serves as a primer on this potentially vast topic. It aims to do the following:

- Explain key concepts.

- Steer firms through key steps and considerations for data collection and analysis.

- Highlight how firms can simplify this task by, for example,

  ◦ Selectively using data collected as part of firms' own management systems

  ◦ Understanding the growing range of tools and devices that make data collection and analysis easier and quicker

  ◦ Recognizing more-complex areas where expert input is advised

  ◦ Drawing upon the many excellent information resources on this topic.

- Offer practical advice, insights, and examples.

Monitoring and Evaluation: Process and Impact

A distinction is usually made between "monitoring" and "evaluation." *Monitoring* (regular checking) covers such questions as these:

- Is the program on schedule?

- Is it meeting its KPIs? Is it proceeding as planned?

These data are generally easier to collect because it is often done through existing systems and processes (and hence sometimes called "*process* evaluation").

Evaluation—in particular, *impact evaluation*—considers bigger questions, generally over a long period, requiring careful design to ensure the validity of the results concerning questions such as the following:

- Did the supply chain investments lead to improved crop or livestock quality and quantity at the times they were required?

- Does the program deliver significant benefits to smallholders?

- Has bank lending to farmers made them good customers for other banking products?

- Has the program had significant unforeseen side effects, good or bad?

In general, impact evaluation can happen only when a project is well advanced or after its conclusion—although regular monitoring data may contribute useful information that can be incorporated into the evaluation's analysis and provide interim pointers on the direction of change.

A baseline survey, which probes specific indicators for the development intervention or partnership, provides a useful reference point against which both monitoring and evaluation data can be compared (Samji and Sur 2006; Save the Children 2014), as the next section explores.

Strategies and Best Practices for Supply Chain Data Collection and Analysis

Identify and Plan for Information Needs from the Outset

The first consideration is to identify *what* to monitor. This relates directly to the question: how do you define success? The answer helps to identify how success can be assessed or measured. It is also useful to consider the obstacles that might block success. These two aspects—how success can be measured and the obstacles that might impede success—form the building blocks of a monitoring framework.

It is much easier to identify and plan for data collection at the outset than to "retrofit" monitoring into a program later, particularly if the opportunity to gather baseline data has been missed. If necessary, forms that field agents routinely fill out (including electronic forms on mobile devices) can be adjusted to include additional monitoring data, and farmer training can also emphasize the importance of particular farm records and how data may be collected or recorded.

To measure change, a baseline is needed. Baseline surveys should be conducted before the intervention begins, although in practice, they are often conducted in the early stages of an intervention. They can vary enormously in scope, but the basic principle is the same: if change is expected in certain variables and the firm wants to measure that change (for example, in coffee yields per hectare, number of farmers using fertilizer on target crops, farm household income, women's nutritional status, and so on), the information must be collected both initially and at subsequent periodic intervals. Depending on the topics of interest, this could be relatively straightforward or a huge undertaking, but recent developments in rapid assessment tools are simplifying this task.

It is almost inevitable that additional data needs will be identified during implementation; the point is simply that it is best to identify as much of this as possible, as early as possible. Keep in mind the two broad categories of information: First, *monitoring* of activities and their immediate or straightforward outcomes (such as sales of fertilizer, number of farm visits, and number of training events held). Second, more *evaluative* data, which will help answer bigger-picture questions, but may be harder to obtain and involve specific "one-off" or sporadic data collection.

Also note that initiatives involving multistakeholder partnerships (as covered in chapter 8) may entail reporting and data collection obligations that differ from normal firm practice. Even a firm with strong corporate social responsibility (CSR) capability may find that the level of reporting rigor and scope for donor-funded projects is more demanding.

SMART Indicators and Objectives

SMART is a useful acronym to remember the nature of good indicators and objectives:

- **S**pecific
- **M**easurable
- **A**chievable
- **R**elevant
- **T**ime-Bound

An example of a non-SMART objective is "to increase farmer coffee yields." A SMART objective, however, might be "to increase yields of coffee of participating farmers by 30 percent by the end of the 2019/20 season, as measured by sales of green bean equivalent (50 percent processing loss and 12 percent moisture content) in kilograms per hectare."

SMART objectives or indicators are much easier to monitor and will yield results that can be compared across regions or programs, because they are so precise.

A Logical Framework for Planning and for Measuring Results

For decades, the development community has used a tool called a "logical framework" or "logframe." The inclusion of such a framework is a requirement for many donor funding applications (Jensen 2013). Developing a good logical framework is not necessarily easy or quick—and it is not a perfect solution—but it nonetheless has some advantages for planning and for monitoring and evaluation (M&E), and it should be developed early in the planning process, following several guidelines:

- The framework summarizes the logic of an intervention—identifying a goal (or overall objective) and planning the lower-level results or outputs to contribute to its achievement, with activities in turn contributing to the achievement of each of those outputs. This is sometimes referred to as the "theory of change" (that is, a representation of the intended goal and then mapping backward to identify the preconditions for its achievement, as illustrated in table 9.1).

- The range, quantity, and nature of inputs or resources needed for a project can also be estimated during the preparation of a logframe.

- Key assumptions are identified, with the logic sequence, "if those outputs are achieved and if those assumptions hold true, then the goal will be achieved."

- That logic should be developed by a team (often during a facilitated workshop), drawing on its combined perspectives and expertise while fostering understanding and ownership of program goals and strategy.

- Developing the logframe subjects the logic and the assumptions to intense scrutiny: if we do x and y, will that really be enough to make z happen? The integrity of the framework means that all its components and their precise wording are critical; it also makes it easier to identify elements that contribute little to key objectives.

- The framework requires that the objectives be described by SMART indicators (described earlier), for which sources of information must be identified—so M&E is built into the program design. The focus on how achievement can be measured injects realism, simultaneously reducing the scope to defer measurement or be vague about how results will be measured.

TABLE 9.1 Sample Logframe for a Coffee Off-Taker

Logframe component	Summary	Indicators	Verification	Assumptions
Goal	Increase volume of coffee purchased	Metric tons purchased	Purchase receipts	
Objective	Increase productivity of coffee suppliers from X to Y within Z years	Tons per hectare	Logbooks maintained by farmers	• Coffee prices remain above X • Farmers do not side-sell to other buyers
Outcomes	Farmers adopt improved coffee growing practices	Number of farmers using improved pruning practices and replanting with new seedlings	Logbooks maintained by farmers, supported by field survey	• Extreme weather events do not affect yields • No unexpected incidence of coffee pests and disease
Outputs	• X seedlings sold per year • X farmers trained in correct pruning methods	• Number of trees sold • Number of farmers trained	• Records of nursery owners • Reports of field staff	• Farmers' interest in improved coffee sustained • Farmers can access sufficient labor to follow improved practices
Activities	• Establish X coffee seedling nurseries • Conduct 15 on-farm training events on pruning	• Number of nurseries established • Number of training events held	• Weekly reports from field staff • Monitoring visits by supervisors	• Bad weather does not delay establishment of nurseries • Timely purchase of motor bikes enables field staff to meet training targets

Choice of Metrics

The hierarchy of logic in the framework mirrors the nature of the M&E data required: at the lower level, activities are monitored, whereas at the higher level, the broader questions are in focus. (For example, is the program achieving its aim? Is the project design right?)

The term "metrics" refers to what will be measured. Figure 9.1 shows how the appropriate choice of metric changes, depending on the level of achievement described. For each level of achievement, the metric should

FIGURE 9.1 Sample Process of Choosing Metrics to Measure Results

INPUTS	ACTIVITIES	OUTPUTS	OUTCOMES	IMPACTS
• The resources that went into the project • Example: Funding, technical expertise, administrative and logistical support	• The specific actions undertaken within the project • Example: 15 on-farm training sessions on proper pruning techniques	• The activities' immediate results • Example: 250 farmers trained on proper pruning techniques	• How the outputs changed participant behavior • Example: The percentage of farmers adopting new pruning techniques	• How the outcomes affected the overall program goals • Example: The percentage increase in productivity after three years

closely describe what is expected to happen. These metrics provide a measure against which the achievements can be assessed. Choosing the right metrics for the logframe can be essential to ultimately improving the business's practices.

Data Sources

There can be many sources of data, and it is not always necessary to conduct in-depth surveys. Useful information may be contained in the firm's own records; producer organizations or farmers may keep (or be encouraged to keep) certain records; local information may be available from the district authority or from surveys conducted by other organizations; and information may also be available from satellite imagery, drones, or remote sensing.

Even if further information is needed, there may be some shortcuts. For instance, it is not necessary to ask all farmers about the frequency of bus services to the market town or about traders coming to the area. It may be easier to obtain this information from other sources, including the traders themselves.

If a survey is conducted, a carefully drawn, robust, representative sample may be quite adequate, without the necessity to survey all farmers. Focus group discussions with selected groups can be useful in probing complex questions. (Qualitative approaches are discussed in greater detail in the "Tools Available for Data Collection" section that follows.)

Results Measurement

Monitoring: Management Information for Firms and Other Stakeholders

Most agribusinesses will already have in place appropriate systems for the collection and analysis of routine monitoring data, perhaps including digitized systems. When working with smallholders for the first time, existing tools may need to be adapted—particularly if the field agent is to play a greater role in collecting and verifying farmer data, because smallholder farmers' own records are likely to be poor.

Many suitable off-the-shelf systems are now available to support the operation and management of agribusiness value chains with small-holder suppliers. This is a rapidly developing field, but examples of agri-business supply chain management software include Cropin SmartFarm, FarmERP, Farmforce, SAP Rural Sourcing, and SourceTrace (also see chapter 6).

Aside from the management information generated, these types of farm management records can help firms answer questions such as "What percentage of farmers in the supply chain are pruning their cocoa trees correctly?" It provides a means of assessing the implementation of the program but does not explain how the results were achieved, nor can the results be generalized beyond the direct beneficiaries being evaluated.

Firms may also collect data to check for compliance with standards and certification. For this, digital systems are available that can dramatically reduce costs (as covered in chapter 4).

In summary, the information collected from a firm's system of monitoring is useful in several ways:

- Data collected before and after an intervention can be used to assess a change in behavior or outcome.

- This monitoring is useful for telling stories about a firm's smallholder strategy and for demonstrating results that contribute to improved livelihood outcomes.

- The assessment may help to identify which aspects of implementation were more successful than others.

- It may also give firms an indication of a strategy's cost-effectiveness, particularly with digitized, integrated data systems and depending on the analysis conducted.

Impact Evaluation

Distinct from monitoring for management and for standards compliance, as noted, impact evaluations take place less frequently; seek answers to bigger, more complex questions; and may need careful design if they are to generate valid information. Evaluations may assess outcomes and impact but can also review the intervention strategy (such as whether it was effective).

There is no single one-size-fits-all methodology; the approach used depends on the scope of the evaluation; how the information will be used; the complexity involved (such as the extent to which multiple factors must be considered); the resources (including the skill set) available; when the results are needed; and the degree of reporting rigor required (depending on, for instance, whether the firm wishes to make public claims about its achievements). In rural societies, where obtaining accurate data can be difficult and multiple factors affect outcomes, evaluations often combine multiple methods to better understand processes and outcomes.

Although evaluations tend to take place once an intervention is reasonably well advanced, they seek to answer questions that may also be important to answer at an early implementation stage. Early assessments, whether they are termed "evaluations" or not, nonetheless seek preliminary answers to important evaluative questions—and those results may be used to adapt program design. Evaluations may entail specific survey work and also draw upon data that is collected over a longer period (including monitoring data).

If firms lack specific in-house expertise in evaluation, they should seek outside expert advice. Moreover, if the firm wishes to make public statements based on such investigations, the use of independent external evaluators will underscore the impartiality and validity of those results.

Farm trials can be used for impact evaluation. Randomized control trials (RCTs), sometimes used in an evaluation, seek to compare participant outcomes with the outcomes of nonparticipants. The results may enable the firm to make a claim attributing changes in the participant outcomes to a particular project, program, or intervention. However, undertaking RCTs in agriculture can be challenging and costly because large sample sizes (as many as 400–500 farmers) may be needed in each group to ensure statistical validity.

To establish a control group, one strategy is to stagger implementation into two or more rounds. Farmers who will receive training or other interventions in subsequent rounds serve as a control group for the farmers receiving training in the first round, but this is still challenging because the "control" group may still learn some of the new techniques and change their practices as a consequence of contact with the first group. This approach also requires sufficient time lag (at least one crop cycle) between implementation rounds to assess the program results.

Quasi-experimental studies can also be used to compare the group receiving program assistance with a group of nonparticipants. However, unlike in RCTs, the two groups are not randomly assigned (so there may be less "purity" in the control group). Instead, program managers identify a group that is similar enough to the participant group that it may serve as the counterfactual. Quasi-experimental methods can be particularly useful in agricultural interventions because they are more cost-effective when working with groups of farmers (as in the India case study, box 9.1).

BOX 9.1

In Practice: Powerful Evaluation Results Scale Up Sugarcane Farmer Training in India

Background

DCM Shriram Ltd. produces sugar in four mills operating in northern India. It buys cane from farmers and supplies sugar to Coca-Cola in India. As part of an advisory service project with International Finance Corporation, DCM Shriram undertook a quasi-experimental evaluation of a program to improve low sugarcane productivity among its smallholder suppliers.

The program taught farmers improved farm-level practices using classroom training and tools such as extension manuals and farmer flip charts. The goal was to train 2,000 farmers in DCM Shriram's supply chain on new agronomy practices and increase productivity of trained farmers by 25 percent over three years.

Evaluation Method

The evaluation matched groups of 207 participating and 207 nonparticipating (control group) farmers. The control group was constructed based on field size, financial status (no overdue loans), and distance from the mill. Evaluators compared the two groups' productivity at key implementation stages, using crop-cutting surveys among a subsample. Qualitative analysis (farmer case studies and focus group discussions) supplemented the trial data.

Results

The results of the evaluation showed an 86 percent increase in productivity among farmers who received training versus a 19 percent increase in productivity for the control group. The results were so powerful that DCM Shriram's management initially scaled up the training to reach 12,000 farmers. By 2017, DCM Shriram was engaged with 150,000 sugar farmers, all of whom it trains to increase sugarcane yields.

Impact Metrics for Smallholder Supply Chain Interventions

Number of Farmers Reached

The most aggregated and basic metric a firm can use is "farmers reached," which counts the number of farmers who participated in a supply chain intervention. For firms with multiple supply chain interventions affecting farmers across various sectors using diverse methodologies, the "farmers reached" metric provides a single summary indicator of the scale of the firm's work with smallholder farmers. If more detail is required, it can be broken down, for example, by gender, district, and type of intervention or approach.

However, this metric does have some limitations. "Farmers reached" does not quantify the improvement in farmers' livelihoods or indicate how their agricultural production changed. Nor does it give firms information about how the supply chain was strengthened as a result of an intervention. Therefore, although "farmers reached" is a useful summary of reach or scale, it should not be the sole impact metric used on a single project.

Productivity Gains or Losses

Most farmer training programs intend to increase productivity (for example, tons of wheat per hectare, tons of fish per unit of pond area, or liters of milk per cow). Firms building traceable supply chains usually want to determine their suppliers' productivity to forecast crop procurement and calculate farm income. However, measuring productivity can be challenging for many reasons:

- Productivity data self-reported by farmers are not always reliable (Beegle, Calogero, and Himelein 2012). Hence, triangulation is advisable (adding some combination of farmer interviews, crop-cutting, farmer records, and buyer interviews).

- When smallholders sell crops, the crops may not be properly dried, which may lead to discrepancies in reporting. Crop weights at farm level should be adjusted to the standard moisture levels for the crop, to be comparable with the data of the Food and Agriculture Organization of the United Nations (FAO) or other published statistics.

- Because crops are often sold wet, many traders use volume measures, which may not correspond to standard metric volumes. To ensure data accuracy, firms should determine the correct conversion factors.

- Most tree crops are harvested a few kilograms at a time, over the course of several months or the entire year. Unless farmers keep written records, it is difficult for them to remember each sale.

- If farmers are part of an outgrower scheme that provides inputs in exchange for crops at harvest, they may be reluctant to report crops that have been sold to other buyers (side-selling).

- Many smallholders plant more than one crop on the same land (intercropping). If the planting density for each crop is not optimal, yields will be lower than expected and not easily comparable with yields reported elsewhere. Nonetheless, producing two crops from the same land may increase overall profitability and reduce risk for the farmer.

- Smallholders often do not know the exact size of their farms, especially if they have irregularly shaped plots or more than one plot. Even within a single plot, some areas may not be planted, because of the terrain. Without accurate area measurement, productivity cannot be determined accurately.

Crop Quality

As with prices, firms usually collect data on the quality of the crops they purchase. These data can be used as part of impact measurement. The challenge is to maintain the data in a form that facilitates program design and helps to measure the results of training interventions. Examples of quality metrics include moisture content, grain size, percentage of broken grains, or presence of foreign material.

Farmer Income

Reliably tracking farmer incomes is challenging but important. If new practices or inputs do not improve household well-being, farmers are unlikely to keep using them (unless there is an enforceable regulatory requirement). Yet farmers rarely keep track of the costs associated with growing each individual crop on their plots, and their self-reporting information on net income may not be reliable.

Standard monitoring systems (further discussed below in the "Tools for Data Collection" section) will enable the calculation of net revenue from the firm (output purchases net of input costs) per farmer or per unit area of crop—and allow that metric to be tracked over time. Specialized tools are also available to track changes in farm household income.

Special Investigations or Research

Aside from program monitoring and evaluation, from time to time the need may arise to better understand a particular issue. Although other information collected during program implementation may be useful, it is hard to predict in advance what sort of information may be needed. However, if the issue is potentially sensitive, it is important to engage appropriate expertise and demonstrate commitment to an impartial external process.

Sometimes this need can arise on short notice. For example, a documentary shown in the United Kingdom in 2000 that highlighted child slavery on West African cocoa plantations (Woods and Blewett 2000) led chocolate and cocoa companies to rapidly commission research to better understand the situation. (For more about this case, see chapter 4.)

Tools Available for Data Collection

Until recently, surveys were conducted using small armies of enumerators, equipped with clipboards and forms. The information collected was subsequently input into a computerized database, which could then be analyzed to generate information and answer specific questions. That has changed, and enumerators are now much more likely to use tablet computers or even smartphones. Surveys are conducted directly by phone, too, often in an automated way.

Global Positioning System (GPS) coordinates can now identify a farm or a field, making repeat visits and follow-up easier. Questions about farm size and yield can also be supported with the use of GPS tools. Careful survey design and training of enumerators is still important, but the direct use of computers short-cuts the process of data input and analysis (and sometimes recommendations, too). Scope for human error is also reduced.

Standard Farm Management Packages for Monitoring Data

As the use of digital technology becomes more ubiquitous in everyday tasks, firms can access important monitoring data in real time. Field agents regularly record information. Companies track input sales or crop purchases—and use GPS or smartphone apps and software to monitor the day-to-day activities of their field teams, generating real-time analysis and graphics. The collection of georeferenced data is also important because it permits spatial analysis.

These tasks (data collection, analysis, and the development of recommendations) are being transformed by the use of smartphones, tablet computers, and faster internet with wider reach, combined with rapid software development. In addition, there is now scope to interface with landscape data derived from remote sensing or drone surveillance, as well as with site data captured via handheld devices, for example, for soil and water testing.

Agribusiness as a whole has embraced this digital revolution, and many digital systems are now available to support firms working with multiple smallholders, covering the following areas:

· Supply chain management and traceability

· Supervision and management of field staff

· Extension management

· Precision agriculture.

Firms are using these systems for data collection, analysis, and reporting; to make payments and monitor loans; to track goods and services; to connect service providers with clients; for inventory; to support farmers with advice and weather forecasts; for targeted marketing, and so on. This digitization short-cuts much of the more-routine monitoring data collection. Standard systems for supply chain management and traceability will, for example, do the following:

· Allow entry of basic farmer identity information, such as address and plot size

· Track farmer use of inputs and cost of inputs

· Show sales of output per unit area

· Record payments made to the farmer.

Many standard systems include the option to customize data collection and surveys—to address particular issues that fall outside the standard list of variables. It is then easy to generate farmer-level and campaign-level monitoring reports, covering variables such as these:

· Number of farmers reached

· Quantity of inputs used per farmer (averages and measures of distribution)

- Farmer yields (productivity)—again, averages and distribution
- Farmer net income from the activity per unit area (or per unit animal and so on).

Records can be separated or disaggregated for different groups of farmers (in different zones, possibly also identifying males and females) or for farmers using different technologies (for example, with or without irrigation). Monitoring reports can be produced almost instantaneously, covering a selected set of variables with visualization choices, and they are remotely available to supervisors once the field officer has entered the data and connected to the internet.

Survey Tools to Measure Farmers' Household Income

Household Surveys

Large surveys can be used to collect data on household consumption, which is a proxy measure for household income (as in the World Bank's Living Standards Measurement Study [LSMS]). Responses to questions about consumption (including consumption of food produced on-farm) tend to be more reliable than responses to questions about income. Their purpose is generally to understand income patterns and trends in a large area or across an entire country (showing differences among different household types or areas, changes over time, and so on) but not to monitor an individual household's well-being.

To generate reliable results, these surveys cover 1,000 or more households with questionnaires that could take several hours to complete. Ideally the survey would be repeated after 5–10 years. Given high poverty (especially rural poverty) in low- and middle-income countries, these surveys are important but are mostly undertaken by governments, possibly with donor support. In a sense, the detailed information they provide substitutes for much of the data collected in high-income countries by a variety of other means (such as aggregate data from tax returns, market research by telephone, and metadata on the use of services). For rural populations that still operate largely in the informal (unrecorded) sector, LSMS surveys still have a place.

The planning, design, field testing, data collection, and analysis of traditional household surveys is a specialized field—and one that is generally costly and time-consuming. Government permissions may be required, teams of enumerators will need to be trained, and it may be several years before the full report of the survey is available.

SWIFT Rapid Assessment Tool

The Survey of Well-being via Instant and Frequent Tracking (SWIFT) was developed by the World Bank Group to estimate household income and expenditure data in a cost-effective, timely, and user-friendly manner (figure 9.2). LSMS data (from an earlier survey) and advisory input

FIGURE 9.2 Survey of Well-Being via Instant and Frequent Tracking (SWIFT)

WHY SWIFT?

Income data is scarce. Collecting reliable income data is costly, time-consuming, and complex. Countries spend millions to collect data and it takes them more than two years to produce poverty statistics. Lacking data often makes the poor invisible, marginalized, and voiceless.

SWIFT measures poverty rates for your project. So you don't have to.

SWIFT IS QUICK, RELIABLE, AND LOW-COST

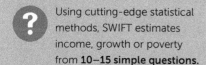 Using cutting-edge statistical methods, SWIFT estimates income, growth or poverty from **10–15 simple questions.**

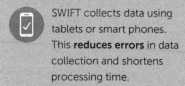 SWIFT collects data using tablets or smart phones. This **reduces errors** in data collection and shortens processing time.

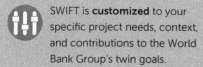 SWIFT is **customized** to your specific project needs, context, and contributions to the World Bank Group's twin goals.

SWIFT FOLLOWS 4 SIMPLE STEPS

 Survey design and data collection
Enumerators interview the household members either face-to-face or over the phone.

 Data recording and formatting
Results are recorded on tablets and sent to a cloud server.

 Analysis and reporting on results
Data are downloaded and analyzed.

 What you can do with the data
Results can help you monitor and report on your impact, and better target your project design.

Source: ©World Bank, n.d. Further permission required for reuse.

are required to identify poverty correlates and use those in the design of a short questionnaire, which is then administered using computer-assisted personal interviewing (CAPI) software (further discussed in the CAPI section below and in box 9.2). A World Bank team supports the survey design and process, while the firm arranges for the survey to be implemented.

Questions and reporting can be tailored to the client's needs, but a typical output would be a short report with graphics of 5–10 pages. SWIFT can be used to collect socioeconomic baseline data or to answer specific questions. For example, one firm wanted to know whether side-selling was associated with poverty. The survey established that there was indeed a link and was able to use the information to adapt its approach to reduce side-selling.

Poverty Scorecards

Scorecards are a simple and quick tool that assesses whether households are above or below a "poverty line" (either a national poverty line or an internationally accepted standard) or even a program target. A score is generated based on the response to a short set of questions that probe characteristics of the household and the things they own, tailored to local circumstances (as shown, for example, in figure 9.3).

The scorecard results can be used to do the following:

· To indicate whether a household is above or below a poverty line

· To measure a group's poverty rate at a point in time, and hence to track changes in poverty rates for a group over time

· To target services or interventions.

The scorecard does not measure changes that occur above or below the poverty line.

Survey Tools to Measure Food and Nutrition Security

Food security is a key concern among low-income groups, including smallholder farmers. Changes in farming practices can affect food security unpredictably. Land may be diverted from food crops to cash crops, but increased income may not necessarily be used to meet food needs. It can be important to consider the food security impacts of an agricultural program—and build in mechanisms to ensure positive outcomes.

IFC projects employ two tools that measure diet diversity and food insecurity at the household level. These can be incorporated into data

FIGURE 9.3 Poverty Scorecard Example for Mozambique

Simple Poverty Scorecard for Mozambique				

Entity	Name	ID	Date (DD/MM/YY)	
Member:	_____	_____	Date joined:	_____
Field agent:	_____	_____	Date scored:	_____
Service point:	_____	_____	# Household members:	_____

Indicator	Response	Points	Score
1. How many members does the household have?	A. Eight or more	0	
	B. Seven	2	
	C. Six	7	
	D. Five	9	
	E. Four	15	
	F. Three	23	
	G. Two	30	
	H. One	34	
2. What is the main material of the floor of the residence (excluding kitchen and bathrooms)?	A. Uncovered, or other	0	
	B. Packed earth, wood/parquet, marble/granite, cement, or mosaic/tile	6	
3. What is the main material of the walls of the residence?	A. Reeds/sticks/bamboo/palm, wood or metal sheets, tin/cardboard/paper/sacks, or other	0	
	B. Adobe blocks, wattle and daub, cement blocks, or bricks	7	
4. What toilet arrangement does the household use in its residence?	A. None, or other	0	
	B. Latrine of any kind	6	
	C. Toilet connected to a septic tank	14	
5. What is the main source of energy for lighting in the residence?	A. Firewood, or batteries	0	
	B. LPG, oil/paraffin/kerosene, or candles	1	
	C. Other	3	
	D. Electricity, generator, or solar panel	5	
6. Does the household have a nonelectric or electric clothes iron?	A. No	0	
	B. Yes	3	
7. Does the household have a clock (wall, wrist, or pocket)?	A. No	0	
	B. Yes	4	
8. Does the household have a radio, stereo system, or cassette player?	A. No	0	
	B. Radio only	5	
	C. Stereo system or cassette player (regardless of radio)	7	
9. Does the household have a bicycle, motorcycle, or car?	A. No	0	
	B. Bicycle only	5	
	C. Motorcycle or car (regardless of bicycle)	15	
10. How many beds does the household have (single, double, bunk beds, or for children)?	A. None	0	
	B. One	2	
	C. Two or more	5	
Microfinance Risk Management, L.L.C., microfinance.com		Score:	

Source: Schreiner and Lory 2013.
Note: LPG = liquified petroleum gas.

collection for projects that are expected to affect households' ability to access sufficient, safe, and nutritious food to meet their dietary needs and food preferences. Diet diversity can be a good proxy measure for household food security, per capita daily caloric availability, household assets and education, and household income (Morseth and others 2017).

To measure food insecurity, IFC projects rely on the Food Insecurity Experience Scale (FIES) developed by the FAO. The instrument incorporates eight key questions, which may be available in local languages on the FAO website along with additional information to help enumerators (FAO 2017).[2]

To measure diet diversity, IFC has adopted the Food Consumption Score (FCS) tool from the United Nations World Food Programme. Before implementation of the baseline survey, the consultant firm (in consultation with IFC and its client) will be required to provide localized food examples for each of the dietary categories mentioned in the FCS tool (WFP 2008).

Qualitative Approaches Including Participatory Rural Appraisal

Qualitative methods are generally better at teasing out cause, process details, and variation within a group (for example, farmers describing the factors that affect their maize yields). With qualitative methods, enumerators use checklists and a set of tools and skills to elicit information. They include focus group discussions; key informant interviews; case studies; direct observation (for example, walking along a transect through a village and systematically recording certain types of detail); and other methods.

Participatory (or rapid) rural appraisal (as further discussed in chapter 7 on women's participation) uses these methods, which are sometimes good at establishing trends and orders of magnitude. They also provide the flexibility to probe an unexpected issue that emerges during fieldwork.

Moreover, participatory approaches centrally engage the stakeholders in the evaluation and in teasing out the lessons. This engagement may yield more accurate and richer insights, and stakeholders may take more ownership of the results and be more likely to address the lessons that emerge.

Almost all evaluations of rural interventions tend to be participatory, at least in part. Although this may appear straightforward, in practice, conducting a focus group discussion, for example, demands good facilitation skills and careful attention and interpersonal skills to probe the views of those who are quieter or less visible but whose perspectives may still be important. It is all too easy to hear only the voices of those who are most dominant or whose performance is apparently strongest.

It is often useful to use mixed methods. For example, initial qualitative work may inform the planning of a quantitative survey, to make sure it covers key issues. In certain circumstances, it is also considered good practice to follow up on quantitative results with qualitative research for a better understanding of those results—such as to probe *why* a certain trend is evident.

Computer-Assisted Personal Interviewing (CAPI) Systems

Quantitative surveys can now be supported and conducted using CAPI systems, including survey options available with supply chain management systems, such as Farmforce. These systems use handheld tablet computers or smartphones, eliminating the need to manually transfer data to a database, speeding up review and analysis, and reducing human error (for an example of one such system, see box 9.2).

BOX 9.2

SurveyCTO CAPI System Features

The SurveyCTO mobile platform (a product of Dobility Inc.) represents one example of the features that CAPI survey software can offer.

SurveyCTO includes these primary components:

- A central repository for both blank and filled-in survey forms, a website to assist in designing and managing surveys, and a universal web interface for users filling out forms online
- An Android app enabling data collectors to fill out forms on Android phones or tablets and to upload data after data collection to the SurveyCTO server (or, for more advanced offline setups, synchronized over local Wi-Fi networks)
- A desktop application that enables safe data downloading, transport, export, and processing, as well as data decryption, including on cold-room computers for the most sensitive data
- A built-in data monitoring and visualization tool that enables quick review of data (even encrypted data) as it comes in, right in a browser.

Source: SurveyCTO (accessed April 4, 2018), https://www.surveycto.com/.

Practical Considerations for Data Collection and Analysis

Adoption of a Learning Culture

A firm's staff should be a key source of information, and their knowledge of critical issues can help shape the focus of an evaluation. If possible, it is good to encourage a "learning culture" among staff. This means taking the time to understand disappointing outcomes and teasing out the lessons, applying the adage, "it is only a failure if we fail to learn from it." This is not always easy, because sometimes staff fear retribution if the results are poor and may try to cover up or transfer blame.

At the extreme, the absence of a learning culture can really obstruct understanding, innovation, and improvement by masking outcomes and contributory processes. Developing a learning culture usually requires deliberate actions—and clear management support—to make the time for the necessary processes and to explicitly recognize and value the learning.

Choice of In-House or External Teams

Several factors will affect a firm's decision to field the necessary skills in house or to look for external assistance:

- Scale of field operation and frequency of data collection and analysis tasks

- Skill set needed, depending on the issue to be probed and type of data to be collected and analyzed

- Whether the use of in-house teams will affect the reliability of the data collected or bias farmer responses (any more than would an external team)

- Genuine desire for external insights and perspectives

- How important it is that the work be seen as impartial, irrespective of the competence of in-house teams.

Normal monitoring can be competently handled in house, but evaluations and special studies often benefit from external assistance. Sometimes there is merit in a dual approach—using external assistance to help with design and analysis (and it is important to design the survey in the light of the planned analysis) and using in-house teams to carry out some of the data collection.

Although technological developments are making surveys easier to conduct and analyze, there is still a role for specialists in the design of questionnaire surveys (asking the right questions, of the right people, in the right way) and other survey instruments.

In partnerships, it is important that there be clarity on which partner is responsible for results measurement, and this should be mentioned in the memorandum of understanding (as further discussed in chapter 8 on partnerships).

Preparation of Enumerators, Surveys, and Special Considerations

Enumerators need training on conducting a survey so that they can go through it quickly, without misunderstanding the questions or asking them in a leading way—"You don't use fertilizer, do you?" versus "Do you use fertilizer?"—and so that they know how to record certain types of responses. It is useful to check that concepts, not just words, are well understood (for example, "access" can be understood in very different ways). They may need training in how to interact with respondents, too.

If a survey is to be conducted in a local language different from the language in which it has been developed, it is important that the translation be agreed upon. Surveys should also be tested before they are implemented. Certain questions may not work well in different languages and need to be changed. Questionnaires may need to be shortened if the interview takes too long.

Finally, the preparation may require special considerations for surveying particular groups (regarding language, gender, or indigenous peoples). For example, enumerators may have to work unusual hours to fit the respondents' schedules.

Choice of Data and Methods: Be Judiciously Pragmatic

It is often difficult to measure exactly the variable of interest—and to try to do so would be costly, with no guarantee of success. Smallholder income is an obvious example. Impacts may also take time to emerge. A scorecard measuring change in household assets may not detect immediate change because there may not *be* immediate change.

Often, the best option is to try to understand outcomes and results by considering a number of different measures and what they mean, when taken together. That implies choosing measurable metrics and mixing methods—particularly combining qualitative and quantitative approaches—to both measure and explain. It also requires experience to interrogate and interpret those results.

In the same vein, it is important to be discriminating in survey design—by asking only those questions likely to yield reliable answers and not asking those that can be answered by other means. Questions requiring farmers to recall detail are not likely to be answered well ("What was the price last year?" "How much crop was sold last year?"). Both farmers and enumerators can find long surveys tedious. Keeping them as short as possible will help ensure that they are completed properly.

It is always possible to dig deeper, to extend the scope of the survey or analysis, and to implement it with a larger sample. With any data collection, a cost-benefit perspective is helpful:

· Will a pragmatic approach deliver sufficient information?

· What would be the additional cost of obtaining more accurate data?

· How much additional benefit would that deliver?

It may be more cost-effective to triangulate data from multiple sources to generate more certainty than to seek a definitive and possibly elusive answer from a single elaborate survey.

Notes

1. "Kaizen," Japanese for "improvement," refers in many industries to a strategy or activities to continuously improve all functions, applied to all employees and processes daily.
2. For more information about the FIES instrument, including available languages and other information to help enumerators, see "Using the FIES" on the FAO Voices of the Hungry (accessed July 8, 2017), http://www.fao.org/in-action/voices-of-the-hungry/using-fies/en/.

References

Beegle, K., C. Calogero, and K. Himelein. 2012. "Reliability of Recall in Agricultural Data." Brief, Living Standards Measurement Study: Integrated Surveys on Agriculture (LSMS-ISA), World Bank, Washington, DC. http://siteresources .worldbank.org/INTSURAGRI/Resources/7420178-1294259038276/RecallBrief.pdf.
FAO (Food and Agriculture Organization of the United Nations). 2017. "The Food Insecurity Experience Scale: Measuring Food Insecurity through People's Experiences." Basics of the Food Insecurity Experience Scale (FIES), FAO, Rome.
Jensen, G. 2013. "The Logical Framework Approach." How-to guide, Bond, London. https://www.bond.org.uk/data/files/resources/49/The-logical-framework -approach-How-To-guide-December-2013.pdf.

Morseth, Marianne Sandsmark, Navnit Kaur Grewal, Ida Sophie Kaasa, Ann Hatloy, Ingrid Barikmo, and Sigrun Henjum. 2017. "Dietary Diversity Is Related to Socioeconomic Status among Adult Saharawi Refugees Living in Algeria." *BMC Public Health* 17: 621. doi:10.1186/s12889-017-4527-x.

Samji, S., and M. Sur. 2006. "Developing a High-Quality Baseline." PowerPoint presentation, World Bank, New Delhi, June 21.

Save the Children. 2014. "Baseline and Evaluation Design and Management." Session 5 of Monitoring, Evaluation, Accountability, and Learning (MEAL) introductory course, Save the Children in collaboration with the Open University, London.

Schreiner, M., and H. N. D. Lory. 2013. "A Simple Poverty Scorecard for Mozambique." Paper, Microfinance Risk Management LLC, Kansas City, MO. http://www.microfinance.com/English/Papers/Scoring_Poverty_Mozambique_2008_EN.pdf. (Accessed July 8, 2017)

WFP (World Food Programme of the United Nations). 2008. "Food Consumption Analysis: Calculation and Use of the Food Consumption Score in Food Security Analysis." Technical Guidance Sheet, Vulnerability Analysis and Mapping Unit, WFP, Rome.

Woods, B., and K. Blewett. 2000. *Slavery: A Global Investigation.* Documentary film, produced by True Vision of London.

World Bank. n.d. "SWIFT Rapid Assessment Tool." Brochure, World Bank, Washington, DC.

Additional Resources

IFPRI (International Food Policy Research Institute). http://www.ifpri.org/impact-assessment. [Resources on impact assessment]

Kessler, Adam, ed. 2015. "The 2015 Reader on Results Measurement." Update of the Donor Committee for Enterprise Development (DCED) Standard for Measuring Results, DCED, Cleveland, OH.

Kumar, K. 2006. "Conducting Mini Surveys in Developing Countries." Paper for the U.S. Agency for International Development Program Design and Evaluation Methodology Report, USAID, Washington, DC.

NRI (Natural Resources Institute). 1998. "Socio-Economic Methodologies: Best Practice Guidelines." NRI, Chatham, UK.

Poate, C. D., and P. F. Daplyn. 1993. *Data for Agrarian Development.* Cambridge: University of Cambridge Press.

SurveyCTO. https://www.surveycto.com/index.html.

Sustainable Food Lab. 2015. "Towards a Shared Approach for Smallholder Performance Measurement: Common Indicators and Metrics." Paper, Sustainable Food Lab, Hartland, VT.

USAID (U.S. Agency for International Development). "Livelihood Measurement and Assessment Tools" (last modified January 29, 2013), USAID Natural Resources Management and Development Portal, https://rmportal.net/library/content/tools/livelihood-measure-and-assessment-tools.

World Bank. Living Standards Measurement Study (LSMS), http://surveys.worldbank.org/lsms.

CHAPTER 10
FUTURE OUTLOOK

KEY MESSAGES

⇒ The agribusiness sector directly affects 8 of the 17 Sustainable Development Goals (SDGs) and has relevance to all the other SDGs.

⇒ Population growth and urbanization are driving significant changes in food markets in low- and middle-income countries.

⇒ Smallholders will take on growing importance in agribusiness supply chains, where the roles of women and youth are likely to expand and help transform the sector.

⇒ Farmers will become more professional with stronger links to local and international markets.

⇒ Global firms will be able to identify suitable rural business partners (producer organizations and other entrepreneurs) who meet accepted business standards.

⇒ Climate-smart agriculture is a growing focus and needed for both climate change mitigation and adaptation.

⇒ Technological advances are contributing to climate-smart solutions, simultaneously opening an astonishing menu of precision agriculture options—possibly even at the smallholder level.

➡ Technology is also transforming the possibilities for agribusiness to engage with smallholders—making traceability easier, reducing the cost and time required for communications and advisory input, making coordination easier, and opening new ways to aggregate dispersed smallholder output and demand for inputs.

➡ Parallel developments are improving the affordability of index-based insurance, in which there is increasing interest in the context of climate-change-related risk.

➡ Insurance nonetheless remains expensive, but take-up is expanding, supported by strategic "smart" public subsidies.

➡ Interest in healthy, nutritious, and safe food will continue to be an important focus.

➡ Strong partnerships will drive the development of more resilient and inclusive agribusiness to meet the food and socioeconomic needs of future populations.

Force Majeure: Challenges to Feeding the World in 2050

A convergence of economic, demographic, and environmental concerns has focused attention on how the world will feed itself in 2050. Volatile food prices since 2007 have underscored the frailty of the global food system, after a 30-year period of relative stability (figure 10.1). The world food crisis of 2007–08—followed quickly by further price rises and compounded by growing concern about climate change, competition for agricultural resources to produce biofuels, and degradation of environmental resources—exacerbated concerns about world food supplies.

Add to these exigencies the persistence of poverty and hunger, particularly among the rural poor in low- and middle-income countries. Malnutrition has also become a concern, in different ways, for both the poor and the less poor. Further pressure comes from youth unemployment and underemployment, including whether agriculture and agribusiness can provide sufficient (and sufficiently attractive) work for a large part of the world's expected 1.2 billion youths (ages 15–24 years) in 2050.

In the face of these collective conditions, an unprecedented coalition of interests—across and within countries and regions, in commerce, in government, in the not-for-profit sector, and among very different disciplines and sectors—has emerged to address the challenge of meeting the food needs of 9.8 billion people in 2050 (UN DESA 2017).

FIGURE 10.1 FAO World Food Price Index, 1961–2017

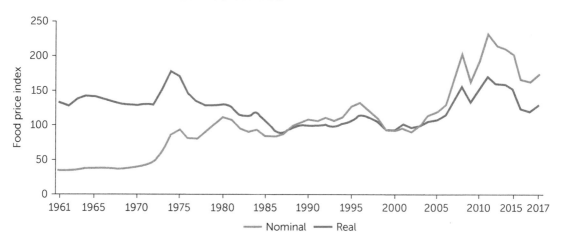

Source: FAO 2018, https://esa.un.org/unpd/wup/Publications/Files/WUP2014-Report.pdf.
Note: FAO = Food and Agriculture Organization of the United Nations. The nominal food price index is estimated by aggregating the international prices of a basket of five groups of food commodities, weighted by the average export shares of each group for 2002–04 (= 100). The real price index is the nominal price index deflated by the manufactures unit value index as reported by the World Bank (FAO 2017b).

The agribusiness sector has potential for wide-reaching development impacts. It directly affects 8 of the 17 United Nations (UN) SDGs for 2030—poverty, hunger, good health, clean water and sanitation, responsible consumption, protect the planet, life below water, and life on land—but it can contribute in all 17 areas (FAO 2017a). Areas of emerging development, with the potential to become increasingly important over the coming decade or more, are explored in this chapter.

Food Market Growth and Change in Low- and Middle-Income Regions

Although population growth has slowed in most higher-income regions, populations are still increasing in the low- and middle-income regions where most of the additional 2.2 billion people in 2050 (compared with 2015) will live, especially in Asia and Africa (UN DESA 2017). Some countries will see especially steep population growth: for example, the combined population of 12 Sub-Saharan African countries—320 million in 2015—is expected to double by 2050 and to double again by 2100 (FAO 2017b).

Moreover, with increasing urbanization, the global population increase will be seen mostly in urban areas, where an additional 2.4 billion people will live by 2050 (FAO 2017b), as shown in figure 10.2. (In contrast, the global rural population will show a net *decline* of roughly 200 million people in 2050 compared with 2015.)

FIGURE 10.2 Global Urbanization Growth and Projections, by Country Income Level, 1950–2050

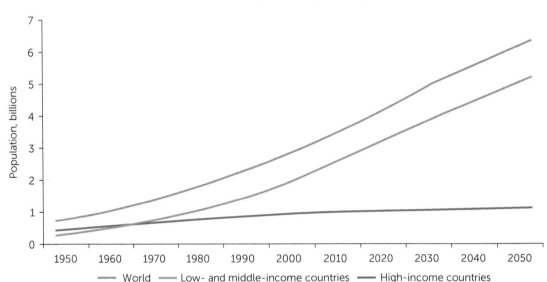

Source: UN 2014.

Wide geographical disparities in income will also continue (figure 10.3). This means that low- and middle-income regions will have large low-income urban populations. "Business as usual" investment would leave an estimated 650 million people (8 percent of the global population) undernourished in 2030 (FAO 2017b). This projection drives much of the interest in public-private partnerships and other means to increase supplies of affordable food, particularly for poor urban populations.

That overall trend notwithstanding, the urban middle class is growing rapidly—and, with it, increased demand for animal-source foods, processed and convenience foods, and supermarkets. For example, between 2016 and 2025, meat consumption in Sub-Saharan Africa is expected to grow more than in any other region (and, unusually, growth in consumption of beef is expected to almost match that of poultry) (OECD and FAO 2016).

As these trends emerge in low- and middle-income regions, the structure of the food industry is also changing—toward more vertical integration. Smallholders can benefit from these shifts wherever there are fair contracts between processors and producers. Those links are most effective where there is good infrastructure as well as strong producer organizations and related institutions (FAO 2017b).

FIGURE 10.3 Global Per Capita GDP Growth and Projections, by Country Income Group and Region, 2005–50

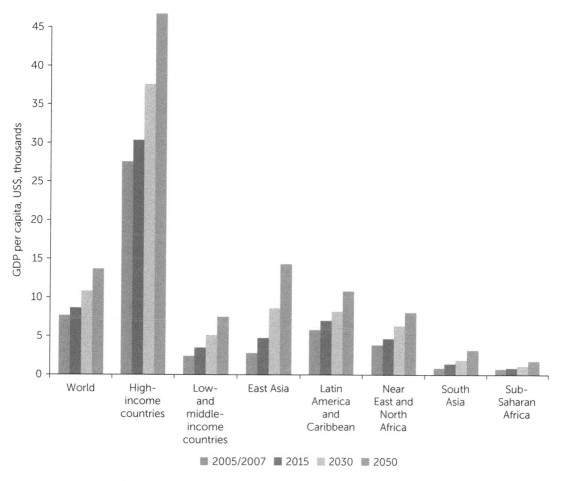

Sources: Alexandratos and Bruinsma 2012; FAO 2017b.
Note: Regional groups do not include high-income countries. Per capita GDP shown at 2005–07 exchange rate.

Advances Boost Potential for Climate-Smart and Precision Agriculture

Climate-Smart Agriculture

Agriculture, forestry, and other land uses account for about 24 percent of global greenhouse gas (GHG) emissions (of which roughly 20 percent is offset by the removal of greenhouse gases by carbon sequestration from forestry and other land uses) (Edenhofer et al. 2014). The emissions from agriculture come primarily from enteric fermentation

---

BOX 10.1

The World Bank Group Approach to Climate-Smart Agriculture

The World Bank Group describes climate-smart agriculture as an integrated approach to managing food-producing landscapes—cropland, livestock, forests, and fisheries—that addresses the interconnected challenges of food security and climate change. Climate-smart agriculture promotes a set of practices and business models that can help reduce emissions and build resilience. It aims to address both food insecurity and climate change by improving resistance to climate impacts, reducing greenhouse emissions, and increasing farm productivity. International Finance Corporation provides investments and advice that contribute to the three pillars of climate-smart agriculture."

*Source:*https://www.ifc.org/wps/wcm/connect/71c0bfd9-30ff-408c-af94-8907c262ddf6/Making+Agriculture +Climate-Smart_FINAL.pdf?MOD=AJPERES.

(methane from the digestive processes of livestock, making up about 40 percent of the agriculture emissions); manure being left on pasture (about 16 percent); and fertilizer use (about 13 percent).

Fueled in part by many decades of escalating GHG emissions worldwide, climate change is causing shifts in temperature and rainfall patterns and increasing the intensity and frequency of extreme weather events. Adaptation to these changes requires new agricultural practices, new varieties, and even new crops—as well as new risk management strategies. Several examples illustrate how smallholder crops are being affected:

- Extended rainy seasons in South Asia are altering cocoa and coffee drying practices.

- Drought in southern Africa is accelerating a shift toward minimum-tillage maize farming.

- Saltwater intrusion in coastal areas of Asia is causing a shift toward salt-tolerant rice varieties.

- Flooding in Asia is increasing demand for immersion-tolerant rice varieties.

The World Bank defines climate-smart agriculture (CSA) as an approach to managing landscapes—cropland, livestock, forests, and fisheries—that aims to achieve three "wins" (World Bank 2017):

- Increased productivity to improve food security and boost farmers' incomes

- Enhanced resilience to drought, pests, disease, and other shocks

- Reduced GHG emissions.

FIGURE 10.4 Climate-Smart Agriculture Opportunities for Agribusiness, by Crop Sector

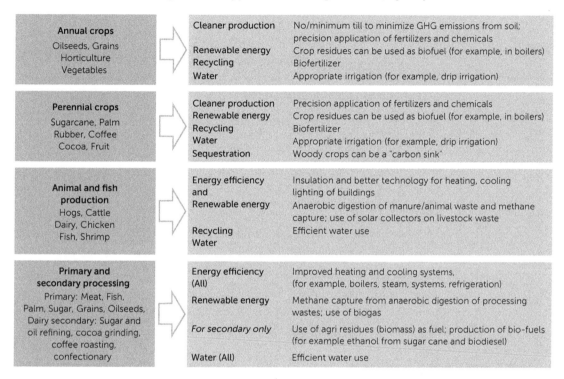

Annual crops Oilseeds, Grains Horticulture Vegetables	Cleaner production Renewable energy Recycling Water	No/minimum till to minimize GHG emissions from soil; precision application of fertilizers and chemicals Crop residues can be used as biofuel (for example, in boilers) Biofertilizer Appropriate irrigation (for example, drip irrigation)
Perennial crops Sugarcane, Palm Rubber, Coffee Cocoa, Fruit	Cleaner production Renewable energy Recycling Water Sequestration	Precision application of fertilizers and chemicals Crop residues can be used as biofuel (for example, in boilers) Biofertilizer Appropriate irrigation (for example, drip irrigation) Woody crops can be a "carbon sink"
Animal and fish production Hogs, Cattle Dairy, Chicken Fish, Shrimp	Energy efficiency and Renewable energy Recycling Water	Insulation and better technology for heating, cooling lighting of buildings Anaerobic digestion of manure/animal waste and methane capture; use of solar collectors on livestock waste Efficient water use
Primary and secondary processing Primary: Meat, Fish, Palm, Sugar, Grains, Oilseeds, Dairy secondary: Sugar and oil refining, cocoa grinding, coffee roasting, confectionary	Energy efficiency (All) Renewable energy *For secondary only* Water (All)	Improved heating and cooling systems, (for example, boilers, steam, systems, refrigeration) Methane capture from anaerobic digestion of processing wastes; use of biogas Use of agri residues (biomass) as fuel; production of bio-fuels (for example ethanol from sugar cane and biodiesel) Efficient water use

Source: IFC 2016.
Note: GHG = greenhouse gas.

Many agribusiness firms are setting carbon-neutral or carbon-positive targets, and International Finance Corporation (IFC) is supporting their commitments through investments and advice that contribute to one or more of the three pillars of CSA. Certain agribusiness sectors present opportunities for CSA and smallholders, particularly in relation to the annual and perennial crop sectors identified in figure 10.4 (IFC 2016).

Precision Agriculture

USDA's Agronomical Note No. 1 defines precision agriculture as "a management system that is information and technology based, is site specific and uses one or more of the following sources of data: soils, crops, nutrients, pests, moisture, or yield, for optimum profitability, sustainability, and protection of the environment." It implies the most efficient and sustainable use of land achieved through the use of technological advances (for example, systems powered by Global Positioning System [GPS] and Geographic Information Systems [GIS]) (NCRS 2007).

Technological advances are revolutionizing analytical capacity, as well as its granularity, cost, speed, and communicability. This is particularly true in the following areas:

- Communications (satellite and cellular)

- Surveillance (drones and satellites)

- Microtechnology for testing, monitoring, and mapping (handheld devices for soil, water, and leaf nutrient analysis, as well as sensors and GPS)

- Powerful computing capability (centralized and portable) supported by software development.

It may not be easy for smallholders to participate in all aspects of this agricultural revolution, but soil-testing devices are already being tried out with smallholders (as noted in box 10.2, among other examples of new technological potential). A subscription service even provides

---

BOX 10.2

Affordable Technology for Precision Agriculture: A Game Changer

Handheld Devices and Tools for Soil Testing

International Finance Corporation is working with partners in Papua New Guinea on a trial of small, handheld soil-testing devices that can be used by extension agents and lead farmers. There are now far more tools for soil analysis that can be used at the local level.

Crop Surveillance by Drone

Drones are now providing an affordable "eye in the sky," making aerial views (for example, of water-logging or patchy fertilizer application, neither of which may be sufficiently evident at ground level) accessibly priced. When used in conjunction with the mapping products now available (such as crop assessment and fertilizer recommendation maps), drone technology becomes even more powerful and cost-effective ($2–$15 per hectare), because it leads to efficiencies in input use (one client recorded increased earnings per hectare of $107).

box continued

Data from Sensors and Satellites

Topic-specific packages are available that use geographic information system (GIS) data, updated from sensors and satellites, to derive maps that are detailed to the field level. The maps give precise weather, water, solar radiation, and other information—in turn informing detailed, week-to-week decisions on agricultural operations (on timing, input use, and so on).

More Opportunities for Insurance

These developments in information and communication technology also help provide timely, localized, and objective data and maps on which weather-indexed insurance products can be developed and refined.

smallholders with a package combining real-time satellite data with a crop insurance policy (box 10.3).

From Big Data to All Data

"Big data" are extremely large data sets that may be analyzed computationally to reveal patterns, trends, and associations, especially relating to human behavior and interactions. They are being used increasingly in multifarious ways: Consumer purchase data can be used to quickly identify a pricing error or items that are in demand following, say, a hurricane. Google search patterns have been analyzed to help predict global flu trends, and big data analysis is one of the enablers for precision agriculture.

Large volumes of data are being ever more rapidly generated from a variety of sources, including mobile telephones, business transactions, social media, and information from sensors.

"The exponential growth of the digital economy has enabled the rise of business models based on the collection and processing of 'Big Data.' The use of big data by firms for the development of products, processes and forms of organisation has the potential to generate substantial efficiency and productivity gains, for instance by improving decision-making, forecasting and allowing for better consumer segmentation and targeting" (OECD 2016).

BOX 10.3

Weather Alerts, Agronomic Tips, and Crop Insurance for Smallholders

A new package deal combines agronomic tips (texted via short message service [SMS]) and weather-indexed insurance into a single product. Launched in March 2017, MUIIS—for Market-Led, User-Owned, ICT4Ag-Enabled Information Service—enables subscribing farmers to receive preseason tips to help them prepare their fields using best practices. Once the planting season begins, the MUIIS system uses real-time satellite data from partners like aWhere to evaluate each farmer-customer's field for risk, based on crop, weather, and growth stage. Farmers whose fields are forecast to have adverse weather conditions or to be at risk for poor performance based on agronomic metrics receive customized alerts warning them of the danger and recommending actions.

Subscribing farmers also receive a crop insurance policy covering their season's production. Unlike traditional crop insurance, where damages are assessed and payouts approved through site visits by agents, MUIIS insurance is weather-indexed. This means that payouts are approved based on satellite data readings on the weather at the farmer's field—eliminating the need for expensive site visits to farmer fields, which are particularly costly when farms are located in hard-to-reach areas.

Together, these two components of the MUIIS product give farmers the information they need to make climate-smart farm decisions and the confidence that if their crop fails, they will be compensated.

Source: Camp 2017.

However, dependence on big data alone can generate a distorted picture unless it is used in combination with careful sampling and design to make sure that it is representative of the group of interest. That is the underlying principle on which the development of the World Bank Group's SWIFT rapid assessment tool is based ("SWIFT" for Survey of Well-being via Instant and Frequent Tracking, as described in chapter 9).

This is an area of rapid development and change, but more sophisticated and accurate uses of big data in the future are likely to draw on such blended big data/small data approaches.

Smallholders: Standardized, Market-Integrated Business Partners

Rapid population growth in frontier and emerging markets, high incomes, and urbanization as well as improved infrastructure and technological advances are all contributing to the improved market integration of smallholder farmers—be they linked to domestic markets, where there has been transformation in recent years, or to global value chains.

An interesting new development, still at an early stage (and more thoroughly discussed in chapter 3), is to independently assess and establish a standard for farmers' organizations as well as other rural entrepreneurs such as agrodealers and crop collectors, based on their financial literacy and business management capacity.

Among these new efforts is the Agribusiness Market Ecosystem Alliance (AMEA). With support from IFC and other partners, AMEA aims to build a global quality system, bringing together complementary and like-minded organizations all sharing a belief in "farming as a business" and the promotion of more professional farmer organizations. Through its partnerships, AMEA provides a vehicle for the *certification* of assessors, trainers, and coaches and for the development of appropriate curricula for farmer organizations and other rural businesses. It also plans to keep a register of those accredited service providers. AMEA's goal is to promote farmer professionalism sustainably and at scale.[1]

Women: Key Players in Supply Chains—as Producers and Processors

Women's roles in agribusiness are receiving increasing attention—and in some regions, rural male outmigration is leading to the increasing feminization of agriculture. Firms are increasingly recognizing the considerable role that women play in supply chains as well as the specific areas in which women excel and can contribute more.

With this recognition comes increasing adoption of gender-smart approaches that address the inequalities that women face in access to the resources they need to improve their productivity. This is likely to be a growing focus over the coming decades.

Increasing Focus on Food Safety, Healthy Foods, and Nutrition

Reducing the triple burden of malnutrition (hunger, micronutrient deficiency, and obesity) and ensuring food safety will remain important concerns. Biofortification of crops and food is likely to grow in importance. Agribusiness firms will be under pressure to show that they are delivering in these areas—be it via their safe and healthy food or the impacts of their value chains on food producers in frontier and emerging markets.

Sector Transformation

Sector transformation is a new area of interest, emerging in response to a concern that smallholder performance often reaches a certain level of development that can be driven by the market but shows insufficient capacity for the *self-renewal* needed for ongoing growth and adaptation. Sector transformation approaches are a further step on the continuum to more professional and sustainable smallholder production. In a sense, they combine the ambition of traditional government-led sector development programs with strong market integration, to exploit synergies potentially capable of driving sustainable development at the farm level and in the sector, as characterized by the following:

- Functional partnerships among public and private sector stakeholders

- Demand-driven services

- Complementary sectorwide investments and regulation

- Sectorwide monitoring and learning.

The sector transformation approach is based on two principles: (1) that transformation only occurs if the incentives in the market encourage continuous improvement; and (2) that there must be sufficient value retention at the production base to reinvest in the sector with limited external assistance.

This effort faces multiple challenges—including alignment of stakeholders, resource mobilization, accountability, and safeguarding of a long-term strategy—but nonetheless represents a logical "next step" in the development of global agribusiness supply chains in which smallholders must play an increasingly important role (table 10.1).

Coalitions and Concerted Action on Challenging Issues

Chapter 8 explored the drivers and functioning of multistakeholder partnerships in agribusiness supply chains. The public-private interface is becoming increasingly blurred as recognition grows that the greatest scope for advance involves a vision and partnerships that cross those public-private boundaries (as required for the sector transformation discussed above, for example).

Firms are also likely to form coalitions to address issues that pose sectorwide or multisectoral challenges. Such coalitions could adopt multistakeholder strategies to correct poor or exploitative labor

TABLE 10.1 The Five Pillars of Sector Transformation

Sector alignment and accountability	Strengthening of demand	Public sector governance	Organization of the production base	Organization of the service sector
• Platform for sector dialogue, alignment, and coordination • Shared vision and interest: FQ and SQ • Joint strategy toward vision • Alignment of investments, technology packages, and farmer support measures • Monitoring, assurance, and learning	• Market alignment and discipline • Good buying practices • Product traceability	• Regulation and governance of market • Support mechanisms by the government	• Effective producer organization for the service market • Effective producer organization for the product market	• Technical assistance • Input provision • Financing

Source: Adapted from Molenaar et al. 2015.
Note: FQ = farm quality; SQ = sector quality.

conditions (including slave or child labor), address environmental concerns, or create employment opportunities for youth.

Building Resilience in Global Food Supply Chains

The ultimate goal, and shared interest, of these different stakeholders is to build resilience in global food supply chains to meet the needs of the world's population. This is in the interest of consumers—everywhere—as well as that of agribusiness firms, primary producers, other value chain players, and governments. Working with smallholders is just one way in which agribusinesses are rising to that challenge. IFC, in its work with private firms, aims to support that process with this handbook as one among many initiatives.

Note

1. For more information about AMEA, see https://www.ameaglobal.org/.

References

Alexandratos, N., and J. Bruinsma. 2012. "World Agriculture towards 2030/2050: The 2012 Revision." ESA Working Paper No 12-03, Food and Agriculture Organization of the United Nations, Rome.

Camp, Hanna. 2017. "New Farmer Service Launches in Uganda Using aWhere Data: Packaged Weather Alerts, Agronomic Tips, and Crop Insurance Marketed to

Smallholders." *aWhere* (blog), April 18. http://blog.awhere.com/new-farmer
-service-launches-in-uganda-using-awhere-data.

Edenhofer, O., R. Pichs-Madruga, Y. Sokona, E. Farahani, S. Kadner, K. Seyboth,
A. Adler, et al., eds. 2014. *Climate Change 2014: Mitigation of Climate Change.* Working
Group III Contribution to the Fifth Assessment Report of the Intergovernmental
Panel on Climate Change (IPCC). New York: Cambridge University Press.

FAO (Food and Agriculture Organization of the United Nations). 2014. "Greenhouse
Gas Emissions from Agriculture, Forestry and Other Land Use." Infographic, FAO,
Rome.

———. 2017a. "Food and Agriculture: Driving Action across the 2030 Agenda for
Sustainable Development." Report, FAO, Rome.

———. 2017b. *The Future of Food and Agriculture: Trends and Challenges.* Rome: FAO.

———. 2018. "FAO Food Price Index." http://www.fao.org/worldfoodsituation/food
pricesindex/en/.

IFC (International Finance Corporation of the World Bank Group). 2016. "Building
Climate Smart Agriculture Business & Impact." PowerPoint presentation to
Climate Smart Agriculture Workshop, The Hague, October 28.

Molenaar, J. W., J. Gorter, L. Heilbron, L. Simons, B. Vorley, E. Blackmore, and
J. Dallinger. 2015. *Sustainable Sector Transformation: How to Drive Sustainability
Performance in Smallholder-Dominated Agricultural Sectors?* White Paper 1 commis-
sioned by the International Finance Corporation of the World Bank Group.
Amsterdam: Aidenvironment; Utrecht, Netherlands: NewForesight; London:
International Institute for Environment and Development (IIED).

NRCS (Natural Resources Conservation Service). 2007. "Precision Agriculture: NRCS
Support for Emerging Technologies." Agronomy Technical Note No. 1. United
States Department of Agriculture, Washington, DC. https://www.nrcs.usda.gov
/Internet/FSE_DOCUMENTS/stelprdb1043474.pdf.

OECD (Organisation for Economic Co-operation and Development). 2015. "The
Impact of Various Farm Management Practices on Resource Efficiency and
Productivity." Report, Joint Working Party on Agriculture and the Environment,
Trade and Agriculture Directorate and Environment Directorate, OECD, Paris.

———. 2016. "Big Data: Bringing Competition Policy to the Digital Era." Background
note by the OECD Secretariat for Meeting of the Competition Committee,
November 29–30, OECD, Paris.

OECD and FAO (Organisation for Economic Co-operation and Development and the
Food and Agriculture Organization of the United Nations). 2016. *OECD-FAO
Agricultural Outlook 2016–2025. Special Focus: Sub-Saharan Africa.* Paris: OECD.

UN (United Nations). 2014. *World Urbanization Prospects: The 2014 Revision.*
New York: UN.

UN DESA (United Nations Department of Economic and Social Affairs). 2017. *World
Population Prospects: The 2017 Revision.* New York: United Nations.

World Bank. 2017. "Climate-Smart Agriculture." http://www.worldbank.org/en/topic
/climate-smart-agriculture.

Yoshida, N. 2014. "Revolutionizing Data Collection: From 'Big Data' to 'All Data.'" *Let's
Talk Development* (blog), December 11. http://blogs.worldbank.org/developmenttalk
/revolutionizing-data-collection-big-data-all-data.